867-5309 JENNY

THE SONG THAT SAVED ME

THE MEMOIR OF LEGENDARY 80'S ROCKER

ALEX CALL

867-5309 Jenny: The Song That Saved Me / Alex Call
First Edition Hardcover: August 2011
ISBN 10: 1-936185-55-5
ISBN 13: 978-1-936185-55-9
Editor: Karen Adams
Cover and Interior Design: Laurie McAdams
Editor in Chief: Jonathan Womack

Readers may contact the author at:
www.alexcall.net
www.twitter.com/alexcall8675309
www.youtube.com/thealex8675309

Published by Charles River Press, LLC.
www.CharlesRiverPress.com

Acknowledgments
of a Book Virgin

Writing a book and bringing it to print is a lot like recording and producing an album. Both are made up of different parts that all have to be massaged and mixed into a coherent totality. When one records an album, one starts with some good songs, some not-so-good songs that one *thinks* are good songs, an overall concept, and a vision that changes with time and criticism. An album team has an artist, a producer, musicians, and a record company. It turns out that books are quite similar to records.

I originally wrote the draft in present tense. I saw it that way and that's the way I wanted it to be. I thought it worked. I sent it to a few friends and colleagues who I knew would need to see what I had written about them before the book became a reality. Huey Lewis, John McFee, Johnny Ciambotti, my Clover bandmates, were first. They offered encouragement, but I heard the comment that it should be in past tense. Others, such as Joel Selvin and Andre Pessis, said the same thing.

Oh brother, that was too much work to switch it all around. Besides, I was on to writing four novels at the time. I didn't want to go back and do the work. I wrote the other manuscripts and did my music thing. I let a year or more go by.

Finally I took a look at the manuscript and completely got it. Present tense was too taxing on the reader. I started in again and got really fired up with adding more stories, filling in gaps, and repairing omissions caused by laziness. My good pal and local historian of the olden days in Marin County, Danny Morrison, kept coming up with missing tales. His memory for all that is much better than mine. His memory triggered mine. I added one hundred and forty-five pages.

I worked hard on the manuscript. At last I thought I had put together what might be a best seller. My conservative estimate is that one hundred and fifty million people have an instant, fond recognition of Jenny and would enjoy tripping back to those days. I was certain major publishers and agents would be fighting over it and me. Hmmm. Well, that didn't happen. Rejection city. I began to get the notion that some in the literary field just weren't plugged enough to the music world to understand what an impact *867-5309 Jenny* had. Back in the day, they were busy reading great books and perhaps dismissing pop music as blather. They are right. It is mostly blather: loud, fun blather.

After treading a frustrating publishing labyrinth filled with various windings, agents who said no, and dead ends, I encountered Jonathan Womack of Charles River Press. I sent him a proposal for what will be my second book, *Second Childhood*. He actually came back with a yes. I was waiting for the standard line: "This is not for me, but another publisher might see it differently." *867-5309 Jenny* had been with an agent for one year who had gotten nowhere, so it was given back to me and Charles River Press decided to publish both books.

Just like an album, a book is about a team. Jonathan and I have become good friends since then. He gave the manuscript to my editor Karen Adams who wrestled it to the ground and did the job of fixing up my run-ons and improperly placed commas and italics. Poor Karen. Thanks! Laurie McAdams came up with the cover, which I love. Through Jonathan, I met Sherri Rosen, a publicist from New York. Sherri and I share various interests outside of books and music and I am excited to be working with her. My team has been gentle with this book virgin.

I want to thank all my pals, my road companions over the years, and my enemies as well: you've all made it interesting!

None of this would be possible without the support and understanding of my wife, Lisa Carrie, who watched me disappear into my studio every night for years, and for the inspiration and joy that I get from my two sons, James and Aidan.

867-5309/Jenny:

A Backwards Forward

The past exists only in its effect on the future. There is no "real" past, except in arrest records and tax returns and other unpleasant documents. Shit happened, that's for sure, but whose version of said shit is more or less correct is widely open to debate.

The following narrative is my version of what I recall. Others recall some of the same events differently, with interpretations that are as varied as the reflections in a sextillion-faceted mirror. There simply is no one truth. As they say: History is fiction.

That being said, I have tried to create as true a story as possible out of my travels and travails through the wonderlands of music and life. I did background research and asked others what they remembered. I was relieved to find that the recollections of others are as fuzzy as my own. My memory resembles a mad scientist's office, with a filing system designed by drunken, ninth-dimensional imps. Some pictures of the past are as vivid as if I was still in them while other major events and periods simply seemed to vanish. Yet sometimes, when it seemed that certain periods were lost in the labyrinths of time, unlikely keys unlocked whole memory warehouses of well-kept files and records and missing epochs were once again revealed, as if by magic wand.

I thank my past associates for their assistance in unlocking these warehouses and for allowing me to tell these stories without the threat of immediate lawsuits.

I hope that this book will trigger your own memories and take you back to those days of old which often seem like just yesterday. My journey was made in the company of all of you in one way or another.

DEDICATION

We are missing some of the souls who figure in this story:

Johnny Ciambotti, Mike Walter, Bruce Campbell, Bob McFee, and others.

This book is dedicated to them, especially to Johnny.

CANOGA PARK, 1985

Oh mama, can this really be the end
To be stuck inside a Mobile with the Memphis blues again...

BOB DYLAN

The neon light above the store on the corner down the block
was on the blink.

"Liq...Liq....Liq..."

I put the two big bottles of budget merlot on the counter.

"How are you, my friend?" asked the skinny Lebanese owner,
his close-set eyes twinkling above his long aquiline nose. With
his eternal five o'clock shadow, he looked like central casting's
version of an Arab liquor store owner in a cop show. He knew
me well.

"Fine, fine," I said. "Shokran." See, I even knew some Arabic.

I smiled my bloated north-of-Ventura-Boulevard smile and
pushed out into the parking lot. Heavy traffic on Vanowen:
Vans, low riders, Beamers, and pickups with four-foot ground
clearance, exhaust flap covers flapping and clanking as they
gunned their sex-substitute engines, spewing out grey filth into
the hot Valley smog. Grandmas, pachucos, blacks, Asians, and
ancient, trembling white couples staring with frightened eyes

1

at the vanished Valley of their youthful dreams stood at street crossings, watching the dizzy world whizz by at astonishing speed. Latino families, mamas holding the hands of beautiful white-shirted little boys and bright-faced, dark-eyed girls in school uniforms waited for the little flashing green man with the bad back to signal it was momentarily safe to cross the supercharged automotive artery. Tossed butts and blown papers rolled and rattled in the tail-pipe wind gutter. The horizon was orange, brown, purple. The smog made nice sky colors.

No one could see me once I was in my kelly green Chevette, I thought. I pulled the door shut and turned the key. Click. Click. Click. Nothing. *Come on, dammit!* Click. Click. I hit the steering wheel. *Fuck!* The starter caught. On. *Thank you, you fucking piece of shit Chevette.*

I backed out and turned up the side street and made my way home through the alleys. Fewer cops. I couldn't get caught again. The reckless driving charge was a lucky break. The next time I'd be in the slammer for more than just a few hours.

The night in jail—with seventeen poker-playing Mexicans and assorted gang-bangers and other regular drunks like me—had been humiliating, but I'd walked away with only a four hundred dollar fine for the crime of reckless driving. An everyday deal between defense attorney and prosecutor, standard shit in those years before all the brouhaha about DUI. Good thing I hadn't made it to my coke dealer before I got popped. That would have been bad.

My little boy was playing in the living room. I slid the cork out extra quietly in the kitchen and filled a wine glass, and put it behind a row of cookbooks on the counter for later. Drained my other glass, then refilled. I went out the kitchen side door into the alley by the garbage can and fired up a smoke. I pulled the can away from the wall, exposing dozens of violet-red palmetto-bug cockroaches, who scurried momentarily away from the light before brazenly stalking back.

The moon was rising, dull and orange, over the lemon trees. Other people had avocados or oranges, but we had lousy lemon trees. You can only make so much lemonade. There was my garden as well. Ungodly tomato hornworms had destroyed this year's crop of Big Boys. I'd thrown both hornworms and Big Boys over the cinder-block wall into the alley.

The alley was part of the endless grid of streets, alleys, and houses that filled everything. Sometimes I climbed up on the roof to try to get a view of the distant mountains, the red Santa Susanna rocks to the north, which reminded me of Sedona. But Sedona was of another age of the earth, of my life. It was hard to believe I had ever been there.

My Buddha's Childhood Kingdom was a misty, half-remembered Shangri-la. I'd left it but hadn't found enlightenment; I'd found my own limitations and my own and other people's excrement. Who knows? Maybe enlightenment was just another piece of cheap and easy nonsense: a Disney movie with talking monkeys and animatronic spiritual teachers who nodded endlessly and mouthed a reverby "om", while some crappy, lush synth song played over and over.

Over the high-priced hills, the Jewish Alps, there was the vast Pacific Ocean, but here it was a sea of ranch house rooftops and palm trees, all laid out over old orchards of the forties and fifties, bedded down with seething masses of people from everywhere who came to consume and regurgitate America. To the south, Woodland Hills and Tarzana shimmered; the houses across Ventura Boulevard, the houses of the rich and famous, Mercedes driven by awesome women wearing Gucci sunglasses. They passed me by, dentist's wives and their tauntingly cruel, beautiful daughters, incapable of even seeing me as I stood at the corner of Ventura and Winnetka, wearing my sweatpants, waiting for the lights and my life to change.

THE RADIO

Whenever I want you
All I have to do is dream
Dream, dream, dream...

THE EVERLY BROTHERS

Wolf spiders. Wolf spiders on my blankets.

They look like scaled-down tarantulas, chopped and channeled like tarantula hot rods, but unlike their lumbering bigger cousins, wolf spiders are frantically fast. That's part of the problem: you take your eyes off them for a second, to get something to swat or catch them with, and they disappear. But where do they go? Under the other blanket? Back in the corner where the wooden bunk-bed frame doesn't quite touch the wall, that place of unspeakable web-wrapped darkness? Tarantulas, of course, are gentle creatures. You can hang them on your sweater or even let them amble over your slowly-moving fingers. But wolf spiders are lightning killers, even if only of other wolf spiders. Their only other known function is to act as nightmare stalkers of seven-year-old boys.

I lay in the darkness in my little basement room. Off in the distance was the ominous deep rumbling of the new "jet" planes flying somewhere in the night. I was under the covers, drenched in a cold sweat, hiding from wolf spiders and rigid with terror that H-bombs would fall out of the sky. I was waiting every second for it to happen. That was what they'd been feeding us kids: Commies and H-bombs.

I had the blankets pulled up around my head, because besides the H-bombs and the wolf spiders, there were mice and rats and other short- and long-legged crawling, creeping scaries waiting to get me down in that basement room.

My dad never got around to finishing this part of the house. It was on his list, but the list was years long and filled the blue-lined pages of notebook after notebook, each entry neatly written in his crabbed writing, each notebook held closed with a rubber band. There were a great many things on that years-long list that never got done. He was a big starter but not much of a finisher, a man of many dreams, but not so many fully-realized accomplishments. So Charlie Owlbox, the Dog-Faced Boy, as my father called me, number three of four kids, was stuck in this unfinished afterthought of a room. My older brother and sister lived down the hall, in finished rooms. My little sister lived upstairs with my parents.

The basement had a semi-smooth concrete floor that was supposed to be polished but wasn't (that was a fifties thing, polished concrete, very modern; now it's au courant again, as in Whole Foods floors) and there were missing acoustic tiles in my ceiling, which left holes from which mice and rats would sometimes peer down on me as I lay in my bed. I once woke up to find that a big, fat mama rat had brought her newly-spawned brood to nestle in the comfy folds of my satin comforter. At first I thought they were kittens, as we had up to a dozen cats at any one time so there were kittens everywhere, but as I squinted at them in the dim morning light, I suddenly realized that these tiny squirmers were of a more feral species. I ran, probably yelling, from my room. My dad came to the rescue, in typical Hughes Call fashion, with his ceremonial navy sword in one hand and our black cat in the other. He flicked back the covers with the tip of his shiny sword and tossed the cat on the rats, which scattered in all directions. Black Kitty might have caught one of them.

At the foot of my bed was a dirt-floored "alcove" full of dusty, cobwebby cardboard boxes, which was a crawl space that led back under the house. This creepy, dark place was home to many kinds of critters, including the black widows that my older brother and his intrepid pals sought with jars. A flimsy little curtain only partially covered this nasty gateway to a child's night terrors.

But my room was a well-lit refuge compared to what waited beyond my pocket door with its little hook latch. Outside the door, there was a dimly lit, narrow hallway with no wall paneling, just exposed rough joists strung with Romex electric cabling and draped with dusty spider webs. Directly across from my door was the open black hole of the ironically named "playroom," another unfinished space filled with partially-started projects such as my dad's "catamaran," the one he planned to sail to Hawaii, which was never more than a few two-by-fours tacked together, leaning up against the windows, which couldn't be seen out of because of the clutter.

There were piles of cut-up sheets of plywood, stacks of boxes and old newspapers dating back to the thirties, three-legged chairs forever waiting to be re-glued, a couple of eight-inch black-and-white TV sets, an old wind-up Victrola, uncountable broken vintage electric fans and light fixtures, and God knows what else, everything covered in spider webs and a light fall of slightly smelly grime that I called Mummy Dust. I'm sure Indiana Jones would be able to relate to that strange indefinable odor. This unkempt jumble was naturally home to myriad species of arachnids, including my unfavorites, wolf spiders, and all the other web-makers, big and small.

My father was one of those people who couldn't toss anything out, and I mean anything. Each old box full of whatnots, each partially-cut piece of lumber, every hanging garment bag full of old, never-to-be-worn-again clothing—I was sure there were corpses in them—had its own old memory or a future use. At its most organized, the playroom was a place of labyrinthine, box-lined trails through the piles and stacks. It only got worse over time, until the tortuous paths themselves were filled to the ceiling. Nowadays, a person who collects stuff in this fashion would be labeled a compulsive hoarder, which is quite accurate, but the old name is more descriptive: Packrat. Both names are sadly correct.

It might seem like I grew up in the hills of Appalachia or a rotting urban tenement, but this was in Mill Valley, California, one of the most urbane pieces of suburbia that ever was. And my dad wasn't an undereducated hick from the sticks or faceless denizen of a forlorn cityscape. He was quite a complicated man. His mother and father had divorced in 1919 when he was two, leaving him to be raised by his wealthy grandparents. His mother's father, my great-grandfather, George Alexander Hughes, was the inventor of the electric stove, if you can get your mind around that. A third-generation Irish Protestant immigrant, Hughes started an electric appliance company that went on to become Hughes Electric and then he was chairman of the board of General Electric in the twenties or thirties. I keep telling my brother that sooner or later a few hundred shares of GE will be found in an old pile of papers and we'll be rich. The shares have as yet not been unearthed. When we find them, I'll let you know. From Maui.

My dad grew up in a big house near Chicago, where he got more attention from the liveried "colored" servants and cooks than he did from his distant grandparents. He was shunted off at age five to a fancy WASPy school or two and then to Harvard and Harvard Business School. From this high-altitude springboard he could have belly-flopped into a cushy corporate job. All he had to do was toe the line and follow vaguely in Grandpa's footsteps. But while serving as a young Lieutenant Commander, U.S. Navy, in a strictly non-combatant role (no doubt through his grandfather's political connections) as a junior adjutant and tennis partner for Admiral Chester W. Nimitz in Pearl Harbor during WWII—where in addition to his forehand my father finely honed his already considerable cocktail-party skills—my father saw Golden California. When the war was over, he turned his back on his guaranteed-to-be-boring corporate job prospects and left the Midwest for the wide-open sunny life of San Francisco.

He was, despite his blustery protestations to the contrary, a black sheep who tried for a long time in vain to wear white: a lifelong failure at business and a staunch anti-Roosevelt Republican who finally came to his senses during the Vietnam War and became a Democrat and an anti-war, civil rights advocate. Should he have been surprised to have spawned a rock musician?

As for Hughes Electric Company and the George Alexander Hughes "Father of the Electric Range" family fortune: My lovely grandmother, the party-loving, almost-good-enough erstwhile concert pianist, spent all the dough traveling the world onboard Cunard ocean liners, draped in minks and pearls, and on entertaining Broadway's and The New York Philharmonic's stars at her autographed-photo-filled 57th Street apartment, right across the street from Carnegie Hall.

Shirtsleeves to shirtsleeves in three generations: that's what they say.

My dad was also an alcoholic, largely of the charming variety, who couldn't find the time to play catch with me or teach me how to drive. He was always too busy either sleeping a big night off or winding up to become Mr. Gregarious, the guy who lived for the next wild, imaginative party coming down the pike. My parents both sang and my mother played piano. We had three pianos in the house, with back-to-back grands in the big living room, the curves matching like musical yin-yang pieces. Above the pianos was an abstract painting done by an artsy parental friend: an oddly stretched-out rectangle three feet high and fifteen feet long. The male cats got up on the pianos and peed on the painting, their pee trails streaming down the walls from the swirls and splatters of the abstract painting. Life imitates art.

My folks belonged to a theater group that did Gilbert and Sullivan and other light musicals, and our house was party central for the cast. Our parties were legendary. My dad cut an eight-by-ten-foot hole in the living room floor and rigged a "stage" that could be raised with pulleys, up from infamous playroom to the living room. Virtually everyone at the party—

and we often had a hundred people or more at our soirees — was required to have an act, the partygoers singing or doing a funny scene from a play. My father had rigged colored spotlights near the ceiling of the living room that illuminated the performers as they rose from the depths.

As a kid, I could only watch the grown-ups at play, though they trotted me out to sing a Broadway song or two. I had a good voice even as a little boy. But the world of grown-ups was basally off-limits to us kids. We had to go to our rooms early. In the morning, I snuck upstairs and gazed upon the detritus of the parties: glasses everywhere, many with cigarette butts floating in white wine, the kitchen a mess. There were usually two or three snoring bodies on the couches. They must have had a grand time.

Often I'd get a book or two and tiptoe back down to my room. There was a library in our dining room with floor-to-ceiling shelves holding books that came down from both my mother's and father's childhoods. There must have been hundreds of books. I learned to read early and I loved the Greek myths, the Arabian Nights, and anything about history. I still do. I have some of those old books today. I also loved comic books, especially Uncle Scrooge, because of the fantastic adventures, and my favorite, Superman.

Superman is a lonely character. He can't reveal his true identity to even his closest friends. He exists to right wrongs and to save the world from Lex Luthor and Mr Mxyzptlk. Superman's only weakness is deadly Kryptonite, pieces of his home world which are poisonous to him. How true that is. The stuff that follows us around from childhood can be very toxic; it can even destroy us. Superman had a place to recharge his batteries when he was at the end of his endurance, the Fortress of Solitude. Even Superman has his limits. The creators of Superman were brilliant. And I wanted desperately to be Superman. Even then I knew the world needed saving. I spent long hours wandering in the worlds of books and comics. The moral choices and the circumstances of the characters were easier to understand than the real world I saw around me.

You'd think my father could've taken a little of his social energy to fix up my nasty room, but he couldn't find the time. He was the party master: he loved the ladies, he lived for the laughter. His nickname was Hugs. He had a clock that said "no drinks served until five." The clock face was, of course, all fives.

My father was much loved by his witty, creative, and simpatico friends, but his own early childhood abandonment by his mother no doubt left him with deep unfaced issues. Kryptonite. His dark, wounded side found expression in the scary bowels of our house, the basement of Dorian Grey. I needed my own Fortress of Solitude.

Of course, I didn't know any of that when I was a young boy. I only knew that everywhere there were piles of stuff too important to be tossed out, projects too far down on the ever-longer list to ever be dealt with. At night, the door-less playroom was a seething black pit of lurking horrors. The laundry area, with its single, hanging bare light bulb and the dark and creepy old blanket-draped doorway to dad's "workroom" (where he hid his cases of cheap Tom Moore bourbon) were just as frightening. There were two more of those scary, unlit, cave-like alcoves that ran off under the old house. The stairs that went up to the main floor had only steps—no facings—since they'd been built by my dad, who we now know never finished anything. I imagined bony hands reaching out of the blackness for my ankles as I ran up to my parents' bedroom in the middle of the night when I was too terrified to stay downstairs any longer.

All this and H-Bombs and wolf spiders, too.

So, I snuck my hand out of the blankets and clicked on the green plastic Zenith radio. Wish I still had that radio. It looked just like the front of a '55 Oldsmobile, with a chrome-like mesh over the speaker and a pea-green body. Two dials: volume and frequency. I turned it a click, didn't turn the volume up at all. At first, there was only a faint buzzing noise. But after a few minutes, as the tubes warmed, there was KYA coming in, too quietly for anyone to hear but me. The sound of the smooth-talking DJ was reassuring to a child who felt as if he had been abandoned to his cellar-dweller fate, and the comforting top-forty hit singles played all night.

There were songs that I loved: *Don't be Cruel, El Paso, Hello Mary Lou, Bye-Bye Love, Pretty Woman.* There were many more songs I couldn't stand: *She Wore Blue Velvet, Hats Off To Mary, Tell Laura I Love Her, Itsy-Bitsy Teeny-Weeny Yellow Polka Dot Bikini.* But good or not, each song was three minutes long: verse, b-section, and chorus. We were a musical family and I was at a tender age a discerning critic. My older sister was a bobby-soxer who had the latest 45s on her little record player. I listened to them more than she did. I waited for the songs that had cool guitar leads, songs that sounded like a band was playing them: Roy Orbison, Ray Charles, Ricky Nelson (with James Burton on guitar), the Everly Brothers, and Elvis Presley. I switched over to KEWB or the black station KDIA when Frankie Avalon, Neil Sedaka, or another of those horrible teen idols came on. KDIA played Bobby Blue Bland

(Lovelight, one of the best singles of all time), James Brown, Barrett Strong, Mary Wells, Jackie Wilson, the Coasters and Drifters, and my favorite, Ray Charles. I liked the real stuff, no lush strings or oboes.

The songs were my own private musical Fortress of Solitude. If I listened hard enough, the night, the spiders, and the H-bombs went away. Eventually I'd fall asleep, but the old Zenith stayed on while I dreamed. The songs sank into my consciousness. I was terrified down in that room, but as I drifted into dreamland on the waves of the old Zenith I was unknowingly uncovering something inside of me: music, a place of refuge. And it was my own Berlitz course: Learn to write hit songs while you sleep.

THE DANCE

Tell your mama. Tell your pa.
I'm gonna send you back to Arkansas...

RAY CHARLES

Hard guys.

Duck-ass haired, switch-blading, sucker-punching, candy-money-extorting, playground-humiliating, stupid-ass hard guys: worse than wolf spiders, because a wolf spider could be stomped, but hard guys traveled in packs, like nasty dogs. Even if you wanted to fight them, which I had less than zero desire to do, it was pointless. You couldn't take them all on; there were too many. The muscle-headed leaders of the pack cut the spineless kids from the herd and harassed them just for fun. Spineless kids like me.

I didn't have a clue what was going to happen when my mom dropped me off uptown on a fine evening in September of 1960—what magic was about to strike from the heavens—but that night I found my life's calling, and those hard guys had a lot to do with my grand vision.

I was in seventh grade and it was the first dance of fall at the Outdoor Art Club in my hometown of Mill Valley, California.

Though someday Mill Valley would become the ultra dot-com village of multi-millionaires, where young latte-sipping entrepreneurs and their slim wives who drove sleek Mercedes and black Priuses bought ten thousand dollar paintings at the hardware store where I used to get my baseball bats, Mill Valley in 1960 was just a nice small town with a California twist: Middle America meets the Ivy League, with a dash of Zen mixed in its highball (or red wine and the first reefers in certain houses.) In 1960, we were on the borderlands of the future. JFK and Nixon were running for president and the Red Menace loomed over our mushroom-cloud-shaded heads. Vietnam was yet to come. Alan Watts, the Beatniks, and the psychedelic sixties were slowly but surely emerging, but for now the button-down fifties were still in control.

I was eleven years old, five-foot-three, skinny as a fishing rod, and only dimly aware of the big world.

It was a dance for seventh and eighth-graders. For a brief moment, I was excited enough not be afflicted with my usual paranoia about getting hassled by the likes of Allan Acree and the other Elvis-haired hard guys who haunted these events.

The ghosts of my wolf-spider-infested basement were fading away as I discovered the spiders were harmless and the ghosts weren't there. My fears were a more present reality. I was now scared shitless by hard guys.

Hard guys. They were my shadow mirrors, the ones who pointed out to me and everyone else just what a total chickenshit I was. Hard guys liked to fight, or at least threaten to fight. Fighting and being tough was cool. In fact, the word for cool was tough. *That deuce coupe is so tough. The Nueland twins are so tough.* Being the quintessential skinny little runty nerd, I lived in constant fear of getting my ass kicked; almost as afraid of that as the H-Bomb, and I was still deathly afraid of that, by the way.

You know that film clip we all grew up with: that magnificent crown-shaped white-hot Bikini Atoll H-bomb mushroom cloud instantaneously blossoming from the sea. As the film runs, the mushroom head rolls skyward, leaving a massive column of gray-white, the stem of the mushroom. Around the base of that impossibly huge and powerful tower rises a gigantic wave that dwarfs a fleet of mothball WWII warships. Yes sir and madam, that vision scared the crap out of me until my late teens.

But H-bombs were on TV. My immediate daily problem was that there was seemingly no escape from the hard guys. They strutted around at school and at C's drive-in, just aching for any excuse to be shitheads, with their Brylcreemed hair, metal combs like weapons protruding from the back pockets of their Levis. They pushed nerds like me around, demanding quarters or when they thought it would be funny to ramp it up a notch, they'd *call you out* while their grinning thug buddies stood around. If you were called out you were screwed; you'd have to fight in front of everybody down at the tracks. I worked hard not to let that occur.

I had two (both failed) strategies: to escape them by having younger, less threatening friends, which only made me a bigger (or in my runty case smaller) pussy, and conversely by trying to look like I belonged in the hard guy "in" crowd. I used Vitalis or Brylcreem (a little dab'l do ya!) or even Wildroot Cream Oil (the pitchman in the old print ads was the shiny-headed cartoon character Fearless Fosdick) and carried my own grease-slick comb in my back pocket. The goal was to have one curl droop down your forehead from the front of the combed-up pomp, like Elvis or Ed "Kooky" Burns from "77 Sunset Strip." I couldn't quite pull that one off because my hair was too fine, so I finally resorted to goo that you dipped your comb into that made your hair as hard as a helmet when it dried.

Why did guys grease their hair anyway? I think it was because in the fifties, daily bathing wasn't a fully-realized national obsession yet. Old ways die hard. Some adults in that Robert Mitchum–John Wayne–post-WWII–post-Korea era only took the plunge into a tub once a week. It was said that washing your hair too much was bad for it. Of course, it was also said that smoking cigarettes was good for you.

I did have one place where I matched up: on the baseball diamond. Since my dad couldn't find the time to teach me how to play catch, it came down to my Little League coach, Barney Johnson. Barney was a working-class guy who saw something in me even when I showed up at the first practice throwing off the wrong foot, "like a girl" and even though I was afraid of a hard-hit ball. I loved baseball, but I was a chickenshit. Barney wouldn't accept that. He showed me the fundamentals and made me, and all of us American League Tigers, practice very hard. He thought I'd make a good third baseman. He'd put a bat behind my heels and hit hard, scorching grounders at me. If I didn't charge the ball, if I ever touched the bat behind me by retreating, he made me run a long lap around the high school field where we practiced.

I began to play well. I went to the schoolyard next to my house and threw a rubber-coated hardball—an early version of the superball—off the wall of the school and caught hard, crazy-bounce grounders on the blacktop. I got very good at it. My first year in Little League I got only six at-bats and a few plays in the field. The next year I made the all-star team. I learned that passionate practice was a good mental and emotional place to go, and that it produced results. Thanks, Barney. I think he would be pleased to know that I still coach kids in Little League. *Charge the ball, guys. Baseball-ready every pitch.*

But baseball didn't save me with the hard guys. I needed to conform. I tagged along with the in-crowd and greased up and also razored off the belt loops on my Levi's, neatly rolled the cuffs over, and wore a white t-shirt with the sleeves folded twice over my noodle-muscle arms. When I hung out at the abandoned railroad tracks after school, I folded a pack of Pall Malls or Marlboros in my sleeve just like the big boys. I smoked; I swore. I rode my gooseneck-handlebar bike with the big back wheel and small front wheel to my Little League games, with my uniform shirt untucked and pair of shades on my face so I would look cool, tough. But none of that worked.

Because there was no way in hell I could really ever be a hard guy. I wanted to be popular, and I didn't want to get my ass kicked, but my tactics weren't paying off. I was still getting punched, pulled under at the pool, and humiliated on the playground in front of haughty girls who thought it was funny.

I was a dorky enough chicken (did I mention the horn-rimmed glasses my mom picked out for me?) that my friend Dennis Brown even fought a proxy fight with Allan Acree for me.

Acree was a junior thug from the wrong side of town who had a set of muscular one-year-older hard guys for friends, the dreaded, hulking Craig Byrd among them. Acree called me out because I'd formed the Tasmanian Devils Club with my younger friends and chubby Mike Walter, another nerd. It was a TV cartoon thing, for Chrissakes. We had other ad hoc clubs, like the Famous Monsters Club (we kept movie monster mags in a tree fort; ooh, Creature from the Black Lagoon, the Tingler!) and our less well-known but much more exciting Junior Jerk-off Club, which congregated in my older brother's junked cars: he kept girly mags stashed under the seats. Allan Acree said he had his own club, the Acree Devils, and what did I fuckin' think of that? He poked me hard in the chest a couple of times for good measure. I stammered something about that being cool. That wasn't good enough for Acree. He called me out. I had to fight him down at the tracks after school.

Oh shit! I was shaking and near tears. I just wasn't a fighter. Acree would kick my ass in front of everyone, all the hard guys and tough chicks and wannabe hard guys who hung out at the tracks after school. My friend Dennis Brown, who had super-cool Kooky Byrnes hair and was five inches taller than me, said no sweat. He'd take care of Acree for me.

After school I went with Dennis down to the tracks, where the old spur line's rusted rails passed beneath a wooded bluff. It was the place everyone hung out to smoke and socialize and fight. The word was out: fight today. I was as nervous as I could have possibly been. There were a lot of kids there; way more than a usual after-school hang. Acree's gang of six or seven goons came up, strutting in like they were the kings of the place, which they basically were. There was some murmured name-calling. Acree had heard that Dennis was going to fight him. It wasn't unheard of to have a surrogate fight for someone. Dennis was a guy who didn't take crap from anyone, but he was kind of an outsider. That's why he was my buddy, because

I was one, too, but I was way more of a dork than Dennis. He and Acree exchanged the usual "fuck you" and other assorted niceties, like "this ain't none of your business, Brown."

"Oh yeah? Maybe it fuckin' is, Acree."

First names were never used, except maybe when you said a guy's name backwards, like Nibor Snobbig or Xela LLac.

They stepped out into a ring formed by the onlookers. The ratted-haired, popular hard-girl Nueland twins smoked cigarettes and acted bored. There was some tense calling, like at a baseball game.

"C'mon, Alan!"

"Git him."

"Take out the motherfucker."

"Hit him low."

There was more vocal support for Acree; he was the popular thug. But there was respect for Dennis, who had the fighting skills that might enable him to kick Acree's ass, which a lot of kids secretly wouldn't mind seeing happen. I wasn't the only one around school who had been intimidated and harassed by Acree.

The fighters raised their fists and circled, looking for the first punch. Acree rushed in and Dennis pushed him off and got a shot in. Acree came back fast—he was a madman—scratching, kicking. He was shorter than Dennis, so he got in underneath and tried to do some damage. But Dennis stood up straight and punched and pushed Acree off. They kicked up some dust with their black loafers and gravel from the old tracks went skittering around.

The bout was over in a few short minutes: a draw, like most fights. No torn Pendletons. Each guy got a couple of licks in.

ALEX CALL

They exchanged some more salutary "fuck yous" and withdrew into the crowd. So I didn't end up getting my ass kicked, but I was sort of humiliated for not fighting my own fight.

I wish I could have that one back. Getting a bloody nose from Allan Acree wouldn't have hurt me as much as the loss of the self-respect I suffered for having ducked out. Besides, Acree could never have hit me as hard as various music publishers and so-called friends would tag my ass in the coming years.

Despite the Allan Acrees of my world, I went on aping the hard guys. What else could I do? Deep down, I wonder if I wasn't always looking for a permanent way out of all that shit. I'd never be a hard guy or a professional baseball player. Vickie and Bonnie and the other giggling, note-passing popular girls who took delight in slicing open my little heart by ignoring me would keep on doing so.

At least I knew that at the Social Club dance Janey would dance with me. We'd twisted at a well-lit sock-hop on the slick hardwood floor of the Park School gym during the summer. We won the twist contest, the honor bestowed on us, the sweaty, beaming couple, by one of the younger, cooler teachers. Dancing was a blast. Most of my fellow dorks were too shy to dance, but I couldn't stand still when the music started and I found that if I got the courage up to ask, some girls would dance with me. I could feel the beat, the melody, and the shouting choruses of the spinning 45s racing around inside me. I knew all the songs note for note from my midnight radio play.

Something undeniable was waking up within the groveling chickenshit. I was so ready for the dance that night.

The muffled thumping of the music came through the oak trees as I walked nervously up the curving sidewalk to the Outdoor Art Club. I began to twitch. I wanted to get in there.

I got my card punched and went with Mike Walter or someone into the tiny, old hall. There, up on the box stage at the far end of the room, was the first band I'd ever seen. They were typical of those groups: drums, bass, guitar, sax, and one Electro-Voice mic going through a totally inadequate public address speaker. The sound system was designed to handle Outdoor Art Club functions attended by middle-aged men who wore bow ties and smoked pipes. My dad wore a bow tie and smoked a pipe. His naval reserve unit met there, under the banners of flag, WWII, fraternity, and Jim Beam. The little hall was paneled in dark wood. It had hardwood floors and a pale-green-walled, fluorescent-lit kitchen off to one side where during most events curled and coiffed women with top-buttoned sweaters and long skirts laid out baked goods and brewed big aluminum urns of weak Folgers coffee. The stars and stripes and the flag of California stood on brass-eagle-topped stands on each side of the band-box stage. You could almost hear crew-cut men chanting "I Like Ike!" or "Nixon's the One!"

The Elvis-haired band guys in their matching suit jackets and skinny ties stepping together in time to the beat on the little stage looked like grown men to me, though they were likely as old as my brother Lewis, sixteen or seventeen. The amps and guitars were real, honest-to-God Fender. The two-tone dark blue and silver sunburst drums were genuine Slingerlands bought by paper-route earnings plus a loan from daddy. During breaks, guitar and bass hung by their straps over the amps. So tough. Cooler than tough. I wanted a Fender Jazzmaster and a Bandmaster two-piece amp.

The combo thudded away in the little boomy hall. The guitar and sax traded off solo licks; there was a Sandy Nelson drum solo on *TeenBeat*. All the Brylcreemy lads and their bouffant hair-spray or page-boy lassies raised their voices on *What I Say, Tequila,* and *Bony Marony*. The two bands that night were called the Chord Lords and the Opposite Six.

Later on, I would get to know some of those guys—the ones who made the jump to 60s rock, that is. A few would become famous, like Bill Champlin, who would someday play in the super-group Chicago and write mega-hits. Others would go down, flat-top-with-Fenders dinosaurs, Jazzmasters blazing, refusing to get hip, keeping their hair products, pints of cheap bourbon, Saturday-night-big-dance-and-fight, and old Duane Eddy rockabilly guitar riffs clutched in their hot-rod hands to the bitter end.

But back then, for me, these guys were like gods. They played Duane Eddy's *Forty Miles of Bad Road,* Santo and Johnny's *Sleepwalk, I Got a Woman, The Peter Gunn Theme,* the Ventures' *Walk Don't Run* and a bunch of Freddie King-style instrumentals that featured only a handful of notes, mostly pentatonic scale. Good dance stuff.

I let it all hang out that night. Once I finally got up the courage to ask her, Janey and I jitterbugged, twisted, stomped, and even slow danced until I was soaked in sweat and then we danced some more. There were sneaked cigarettes outside and nervous futile attempts at kissing. She was kind to me; she kept dancing. But she wouldn't smooch. Making out was still a year away for me. I just got to hold her hand a couple of times for a lingering moment after the slow songs, which fired my poor, hormone-wracked pubescent body enough to make my post-dance masturbation even more earnest than usual.

I was the original dancing fool. Since I was using a deadly

combo of Vitalis plus that god-only-knows-what-it-is stuff you dip your comb into that turns your hair into a helmet, my sweat melted my hairdo and my would-be hard guy hair failed me, falling lank and wet on my forehead. But while my sweaty, horny manifestation may have driven cute little Janey to keep me at arm's length, I had the time of my life. And I learned something that changed it forever.

The guys in the band had lots of girls staring at them while they played, some girls even sneaking longing, adolescent glances at them over their boyfriends' shoulders during the slow dances. And they watched the band guys when they were done playing, too, the girls giggling and glancing in little groups at the players. Girls, the thing I most wanted. Hard guys of any age didn't fuck with band guys. The musicians had a magic passport to cool. They were above the juvenile Darwinian law of dickhead-beats-up-dork. The band guys hung out by themselves. They were in a world of their own. I wanted to be in that world. And starting right then at that seventh grade social club dance, I, a skinny little eleven-year-old dork with glasses and barely emergent cojones, had a feeling that I would get there. From that dance on, there would be no turning back, I would have no doubts. I was going to be in a rock-n-roll band and get out of the hard guy rat race forever.

There was a nylon-stringed guitar at home. I don't know where it came from, since no one played guitar in my family. The battered Spanish-style guitar only had the bottom two strings on it, but that was enough. I just slid my fingers around, kind of playing bass for the songs I'd heard at the dance. I could kind-of sort-of figure some of them out. *Tequila!* I was on my way.

What's funny is that I still play the same way today.

LEAD SINGER

Well, she was just seventeen
You know what I mean...

THE BEATLES

Zombies.

No, I was never really afraid of zombies, except for a few nights after I saw "Night of the Living Dead." And the Zombies were a great band. Just thought I'd mention them. Where'd they go, anyway?

Despite the wolf spiders and the insufferably moronic hard guys, by any wide-worldly standards my childhood was idyllic. I didn't have to deal with war, racial discrimination, or poverty. I played outside in the dirt with my toy soldiers and engaged in make-believe battles in the dunes at Muir Beach until I was too old for that to be cool anymore. I wandered around Mill Valley, Muir Beach, and Sausalito, riding my bike, fishing on the bay, and playing a lot of baseball. Finally in eighth grade I broke through the girlfriend barrier and snared a real make-out-at-the-movies-and-everywhere-else girlfriend.

But by seventh and eighth grade, my grades were falling. I was going to be a rock and roller, so who needed school? My

Harvard and Vassar-educated parents, in their wisdom, decided that I should be removed from the temptations of public school and the bad influence of my friends, who all seemed afflicted with a common distaste for homework and with dreams of a future that only featured cool hair, Marlboros, and getting detention slips.

So I was shipped off to Verde Valley School in Sedona, Arizona, where my older sister had gone. It was that or San Rafael Military Academy. The military school uniform fitting scared the shit out of me, to say the least. I might have ended up marching around and standing up straight. Maybe my parents were just motivating me. In any case, I wrote an impassioned letter to the school in Sedona, begging them to admit me and promising to change my scholastic ways. After all, my sister was a straight-A student there.

I lied. It worked.

At the rather tender age of thirteen, I anxiously climbed aboard the old Santa Fe Chief in Richmond, California and clickety-clacked off into the night all the way to Arizona, a shoebox full of my mom's deviled eggs cradled in my skinny arms and a smuggled pack of Pall Malls in my coat. The eggs were consumed in a fit of anxiety a half-hour after the train left the station in the East Bay. I lit up the Pall Malls with my trusty Zippo in the open, jostling, clackety space between the coach cars and stared out at the passing Central Valley, hot, brown, and crackly in the autumn sun. The racks of raisins drying alongside the dusty, oily train tracks in Fresno made me not eat raisins for a very long time. When it got dark, I tried to cat-nap in the dome car. I felt abandoned and alone, but not for long.

I arrived at my brave new school by van the next day, driven by a teacher and in the company of a few new companions. We'd found each other on the train during the night. It wasn't hard to guess who they were. Most train travelers in 1962 were old, bald men and tiny, birdlike grannies, members of a generation born before the universal use of the personal automobile, not to mention the commercial airplane. By traversing the coaches of the Santa Fe I met a handful of fellow future Verde Valleyans who I would come to know better than my birth family over the course of the next four years.

Since I am one of those fall birthday kids who are always among the youngest of any class, I felt a bit lost at the school at first. I saw that there were school traditions I needed to figure out quickly. I was a thirteen-year-old in a school with eighteen-year olds. That's a big difference at that age. I was upset at my parents for having sent me into such irrevocable exile. But despite the minor homesickness, I soon made a dorm full of like-minded horny little freshman friends and found myself reveling in a whole new world.

If my childhood, absent the spiders and shithead hard guys, had been largely an idyll, Verde Valley School—VVS as it was called—was even more so. It looked like a little pueblo in its own otherwise-unoccupied valley beneath the majestic loom of Cathedral Rock, one of the seven sacred mountains of the Native Americans and nowadays as ubiquitous a hunk of red rock as ever graced a Sierra Club calendar. The school was run by anthropologists, and had ties to both the Native American communities of Arizona and New Mexico and to academic and community organizations in Mexico proper. From day one, we were taught the virtues of multiculturalism, long before it became a buzzword. One hundred ten coed students lived in a hard-guy-free world of white-washed, red-roofed Southwestern-style buildings peopled by intellectuals, both students and teachers, with high scholastic and moral aspirations.

Verde Valley School was a real tight community. Students were on first-name basis with teachers: Cliff, Tom, Pedro, Maggie, and Ham, and Babs, though oddly the students usually used last names with each other. Hey, Holbert. Hey, Call. You seen Fernandez? The students had responsibilities such as waiting on tables, dishwashing, and basic school maintenance, like whitewashing walls, hauling trash by tractor to the remote dump, and cleaning out the stables, which was a real chore in the winter. I chopped up frozen horseshit and blocks of pee while wading around in fresh, unfrozen glop in my rubber boots.

The studies were rigorous, but also stimulating. Verde Valley was a top academic prep school at that time. Our days started early, with work and dorm inspection and ended late, with evening study halls. I've always been a dawn patrol person, so I got up before five and went in the darkness to the kitchen, where the cooks had an urn of coffee going as they baked the daily fresh bread. I'd take my coffee and go the library, where the math answer books were sitting innocently on the shelves. I'd work my way though math problems from the answer books, making enough intentional mistakes to average a B. I leaned otherwise incomprehensible advanced algebra in that way, so I was able to squeak by on the tests as well. We had some great, great teachers: men and women of real vision who gave us the keys to a larger world of ideas and ideals. I've never felt that I was undereducated by not going on to college. I soaked up a lot, even when I was sitting in the back of the classroom looking out the window at the red cliffs.

We were supposed to learn a wide curriculum of liberal arts and go out and make a difference in the world when we graduated. Our time was one of change; we were on the cusp of a new era, so we straddled the old and new. We still dressed for dinner every night except Saturday: coat and tie for boys. But Bob Dylan could be heard coming from someone's dorm room suitcase record player: "the times they are a-changing." Yes, they were. When we had free time, after Saturday morning classes until Sunday dinner, we had total freedom to hike or race horses through the wide-open fields or climb the sheer, red-rock cliffs that towered above the isolated campus. We found Indian ruins, skinny-dipped in Oak Creek, and slept out under the Arizona stars.

Every year we'd camp our way down into central Mexico in "Brenda," our little bus and these old GMC flatbed trucks with unheated, windowed metal boxes on them. We piled in and lay around on each other's legs for hours on end. We had jobs on the trips as well. Fire, wood, and water was a good one. Collect firewood, find stones to make a fire ring, put out the water jugs. We set up a couple of folding tables and laid out food. We'd eat around campfires: canned sardines, bollios, and hot chocolate. The teachers had "faculty tea." They'd been driving those cantankerous trucks all day on the dusty Mexican roads, dealing with the authorities, with overheating engines and blown tires, and trying to not lose any students at rest stops out in the cholla-studded desert. We camped with tarps—no tents—on the ground under the blazing stars or in the rain or snow. It was hardy and fabulous.

We'd be dropped off singly with Mexican families, where we'd live as guest family members for a few weeks. There were often no VVS teachers in the towns and cities we were left in. We were on our own and were expected to behave responsibly. That was hard sometimes, as in Mexico a fifteen-year-old might get served Cubalibres at a bar. Let's just say we had a blast. I was walking the streets of Guanajuato with Mexican girls when I was sophomore, *promenando* in the Zocalo while mariachis played and older women watched for signs of forbidden hanky-panky.

Spanish was a requirement at school and I had a good ear for it. On one side trip by commercial bus to Leon, a conductor made fun of me for wearing sunglasses. I wore my prescription shades day and night to avoid wearing my big, black-framed glasses. This bus was of a mixed class, schoolgirls in uniforms, farmers with chickens in cages. He joked to the passengers about the gringo movie star, unaware that I understood every word he was saying. I whispered to the Verde Valley girl next to me to lead me off the bus when we got to Guanajuato. The bus rolled to a stop. I stood slowly and played blind, stumbling along, feeling with my hands and feet as my fellow student helped me make my way along the rows of seats. The poor conductor, no doubt a good Catholic, crossed himself and broke out in a visible sweat. He helped me off the bus as I stared straight ahead, seemingly unseeing behind my shades. *Cuidado, chico!* We nearly peed ourselves laughing when we got around a corner from the bus stop.

We took extended trips to the Navajo and Hopi reservations as well. We attended Native American events like healing dances and ceremonies. I was a lucky boy. If I'd stayed in Mill Valley, I'd have missed hearing about the deer-legged woman at the healing dance that the Navajos chased across the mesa in their pickups. I wouldn't have gotten gloriously drunk in that bar above the Zocalo in Taxco with my buddy Ernie. I wouldn't have camped out at the base of the giant statues of Tula or picked up obsidian blades from the grounds of the ruins. I'd have missed out on racing horses across the open lands around Oak Creek in the days before so many people and fences changed Sedona. I wouldn't have had the thrill of having the buttons cut off my shirt at the Indian Arts Institute in Santa Fe by a student Indian painter with a switchblade who'd eaten the stuffing from two inhalers as my friend Big Bruce the Tlingit watched over me with his war club to make sure I didn't get accidentally killed. I was very lucky to go that school.

We heard or knew little of the outside world. There was no TV or radio, though on a Saturday night you could sometimes get a wavering, fuzzy Prescott or Flagstaff radio station playing the hits of the week. It was a sheltered, cloistered world of high ideals and transcendent social vision. There was no fighting, stealing, or any competition beyond friendly inter-class rivalry. Later in my life, I connected to what this paradise was. It was our own little version of Prince Siddhartha's Kingdom.

All this broad, visionary thinking didn't stop me pursuing my dream. In fact, it helped, because there wasn't much competition for what I wanted to do: be a lead singer. The Beach Boys, Dick Dale and the Deltones *(Miserlou)*, the Chantays *(Pipeline)* and surf music were the rage in '63. We had records from home. I listened wistfully on my tiny, suitcase record player with its vinyl-destroying two-pound tone arm, but I no longer had my two-stringed guitar. I didn't know how to get this rock-n-roll band thing going.

Then something incredible happened. A weird British band

appeared on Ed Sullivan when I was home at Christmas my
sophomore year. They wore their hair combed down and their
band was all guitars. They made the cover of *Life* magazine.
They were everywhere. Beatlemania. No more *She Wore Blue
Velvet or Tell Laura I Love Her* on the Top 40 charts. It was real
rock-n-roll again.

Wow, what a rush the Beatles were. I instantly combed my
hair down. I lived in the senior dorm that year, and a bunch of
the older guys with whom I played baseball somehow heard I
could sing. So they started a band and incredibly, they wanted
me to be the lead singer. We had a "rehearsal" in a dorm room.
There must have been twelve guys, ten of whom were seniors,
crammed in there, with nylon-stringed guitars and maybe a set
of bongos or two.

One senior had a skinny gray cardboard guitar case with
black plastic piping around the edges. I burned to know what
was inside. He opened it and there was a Danelectro, a one-
pickup, black-painted electric guitar with knobbly white tape
striping the edge of the body. Unbelievably cool. I asked if I
could try it. I guess I played something that made sense, because
he told me I could keep it in my room. It was like it was mine
for the rest of the year. I couldn't believe it. A real electric
guitar. I started playing and I just didn't stop. I played every
minute I could. It was like learning how to catch grounders off
the schoolyard wall. Over and over and over.

That summer vacation I went home and somehow got my
hands on fifty dollars and took the bus with my childhood
best friend Mitch Howie to a pawn shop in a seedy part of San
Francisco, where I bought a cheapo Japanese electric guitar
(with three pickups and a wiggle stick for bending the notes),

a bass (with a bowed-out neck, and dead-sounding flat-wound strings that were half an inch off the fretboard, but who cared?), and a one-speaker amp with its own microphone and stand (the amp even had tremolo.) All for fifty bucks!

Mitch, a "drummer" (who only had a snare drum) and I practiced every moment we could and played our first gig that summer, just the two of us entertaining a packed kegger thrown by my older brother's friends at a third floor walk-up apartment in San Francisco. Mitch's drum kit was the snare drum and a wire magazine rack that he used as a cymbal. I didn't have a guitar strap, so I put my foot up on the amp and held the guitar on my knee for about three hours while we wanged away. I spray painted the guitar candy-apple blue—a bad, drippy, streaky paint job. We played *Louie, Louie* and *What I Say* until my fingers bled, and then we played some more. The crowd, all college types five years older than us high-school twerps, danced their asses off. It was a powerful experience, to say the least. A few in the crowd even complimented us. Of course, they then puked Budweiser on their loafers.

That fall, my junior year at Verde Valley, five of us formed my first real band, the Urthworms.

Yeah, with a U. I know. Well, the Beatles was taken.

I'd been summoning the beast for five years and now it was rising up out of the earth and taking form: a real band, with bass, drums, and two guitars. We were all obsessed with playing. The Urthworms were always up in the balcony above the dining hall, where our gear was set up, wanging away. Twice a day, at "milk lunch," where the leftovers from breakfast and lunch were put out to be scarfed down by ravenous teenagers, we had mini-concerts, plus we played in the afternoon when we didn't have jobs or sports to interfere. If I'd put half that effort into my schooling, I might have been able to get into Lewis & Clark College or someplace like that. But nooo...

By the end of my junior year, the school was letting us play for events. We played all the school dances, including the one in the tack room at the stables where Eric Detzer got so wound up from the music and dancing that he barfed. Okay, maybe he got some booze somewhere. Some guys made very crude vodka using the distilling equipment in the chem class lab. My friend Bruce Campbell got a silver sparkle set of real Ludwig drums, just like Ringo's. Brian Ruppenthal had a Gibson 335 with a varitone switch and a Magnatone amp with two speakers. God only knows what that rig is worth today. I hope he kept it, at least the guitar. I played borrowed electric guitars, since my cheapo Japanese electric wasn't good enough for the band and my parents weren't onboard with spending a couple hundred dollars on an electric guitar and amp. When I found that some student at the school had a nice electric I basically appropriated it for my own use. *No, you can't join the band, but I am taking your guitar.* It was matter of destiny for me; for anyone else, it was just a guitar.

She loves you, yeah, yeah, yeah...

Mitch Howie and I kept playing during vacations at Christmas tree lots, parties, in his mom's basement. My old friend Mike Walter's dad was a concert violinist and so Mike knew a lot about music. He turned us on to Chuck Berry and other real roots music. I kept learning chord progressions until I knew the basics and kept writing songs. Back at school, our band got better and better. Towards the end of my senior year, the Urthworms scored a real, paid road gig. It was the senior prom for our rival, the Orme Ranch School, out in the desert mountain country seventy miles north of Phoenix. Somehow we got a ride down there.

A cute Orme girl talked to me while Brian, Terry, Bruce, and I set up our gear in the vinyl-floored cafeteria. She was friendly, with flirty eyes. I knew that Orme had a strict boy–girl hands-off policy. Still, I thought she might like me, even though most girls liked Terry or Brian more. It was exciting. We were away from Verde Valley on our own, a rare occasion, and we were going to rock out. It was our first paid road trip and we were getting two hundred bucks. It was spring of '66. Terry, our smooth-talking, dark-haired Latin-lover bass player and I were seniors. The Urthworms' two-year run would come to an end with graduation in a few weeks.

I don't remember how Orme heard we had a band. Maybe it was when they were kicking our asses yet again in baseball, basketball, or soccer by some hideous, yet totally expected, score. Our school excelled in intellect but sucked at sports. But Orme didn't have a rock-n-roll band. So there we were with our guitars and the Orme girls were definitely interested in us.

Orme Ranch School was the mirror opposite of Verde Valley. VVS was progressive, with a curriculum that placed a lot of emphasis on anthropology, Spanish, and American history and literature. Orme was a working cattle ranch, with a conservative, traditional scholastic program. Their hands-off policy was for real. Boys walked on one side of painted lines, girls on the other. Screw that! At VVS it was definitely hands-on, if you could find a willing girl, that is.

Our band was as unconventional as was our school. Of course, I'd started writing songs back in middle school. We'd learned a lot of other bands' songs, too: everything we could get our hands on. Records were hard to come by; they had to be sent to us. The Urthworms played maybe half original songs that I'd written with the other guys: crazy stuff like a raga-rock song that was open-ended and a wacko thing based on the attack of the Nazgul on Weathertop from *The Fellowship of the Ring*. But we also did most of the brand-new first Paul Butterfield Blues Band album, including *I got My Mojo Workin'* and *Born in Chicago*, and a couple of Stones songs, like *Little Red Rooster*.

Everything we did was definitely in our own style. We weren't that good, so our cover songs probably sounded like crap. I know our originals were dumb. But since we didn't have any idea how lousy we sounded, we just let it all out and had fun. We had innocent and wild teen energy. We rocked the Orme cafeteria that night. The girls lined up in front of us did some faux screaming and some interested ogling went back and forth from both parties. Pretty Blythe was both my witness and my evidence.

That is, I think she was named Blythe, or maybe she was *from* Blythe, California? I can't remember. But she was a cute, brown-haired girl, and she showed me around the school in the afternoon, held hands with me against the rules, and even gave me a couple of lingering forbidden kisses in the bushes behind the dining hall before we had to go back to VVS that night. Bruce, Terry, and Brian pretended to be looking for me elsewhere, knowing I was getting lucky, which they knew wasn't an everyday occurrence.

Sweet, sweet, sweet! Being the lead singer was good.

It's true that nerds in bands can score with chicks. As soon as it got around that I was a lead singer, I started doing a little better with girls. I now qualified as an artistic - and therefore vaguely dangerous - band guy. Bye-bye, hard guy. The whole world was changing, thanks to the Beatles and the Stones.

From the first time I saw the Beatles' photos in *Life*, I grew my hair as long as the school would let me have it, just over the tops of the ears. My prescription shades were on my face day and night. I was ahead of the curve in that I already wore black clothes all the time. I'd started doing that by eighth grade. My reason was that I was "in mourning for the world," so in that I concurred with Johnny Cash, though I didn't yet know that was his deal. One of my buddies' Baptist parents thought I was in league with the devil, since black is the devil's color. I suppose that from their perspective, they were quite right. If the devil had a Gretsch and a Fender deluxe reverb amp with tremolo too, and chicks dug him, well, who wouldn't sell his soul for that?

But I just had my own thing. I thought wearing black was cool. John Lennon proved that to be true. And being in a band was way cool. I was set for life. I had found my way outside the system. I was a rock-n-roller. That's just the way it was going to be.

In early spring of my senior year, when we were becoming somewhat accomplished in our own weird way, we pulled off a brilliant move. We signed off campus under the guise of going camping down by Oak Creek on a Saturday night. Instead, we conned a ride to Flagstaff from an unsuspecting campus employee on the pretence of going to buy guitar strings at the only music store in northern Arizona.

We took our guitars along "to make sure we got the right strings." It's amazing how an innocent adult can be conned. Once in Flagg, we slipped off, ostensibly to the music store, but instead we bought bus tickets and jumped on the overnight Greyhound all the way to Los Angeles. The next afternoon, we played the "Teen Fair," a band-showcase extravaganza held in the parking lot of the Hollywood Palladium, right in the heart of the action. Somebody's duped-but-connected mom had set it up with a show biz friend.

There were bands all over the parking lot, playing at booths sponsored by radio stations, car dealers, and surf shops. It was a lot of surf music, Beatles, and Stones. *Time Won't Let Me* by the Outsiders was a big hit; we must have heard that five times in an hour by different bands. Hell, probably the future Doors and the guys who became Buffalo Springfield were there, playing Animals and Zombies covers. Who knows?

Oh, no one told me about her
The way she lied...

We had a good crowd, as our friend's mom had pull, and got us on the main attraction Fender Sound Stage. It was a huge thing built of scaffolding, five feet above the pavement, with twenty-foot-high towers full of enormous P.A. speakers. It was also fully equipped with a set of Ludwig drums and real Fender amps. At last, what I'd always dreamed of: a line of big combo Bandmasters and Bassman amps to play through! There were two gorgeous twenty-year-old go-go dancers wearing Raquel Welch cave-girl-bikini outfits flouncing away on the towers alongside the stage while we played. They even flirted a little. With Brian and Terry, anyway.

We were more than bit weird for the audience, with our originals sounding way out of place echoing off all those simultaneous versions of *Time Won't Let Me*, but we did well enough on the blues stuff. Brian played harmonica in addition to some fairly competent blues leads. The lyrics were pure Urthworms. He had a song that went:

Talkin' to you is like talkin' through a hollow log
Tryin' to love you is like tryin' to love a dead dog...

We had a blast. There were two hundred people there, our biggest audience ever.

A VVS graduate drove us through the night to Sedona in a station wagon. We pulled into the school quadrangle just in time for Monday morning classes. We'd known the whole time that we'd be in deep shit for our stunt. We were almost expelled. But it was well worth it. What's that old prep school phrase? *Carpe diem?*

My studies by this time were an afterthought, and my last semester grades suffered, but hey, unlike every single one of my classmates, who were bound for Stanford, Brown, UCLA, Harvard, Yale, and Berkeley, I wasn't going to college anyway. My poor Ivy League-educated parents had a tough time with it, but I've always been quite stubborn in my own wimpy way. I was going to have a band and make it big, and I was going to write all the songs for the band. I could already make up songs that sounded like real radio songs. They just came to me. I knew it would happen. Remember, I left the radio on all night when I was a kid; it was ingrained in me. I felt that I had no choice.

The rock-n-roll muse was giving me that come-hither look like the dark-eyed Jezebel she is.

But for as long as the seemingly-endless months before graduation prevented me from going off into the wide, wild world of rock music, Verde Valley School was a continuation of my Buddha's childhood. Everyone at VVS was so smart and idealistic. In this incredibly tight-knit community there were never any fights, no bullying, and no stealing. Teachers and students alike were dedicated to the vision of a world shared in common with people of different cultures and skin colors. My parents and teachers wouldn't have seen it the way I did, but I thought my future music would be part of this world, this living goal. Superman with a telecaster.

When we saw a documentary on the growing civil rights movement, in my sophomore year of 1964, I heard a fat, florid, cat-glasses-wearing middle-aged white Southern woman with her hair up in a beehive use the word "nigger" in anger. I was profoundly shocked. I didn't know that people still carried around real racial prejudice. I mean, I'd heard the word used back home in supposedly color-blind Marin, but it was kid stuff. Niggers pissed in the high school pool, so you should swim at the tennis club. Niggers would steal your bike. But I never heard that you should "kill niggers" and blacks weren't banned from public places in California. Schools weren't segregated. Sure, there was de facto segregation, but not like in the South, with its Jim Crow laws. The father of a VVS classmate was a doctor in Yazoo City, Mississippi and the Klan burned a cross on his lawn because he treated blacks in his clinic.

In my house, that kind of talk was strictly not allowed. My Rockefeller Republican parents were progressive when it came to race and religion. My suffer-no-fools mother would have cut me to the quick with one of her withering looks if she'd ever heard me saying that word in anything but a literary setting. As a child, I just didn't hear the race prejudice message correctly. What I had heard in Mill Valley was, in fact, the same old segregationist shit, watered down in the melting pot of California. But the intensity and hatred that I saw in Beehive Woman's face was a revelation. That absolute prejudice was really out there.

I looked at the men in the documentary. I recognized them, tense and mean, with their Elvis pomps or crew-cuts and angry faces. They were hard guys. Those fuckers were out there waiting for us, weren't they? I'm afraid that we VVS grads were set up to be passionate champions of the other way, the way of peace and intelligence. But we were about to be cast out into the world. Vietnam, civil rights, poverty, and hatred: a harsh reality.

On spring break I went home and saw my first Fillmore show. The soon-to-be fabled place had just opened up. It was a Sunday matinee, of all things, with a couple hundred wild-looking hippies kicking around a beach ball in the still-day-lit hall while the bands played. I was super excited because it was the Paul Butterfield Blues Band with Mike Bloomfield, Elvin Bishop, and Sam Lay. They were fuckin' incredible. I already knew their album note for note. Quicksilver Messenger Service, who I hadn't heard of yet, opened the show.

I didn't like their music too much, because in my snobby high-school way I already had a negative attitude about guitarists who bent what I considered to be the wrong notes (bend the four note up to the five or to the bluesy flat five, but don't bend the one note a half-step!) but I sure dug they way they looked. They wore cowboy hippie: fringy shirts, custom hand-sewn bellbottoms, and love beads. They were as skinny as rifle barrels. A couple of them had black cowboy hats thrown back on their shoulders, stampede straps across their necks. Their hair was long, girl long. And let me tell you, they had a lot more girls staring at them than the street-smart Chicagoland Paul Butterfield band guys did.

The night at Orme Ranch School, as pretty Blythe smiled at me as she watched me sing, I'd pictured myself as one of those Quicksilver guys: long-haired, cowboy-hip, dangerous and wild, a psychedelic gunslinger. Oh yeah, man. How do you like me now, hard guys and tough girls? The fifties world of my junior high days might as well have been the Bronze Age, it seemed so long ago and far away.

Butterfield and Quicksilver and the other bands were huge, but the tsunami influences were still the Beatles and the Rolling Stones.

I loved the Beatles, especially John Lennon. He was the coolest guy ever. I wasn't a Paul guy. You're either a John guy or a Paul guy. It was Lennon's obvious insightful intellect and biting sense of humor that came across, plus the wounded artist thing. So deep. I knew that Lennon grew up fighting, but I intuited that he wanted out of that as much as I did. I got a John Lennon cap and wore it around school, the front unbuttoned. Even Bob Dylan wore that cap, but Lennon was first. I wore black turtlenecks and a navy surplus pea coat.

We learned every Beatles single as soon as it came out. The Beatles double-hit-sided 45s were sent to us out in the desert by parents and friends. Brian Ruppenthal, the Urthworms' lead guitarist, was the most knowledgeable about chords and lead parts. He was a pretty good player. We all sat around and played the singles over and over until we had them figured out. I learned a lot about chord progressions from those songs. The Beatles used a lot of progressions that were similar; after a while it was fairly easy to pick out where they were going musically. It's funny, considering all the wood-shedding we did with the Beatles, but I don't remember playing too many of their songs at our dances.

The Beatles and Stones were both gateways to other music: blues and R&B stars like Chuck Berry, Howlin' Wolf, Sonny Boy Williamson, and also country. Ringo singing *Act Naturally* led to someone coming up with a Buck Owens record, which was a real eye-opener for me. I hadn't heard such a cool sound since rockabilly stuff when I was little. That in turn led me to bluegrass, Jim and Jesse, Bob Wills & His Texas Playboys, and later to Merle Haggard and the whole panoply of Country and Western music stars. The "western" part of the music hadn't been surgically removed with a Red-State-Republican-Jack Daniels-powered chainsaw yet. "Country" means "redneck" now, no matter what part of the good old US of A, Canada, Greece, Norway, or Japan you're from.

We did play a couple of Stones songs. They were bluesier and rawer and generally easier to hack through. Besides, the Stones were cooler-looking than the Beatles; more dangerous. They didn't wear the silly little mod suits. And *Satisfaction* is the best rock single ever: it's still my all-time #1 favorite rock song. I loved direct, blunt rock songs. That mid-sixties era produced such great radio hits. *Satisfaction, Gloria,* and *You Really Got Me.* It was burned into my rock consciousness that a great single starts with a cool, distinctive guitar riff. I had absolutely no idea that someday I would write a famous one myself.

As great and cool as the Stones were it was the Beatles' show. Every Beatles album was truly a revelation. No one had ever made records like that before. Each one was something new, something never done before. The Stones records sounded small on our suitcase stereos, but I had the feeling they kicked ass live. When Bob Dylan came out with the band sound on Highway 61, with Mike Bloomfield on guitar, I became a huge Dylan fan too. The Byrds' amazing-sounding record came out right before graduation. It was mind-boggling sonically and had great songs. And of course, who didn't dig the Animals, Them, the Zombies, and the Kinks?

I had acquired or appropriated from some kind soul at school a black Gibson acoustic round-holed flattop guitar with a little pickup, the very guitar that John Lennon sometimes played. But I broke the high E string around Christmas, so I played for the rest of the year with just the lower five, tuned to a G or D chord sometimes. One less string to worry about. The open tuning was cool. It made our insane raga-rock song happen, with the guitar feeding back sonorously, like the opening feedback on the Beatles' *I'm in Love With Her and She's So Fine,* as the entire crazed audience danced through our stage setup, whooping and shouting.

And just think, we hadn't even discovered drugs yet.

Hippies on Haight Street

C'mon people now, smile on your brother
Everybody get together, try and love one another right now...

YOUNGBLOODS

Abba zaba zoom
Babbette baboon...

CAPTAIN BEEFHEART

Hippie chicks. Not scary at all. Oh no, quite the opposite, brother. *Make love, not war.* Moving long-limbed and freely in their granny dresses, long tresses flowing down their skinny backs, tan shoulders exposed to the sun and wind, they looked like Aphrodite's sisters. Some of them were a bit frightening to me in their dazzling beauty, but it was a desire-driven frenzied fear: the kind a moth must feel for a flame.

Brown Derby Beer. Fear the beer.

John McFee slouched on the old cat-barf sofa and let out a whole-quart-of-beer belch, which took the form of moist, gaseous words, "Fuuccckkk yoouuu!" to Mike Walter, who was coming down the steps to our hillside hippie pad at 96 Laverne Avenue in Mill Valley. "Yoouuu ahhsshoole!"

This cracked us all up. McFee could out-belch anyone. Mike smilingly flipped him off and reached into his pocket, then dangled a small bag of pot like a dainty object.

"Here you are, girls!"

Pot! Mitch rolled, we smoked. The gear was set up right in the living room: Mitch's drums, Johnny Ciambotti's bass rig, the two Fender twin reverb amps, telecasters leaning up against them, and our candy-apple blue tuck-and-roll Kustom P.A. It was a setup right out of my old Fender and Gibson catalogs, right from the dog-eared pages of those glossy, color-photograph dream machines.

We were called Clover now. For a year right out of high school McFee, Mitch Howie, and I had a band called the Tiny Hearing Aid Company. Mitch and I had been banging around on guitar and drums for six years. We met McFee through his brother Bob. John was just seventeen, as was Mitch. I had just turned nineteen.

Ciambotti plugged in his bass. Johnny had just joined the band; that's why we'd changed the name. He'd been playing with a band of slightly older guys called the Outfit, but we started jamming and he ended up joining us. He was our resident old man at twenty-five. He was handsome, street-smart, and brought a different vibe to our band. We were legit now.

We jammed and rehearsed our set. McFee broke into an outrageous solo on *Wade in the Water*. We picked up on that song from watching the Charley Musselwhite blues band with the magical Harvey Mandel on guitar. Our rather free-form covers of that and Junior Walker's Shotgun were staples of our gigs at Mill Valley's tiny Browns Hall, one of our regular shows. The hall—almost a dead-on duplicate of my childhood Outdoor Art Club, right down to the pale-green, aluminum coffee-urned kitchen and plastic-brass-eagle-tipped flags— was packed with wildly enthusiastic sweaty teenagers from Tamalpais High School every time we played. Just eight years after my night of musical revelation, we were the young gods on the stage, inspiring new legions of nerds to get telecasters and start singing.

John McFee was a great, uniquely talented guitar player from day one. I don't think he ever played an unintentional bad note in his life. He was capable of playing the world's worst solo, but if he did it was completely intentional. *Make it cry, John.* He was tall and thin, with long brown hair and a broken nose he got from his brother growing up in Orange County. He ditched both high school and his mom, whom he loved, but who was a mess, to come up to San Francisco with his wild older brother Bob, who was my age.

John had country music in his family background along with surf music, the Beatles, Stones, and Kinks and all that. I'd also found country at age fifteen in those Buck Owens records at VVS. Johnny Ciambotti came from a bluegrass background. Mitch and I played a lot of Ray Charles and Kinks. So Clover was really all over the place musically. We didn't think about categorizing ourselves. We listened to and played straight country, blues, and R&B, anything as long as it was roots. We might have been turned on to the blues guys by the Stones, Paul Butterfield, and Charlie Musslewhite, but the real blues guys were still out there: Howlin' Wolf, Sonny Boy Williamson (#1), Muddy Waters, Chuck Berry, and Bo Diddley. A note about Chuck Berry and Bo Diddley: Mr. Berry really is a giant in American pop music. He bridged the gap between black and white music with his accessible lyrics and rootsy riffs. Bob Dylan was part Chuck Berry on acid. *Subterranean Homesick Blues.* Bo Diddley's famous beat has soaked into the roots of pop and rock music. We saw him at the Avalon. What a gas.

Bo Diddley, Bo Diddley, where you been?
Been around the world and I'm goin' again...

James Brown was huge for us, as was Otis Redding, Wilson Pickett, Jackie Wilson, the Coasters, the Staple Singers, and Bobby Blue Bland. For country, we liked Hank Williams, Bob Wills, Buck Owens, Lefty Frizzel, Jim and Jesse, and later Merle Haggard. Our present-day heroes were the Beatles, Stones, Kinks, Taj Mahal, and the greatest guitar player of all time, Jimi Hendrix.

Wow, we pounded those Jimi records. My brother made a star globe: a light bulb inside a rotating ball with holes poked in it and red and green cello paper inside that projected colored dots of light on the walls and ceilings. Our own light show. We got stoned and listened to *The Wind Cries Mary* and the rest of Jimi's amazing stuff. *Are we high yet?*

There were also jazz records like Django Reinhardt, Howard Roberts, and Vince Guaraldi in our hippie house, plus odd-ball stuff like Hawaiian music '78s and the Mills Brothers. Like I said, we were all over the musical map.

McFee took up pedal steel and fiddle and soon was legit, especially on the steel. He got a pedal steel and just figured it out. The man can flat-out play any instrument well. Because we were one of the few bands who had pedal steel and fiddle in our rock music, Clover became known as a country-rock band. That also reflected our non-city lifestyle vibe, the cowboy boots, and shirts, the beer-soaked jam sessions on country tunes. We spent a lot of time going to the City, as any proper San Franciscan calls it, but wide-open west Marin County was home. Clover was never really country-rock; that was more the zone of Gram Parsons and Flying Burrito Brothers. We might've made it work if we'd made a decision to be an actual country-rock band, but you can't be country-rock if you play Merle Haggard and James Brown in the same set, as we did. We were unconscious. We just played what we liked.

John's brother Bob McFee was a real character. He called himself Jim Roberts or something—he had a couple of names and even more life stories—it was hard to sort truth out of the tales he told. It was hippie time, late in the Summer of Love, and who knew who anyone was? People had new names, like Sunshine or Mellow Mike, or Shooter. You name it: Buddha, RJ, Bummer Bob, Rainbow. But John McFee, unlike his brother Jim-Bob-whatever, was a straight-shooter, and he was also extremely smart and highly spiritual. He soon became a teetotaling vegetarian yogi who somehow remained calm through many years of band storms.

McFee's incendiary and original chicken-pickin-meets-Jimi Hendrix guitar playing was the best thing about Clover, though Johnny Ciambotti was a solid bass player and another very smart guy. Mitch Howie played well on drums, sometimes very well. People said I had a good voice; whether I was a good *lead singer* or not was a question I couldn't answer. I wrote most of the songs, some on guitar and some on piano. Johnny wrote a couple of straight country songs. We could all sing, and the Clover harmony sound was a big part of what we did.

By 1968 our cosmically enormous, insane LSD year was behind us. We'd become funky beer-and-pot heads. We liked wearing cowboy stuff; we liked to rock out. We were committed anti-war types but we weren't Peace, OM, Love, and Groovy hippies. We were a little too smart and cynical to be real hippies, plus we liked alcohol a lot. Hippies ate magic mushrooms and chanted. OOOMMM. And said vapid, yet irrefutable things like "I love you so much, man" while stealing your pot stash. We drank Brown Derby beer and belched. We also stole your pot stash, but we didn't rationalize it. We stole it because we deserved and needed it more than you.

Acid was a great mind opener at first. We would drop, and then go in Bruce Campbell's parents' fantastically cool Citroen to the Avalon or Fillmore and check out bands and hippie chicks and other freaks like us. We had good acid trips, like the time the entire city of San Francisco from Bruce's parents' house on top of Twin Peaks looked like thatch-roofed jungle huts and somehow from that I grokked the interconnection of all beings. But we also had bad trips, like the seemingly-endless weekend nightmare that ended our extended hippie family's dalliance with strong psychedelics.

One of us nearly bought the farm from a huge dose. Through one of my brother's connections, we got a small glass bottle that held blue liquid LSD, the kind that ended up as edible dots on blotter paper. The Blue Bottle. All that was left was a scummy residue that perhaps thirty or more of us from our extended Clover family dabbed out with our fingertips and licked. The result was a psychedelic disaster. There was a day and night of group bad-trip bummer insanity, during which one of our family, who I won't name, had to be held down by teams of three strong guys at a time to keep him from injuring himself. He was bellowing like a primordial beast-man and literally throwing himself against the wall of the little cabin at Muir Beach. He was finally "shot down" by a courageous doctor, who administered a large dose of Thorazine. It was a very dangerous decision because Thorazine could have fatally interacted with another drug going around called STP. I stood there in the crowded cabin as the bearded, long-haired doc said, "If it's STP, this will kill him," and then stuck the needle in our friend's leg. Fortunately, it all ended well, but we were all deeply scared. It sobered us up, at least in terms of acid. It was another entry on a long list of incidents I never mentioned to my parents. The things they didn't know, oh my God.

So it was pot anytime and anyhow we could get it and beer when we could afford it. We were totally broke. Our big meal was the occasional taco pig-out, which was generally supplied courtesy of Johnny and John's *old ladies*, Nancy and Ronelle, through their panhandling efforts, usually down in Sausalito. Taco pig-out included a case of Brown Derby beer in those old bi-metal cans (taste that can, man!) and a gallon of Red Mountain wine ($1.50 a gallon!) A lot of the time we plain went hungry. We didn't make much on our gigs. We shared whatever we had communally for the house and for gas for our beat-up Ford Econoline van, a rolling bucket of rust and bolts and duct tape, the floorboards of which were layered with a nice collection of empty beer bottles and cigarette packs and greasy brown paper bags and old oil cans. It was piloted by our opportunistic and rather sticky-fingered road crew. Gas was still only twenty-five cents a gallon, so we'd take up a collection and get two-fifty's worth of gas sometimes. We'd drive all night, just looking for what might be out there.

Mitch's mom rarely surfaced from her alcoholic rambles long enough to charge us the fifty-dollar-a-month rent for the house. In her absence, we transformed it from a catshitinfested, hoarder's trash heap into a nice clean hippie pad, with extra interior rooms created by artistic use of old fence lumber and discarded windows. American flags and beaded curtains served as doors. We had tacked up big National Geographic maps on the walls over the old chipping paint. On the living room wall there was a section reserved for artsy-fartsy felt-pen acid doodles as well.

We drove a faded green '52 Chevy sedan around town, usually with six horny guys in it. A good solid used car like that cost only a couple of hundred dollars back then. It was a little problematic to pick up chicks with six guys in the car, though it did occasionally happen. Tam High School girls were frequent lovely visitors at our pad, before school and after, like every afternoon. There were some hook-ups there. We were trying on each other for size and fit; it wasn't like real dating. I didn't even know what dating was. We just slept with each other, as much friends as anything else. John McFee and Ronelle and Johnny Ciambotti and Nancy were the real couples in the house of twelve.

Andre Pessis lived there for a while. He was a really brainy and funny guy from New York, a former Greenwich Villager, who would be the lead singer in the other Clover family band, the Flying Circus, and later a very successful hit songwriter. The Circus opened for us at Brown's Hall and at the Muir Beach Tavern. Andre slept in a fence-lumber walled-off sun porch in a sleeping bag we dubbed the "cum sack." There was endless needling and cutting, but it was mostly in good fun. Ciambotti was called "Clambottle," I was "Al'C'hol," and Steve Bonucelli, the drummer for the Flying Circus, was "Bowl'o'Chili." We were just kids. Life was an adventure. We were out looking for girls, pot, or beer, in any order. We played crazy gigs for little or no money and ran around the hills of Marin howling under the full moon.

***

There was someone at the door. It was a cop! Shit, there were roaches in ashtrays and on top of amps. Johnny was nearest the door and opened it slightly, still holding his bass.

"Can I help you?" He asked politely, keeping his face between sheriff and room. If the cop couldn't smell the pot his nose must have been shot off.

The sheriff's deputy shouldered halfway into the doorway. There was a big roach right on top of the bass rig, not two feet in front of him.

"There's been a complaint about the noise," he said. He didn't come off as too unfriendly.

"Oh, really?" said Johnny. We were standing by our amps, holding our breath, so freaked out you could've popped the tension in the room with a pin.

"Shoot. Sorry. We'll turn it down, officer."

Johnny was very, very smooth in tight spots, even when he was stoned, or maybe especially then, when others couldn't handle it. It was his L.A. streets upbringing.

The sheriff looked around the smoky room for a moment. "I don't see any reason for an arrest here. You guys keep it down, okay."

We all nodded and mumbled. (Yes sir, no problem, absolutely, won't happen ever again.) Gulp, gasp.

He left, going up the steps to the street above with his partner, their hands on their gun belts. They drove off. We all breathed out. We were still adrenalized, but figured we'd dodged a bullet. We hurriedly cleaned up the roaches and someone stashed them out in the blackberries in a coffee can. After a few minutes we went back to playing, this time at a lower volume.

Wrong. Ten minutes later they were back, maybe eight of them, and we were busted. Cuffs, back of the squad car, jail, the whole bit. We'd cleaned out the obvious stuff, but they found a bag of seeds in Mitch's room, and it was his mom's house, so he was in the worst shape. Busts were common, and we knew they didn't have much on us. *Must bust in early May, orders from the D.A.* It was just the Man being the Man, and us hippies being stoned hippies with our long hair and radical attitudes. They were pleasant enough and let us all out shortly. Nobody even had to spend the night. But it was a real drag. It meant court dates and hassles for Mitch. Nobody wanted hassles. *What a bummer, man.* For Mitch, it was the start of a long, bad relationship with the long arm of the law.

***

We were gigging frequently at the Straight Theatre on Haight Street. One night we opened for the MC5, the infamous bad boys from Detroit. They were insanely loud, notes and lyrics indistinguishable in that cavernous hall. They were also wild men, up for anything. After the gig they came to our house, got quite stoned, and ended up driving their rental car off a steep Mill Valley hillside street and into one of our neighbor's yards. Just another Saturday night.

The Straight Theater was kind of a second-tier Avalon

Ballroom in an old neighborhood movie theater right in the heart of Haight-Ashbury. It'd been the Haight Movie Theater. It was a big old boomy room with most of the seats long-gone, replaced by a very dimly lit dance floor, and the crowds were often only dozens rather than hundreds, but it had a semi-legit vibe. There was a big P.A. and they had nice posters, like those done by Mouse and Griffin and other cool poster artists. The old movie projection booth high in the rafters where you went to get high was called the Yellow Submarine. You had to climb up a ladder to get in. From up there, bands on stage sounded like supersonic cat-and-dog fights inside a huge echo chamber. You couldn't make out the notes too well, and it was very loud. I'll always associate loud, wanky guitar solos with being in that room. There were some really bad guitar players back then. But, it was cool: *Don't Bogart that joint, my friend!*

There were a lot of R. Crumb-like characters at the Straight. There was one guitar player, Joe T., who played solos on his miked-up acoustic while staring balefully out into the dark room, rocking back and forth on his heels like an insane wind-up toy on speed. It was kind of cool, but also edgy-crazy. Or actually crazy. At the end of a song, as the assembled handful splattered the dark, echoey chamber with light applause and few whoops, he deadpanned, "Thanks for the clap."

Carlos Santana and Greg Rollie from the really cool Santana Blues Band were frequently around. At one gig, Carlos spent the entire set lying on stage with his head inside Mitch's kick drum. *Mellow, Carlos?*

There were a lot of wackos trying to be rock stars. Many of them were con men, running a poseur game on anyone they could. One guy had penis pants. He had like an embroidered sock sewn on the front of his pants in which his unit was supposedly housed. This worked for him for about fifteen minutes of Haight-Ashbury fame. It was maddening when you saw one of these guys getting taken seriously. Sooner or later, the fakers were exposed for what they were and faded away. There were others who were good players and had the business part figured out, but we couldn't stand them or their music because it seemed so calculated.

There was veiled aggression going on under the rhetorically correct banners of hippiedom. *Love is the answer, man.* Oh yeah, then why are you trying to screw me behind my back? Contracts sealed with drugs were offered and broken, managers were signed and dumped, players were hired and fired. We kept plugging away, fueled by the belief we had something special; that we'd heard the real call. Okay, so it was something unfinished, but we were a pure band, not one driven by the desire for commercial success. Maybe that's why we weren't making any money.

In order to play the Straight and some of the other clubs around town, we had to join the Musician's Union. We went down to the Union Hall somewhere in the Tenderloin district— not a nice part of San Francisco unless you're drawn to strip joints, whores, junkies, and armed robbers—and signed up. The guy who took our applications and our thirty-five bucks was right out of a noir gangster flick. He wore a pin-stripe suit with a boutonnière, had a pencil mustache and greased-back hair, and was named Vito or something like that. After we auditioned, which consisted of Mitch doing a drum roll with his hands on the guy's desk, Vito said conspiratorially, "Hey guys, wanna see something really cool?"

"Uh, sure, man."

Vito slid open the top drawer on his desk and revealed a shiny black pistol. Later, at a high school auditorium gig in Eureka, a "union rep" showed up and demanded traveling dues from us. We gave him twenty bucks and he stuck it in the pocket of his trench coat. He wrote us a receipt on a paper napkin. Not impressed, I never re-upped my union membership.

Many days we'd get all duded up in our hand-sewn bell-bottoms and cowboy shirts and acid beads, pile into our van, and drive to the city to go walking down Haight Street. Making eye contact with pretty hippie chicks was the game. There were a lot of young girls and freaky, long-haired guys and poncho-wearing street people. Music came out of hippie-pad windows. The latest far-out Fillmore and Avalon posters were up in the windows of the head shops. *The Charlatans and Quicksilver Messenger Service. The Grateful Dead and Jefferson Airplane. Canned Heat and The Doors.* The sweet smell of incense, the disgusting stench of patchouli oil, and the enticing aroma of pot being smoked was in the air.

We got smiles and peace signs, and sometimes a flirty glance that led to conversation. "Hey, we're playing at Muir Beach tonight; you should come out there with us. You can crash at our pad." It was easy to meet girls; sometimes it even went somewhere.

She said, "Are you doing a thing with one particular old-lady right now?"

He answered, "Uh, no. And by the way, I can't help notice that you really don't need the bra you're not wearing."

The hippie chicks were sloe-eyed, lithe, and so beautiful. I was mostly too shy to pull the trigger, but it happened sometimes.

The street people were all young; no one over thirty. *Can't trust anyone over thirty.* The sidewalks were crowded; everybody was cruising, looking for action of some type. Guys whispered as they passed, "Lids? Acid?" We got fantastic greasy, meat-filled piroshki at a Ukrainian bakery we called Mama Khrushchev's. The lady who made the piroshki looked just like Nikita Khrushchev with a bad wig, like a Monty Python character. Twenty cents each, they were the size of big burgers. Down the sidewalk came H.P. Lovecraft, a band from Chicago with huge, wigged-out hair and Sgt. Pepper outfits. What a scene, and not a single hard guy in sight. They'd been magically eliminated, banished from the hippie realm. Good riddance.

There were some future legends walking around. We saw Janis Joplin at free outdoor gigs in Golden Gate Park's Panhandle. She was not very attractive, though she did have the hippie look in spades. In fact, she was an originator of the look: the long, wavy hair, love beads, antique flowered dresses, cool granny lace-up shoes, rose-colored John Lennon shades. Big Brother, her band, was the ultimate hippie band. They were real friendly guys and they looked perfect: skinny, with long, long hair, flower-child chic, everything. But boy, did they bend the wrong notes! It drove me (and others) nuts. But something cool happened when they got on stage. Somehow it all worked. The band was just right for Janis and she got better looking the more she screeched. Within a couple of songs, she was lookin' good. By the time she got to *Piece of My Heart*, she was the best lookin' babe you had seen in a long time and you wanted her. Weird, but that's charisma for you. It was a drag when she left Big Brother for a "better" band. Management and their big-money suggestions: once the record deals start getting handed out, many so-called hippie musicians tossed their scruples and their peace, love, and groovy friendships under the nearest bus, fast. Something magical got lost there, and it wasn't just the unique sound of Janis singing with Big Brother. It was the sound of the idealism of the sixties being strangled with a golden chain.

Jefferson Airplane was about the biggest band in the city. They were sort of folk-rock: nice, but not a real turn-on. They'd become more of a powerhouse when Jack Casady and Grace Slick joined the band. Still, they were never quite my quart of Brown Derby.

We saw the Grateful Dead around a lot. They were accessible. Remember, it was nominally a big hippie family at this point. We caught them at the Fillmore or Avalon every chance we got. The Dead's secret was that they were the only band that made sense when you took acid. Jerry was the leader, the acid-trip hero, but I dug Bob Weir, Phil Lesh, Bill Kruetzman, and Pig Pen. I loved their free-flowing sound. And Jerry bent mostly the right notes, by the way. At one free gig at the outdoor Greek amphitheater-style Mountain Theater on top of Mount Tamalpais, Weir mentioned our gig that night at Muir Beach. We were thrilled to have him say our band's name over the P.A. The Dead were not at this point all the way into the forty-minute solos they'd become famous for. They were much tighter than most of the bands. But then they made their first album, which failed to catch their live vibe. It was a big disappointment for me. Then their solos got longer and longer, and besides, when we stopped taking acid, we didn't go to see them as much. Because without acid, well, let's just say they make more sense when you're on acid and leave it at that. So those who might have wondered what those Deadheads with their Volkswagen busses with tie-dyed curtains were doing at those gigs for all those years, wonder no more.

We saw all the Bay Area bands, and many of the touring ones. The Fillmore and Avalon, of course, were the top venues. The Family Dog, a bunch of semi-business-minded hippies headed by Chet Helms, ran the Avalon Ballroom. It was a big old dance hall up a flight of stairs just off Van Ness Avenue above Polk Street in the city, near the porn shops and crime district called the Tenderloin, the same neighborhood that the Musician's Union was in. The Tenderloin, home of hookers and transvestites, muggers, and heroin dealers: a nice wholesome location for our counter-culture revolution.

The ballroom held a thousand stoned hippies, maybe more. I was there, so of course I can't remember. The stage was angled in one corner of the room. There was a plush-carpeted balcony area upstairs. Strobe lights flashed along the wall under which you could get lost in your trip and swing your beads around in the air. They magically changed color and location. Hippie chicks appeared in freeze-frame, their long hair flashing. The P.A. was huge compared to those bands played through just a few years earlier. When I saw the Ventures *(Walk, Don't Run)*, the Shantays *(Pipeline)*, the Surfaris *(Wipeout)*, and other bands at the Corte Madera Community center in 1964, the P.A. was just one microphone and one Voice of the Theater speaker on the side of the stage. The new venues had big bass speakers and treble horns. The drums and the amps were all miked up; there were monitor wedges across the stage. The lights were regulation theater stage and spotlights, mixed with a big, squishy projected light show by Bill Ham or some other stoned guy pulsing away above and behind the band and on the walls of the hall. Hard guys pushing each other around were not the show anymore. Now it was the band, man, and the lights. Band guys were *stars* now. Not just cool. Not tough. They were *gods*, written about in *Rolling Stone*, our new Bible. It was happening, man. Now I really wanted in, and I was so close.

Chet Helms, the head dog of the Family Dog, was a tall, skinny, gentle guy with long hair and beard and wire-rimmed glasses. He could usually be found near the top of the stairs, arms folded across his chest, welcoming people and talking with his buddies. He gave off a peaceful vibe, and the Avalon was definitely more of a hippie place than the Fillmore.

The Fillmore Auditorium was right on the edge of a tough black neighborhood called, simply, the Fillmore. It was a similar hall to the Avalon, maybe a bit larger, but not by much. Both places had an air of faded glory about them: gilded balconies, carpeted hallways, long bars in the annexes. They must have been WWII-era dance halls. The Fillmore's stage was at the far end of the room. There was a balcony that ran three quarters of the way around the hall, and a room off the balcony where you could catch a breather and tell your compadres how stoned you were. One night we all scared the shit out of each other by talking about the size of the universe and how tiny and alone we were in it. At a time like that, when you and your stoned posse are looking at the edge of a space you are not prepared to gaze fully into, there is nothing else to do but listen to Otis Redding or Van Morrison or Cream.

Greeting you at the top of the stairs when you went in was the one and only Bill Graham. Bill was a compact, tough-looking guy, with shortish dark hair. He had a New York vibe;

cool but passionate, formidable, like your older brother. You got the feeling that he'd kick your ass if you got out of line, so you didn't get out of line. But there was also a feeling that he'd shield you from bad shit, like if the cops came in, as they sometimes did. He probably paid them off. At the end of the night, Bill handed out apples to everyone and told us to *be cool* as we took our stoned selves out into the San Francisco night. We'd see the dawn come up before we came down.

All the big bands played those venues: Cream, Them with Van Morrison, Jefferson Airplane, the Doors, the Charlatans, Otis Redding, the Grateful Dead, Quicksilver, Love, Steve Miller, Buffalo Springfield, Captain Beefheart, Blue Cheer, Canned Heat, Mother Earth, Charlie Musselwhite, the Electric Flag, Moby Grape, the Charlatans, the Youngbloods, Janis Joplin and Big Brother, Taj Mahal, and too many others to remember. When Bill Graham moved the Fillmore to Fillmore West and then to Winterland, a cavernous hall that held 5,000, the shows got even bigger: Jimi Hendrix, Albert Collins, B.B. King, Fleetwood Mac. It was the dawn of the huge concert era.

Bands we really dug were Taj Mahal, with Jesse Edwin Davis on guitar, and Moby Grape, a sensational band—the best in the city, though their career went crazy haywire after two albums. Sadly, a couple of band members became drug casualties and were committed to institutions. The Steve Miller Blues Band with Boz Skaggs and Curly Cook was awesome. They held down a club in the marina called the Matrix for awhile and then Miller went on to big-time stardom. Boz followed later. Carlos Santana with his Santana Blues Band was already doing what would make him a mainstay for the next forty years. On the other hand, the Great Society with Grace Slick made me go on a bad acid trip with their music, and Blue Cheer and the Oxford Circle were just plain so loud and so bad I couldn't take it. Sorry, guys: you sucked. I was more into the blues- and country-influenced stuff. I liked to rock out, but I didn't like aggressive, ugly hard rock.

No hard guys, no hard rock.

For a while there, I thought hard guys were on their way out. At last the myth of progress was a reality. The world was coming to its senses after a long bloody history featuring mainly a lot of hard guys: hard guys in animal skins, hard guys in togas, hard guys in Nazi uniforms, hard guys in white sheets, hard guys on Main Street Anywhere USA. In terms of evolution, hard guys were once necessary; someone had to protect the village and raid neighboring tribes for cattle and women. But the world had become one gigantic village. Slowly, inexorably, people were coming to realize that hard guys aren't the solution, they're the problem. For a brief moment in the sixties, this realization seemed to be coming home to roost on the rooftops, cooing and fluffing its wings.

From the summer of '66 to the end of '68, there was a real feeling among us hippies of a movement, a common counter-culture. R. Crumb had a great cartoon that summed it up: A cosmic meatball falls out of the sky and bonks one person on the head, then another, and then another, and so forth. Each of those bonked, from a busty, hot Crumb chick to a scientist to a pimply, bike-riding kid to an Air Force general, or whoever the Crumb characters were, achieved a measure of enlightenment of some kind. Finally, the meatball rolled out of sight. The script read: *Will Meatball ever come again? Who can say?* Well, we had our Meatball moment, though just like in Crumb's cartoon, it soon rolled out the door.

It was a really exciting scene; a genuine "time and place," but the good vibes faded away far too soon. The moment rapidly morphed into an aggressive, dark, mirror-image centered on the "rip-off" rather than Peace and Love. The angel shape-changed into a demon: Lucifer fell again, from enlightened hipster to low-life, meth-crazed biker. It was all over by 1970, but the Summer of Love would remain a transformational crossroad that would have an effect for the next generation and beyond. Though the forces of reaction still are powerfully tenacious, expectations for the future have evolved and retained a measure of the higher planes of possibility glimpsed by the flower-power people in '67. Will humanity last long enough to see the seeds planted by that rare moment bear fruit? *Will Meatball come again? Who can say?*

At least I was temporarily free of those fuckin' hard guys.

***

We dropped acid in Mill Valley, and once again Bruce Campbell drove everyone across the Golden Gate Bridge to the Avalon in his parents' Citroen station wagon. We were all amazed when the car magically stopped at stop signs and red lights. As we came on, we waved at fellow long-hairs on the streets or in other cars. *Hey, Freaks!* We were really high by the time we got there, with that metallic acid feeling welling up in our throats and eyes, the cosmic electricity flowing in our veins. The Great Society with Grace Slick was playing. I watched them, hallucinating like crazy.

I'd heard they were good, that Grace was a cool singer, and I wanted to like them, I really did. I saw actual musical notation flowing out from the stage, like something out of Disney's Fantasia. It was so beautiful. But then Grace's grating, piercing voice and the twangly guitars became distorted and ugly, and suddenly very, very scary. The notes exploded on the hallucinated staves, like bombs. The red-blue molecular structures that made up my field of vision began to spin. It was an inescapable downward spiral, a twirling vortex, a wormhole to Hell. I turned to Mitch, who now looked like some sort of odd lizard being, and said, "I'm scared." The sound of my own voice sank me at an impossible speed to a place I'd never been. *My mind was blowing! I was flipping out!* Now I knew what that meant.

I stumbled through the insanely babbling crowd of mad-hatters and cardboard cut-out, two-dimensional freaks. Somehow, I made my way up the balcony, looking for a place of refuge, but there was no place to hide from what was happening inside of me. I vomited, and the vomit was fire. From somewhere, my brother Lew and his friend Peter G. found me. They took me out of the Avalon to Peter's Chevy Nomad. We headed toward Marin. Away from the insane, hell-like noise and looking-glass crowd I was calmer, but still deeply scared. The road seemed to roll up under the car like we were driving on a big, rotating metal drum. I didn't know why the Nomad didn't fly off into space.

I crawled from the back seat into the front. A feeling of ice cold seeped in my ass. It was beginning to freeze. My ass was freezing! I was going to die! Wait a minute, I'd knocked over a Coke bottle and it was pouring into my pants. I cracked up, and relaxed somewhat, much to the relief of Lew and Peter, who were no doubt mulling over whether they'd have to take me to the hospital. It was a course of action that might well land them in jail. They were on acid, too.

Instead, we drove all the way to the top of Mount Tam and watched the starry night go by and the dawn come up over the layered, purple, East Bay hills and the steel-gray bay. It was very beautiful. It was very fucked up.

MUIR BEACH

In every heart there is a vision of a simple life…

ALEX CALL

One Saturday noon we were supposed to play with the up-and-coming Creedence Clearwater Revival out on the big front porch at the Muir Beach Tavern. I'd seen Creedence out there before. Their P.A. system was just bull-horns on tall stands, no speakers. It made John Fogerty's voice like that nasty, squawky bit on *Susie-Q*, the song that got the unstoppable Creedence ball rolling. I couldn't stand it, it sounded so phony to me at the time, some white guy affecting this blues style, but what did I know?

If Haight was the center of the hippie galaxy, one of the far outer-rim planets was Muir Beach, five twisty, cliff-hugging, death-defying Pacific Coast Highway miles west of Mill Valley. The beach was sort of our home base. It's a smallish grey-sand cove a half-mile across, set in the midst of towering headlands that plunge into the wild Pacific. From the beach you can see the whitewashed western part of San Francisco, the Sunset district, stretching out onto the ocean twenty miles to the south. Beyond this low-lying finger of the city are the dark, wooded coastal hills that rise to the west of the San Andreas Fault. Muir Beach is just east of that fault line. At the north end of the beach, above the tiny adjoining cove of Little Beach is a classic dragon-spine cliff-faced point that snakes its way down from the flanks of Mount Tamalpais, the highest peak in Marin County, to stick its nose in the mighty swells of the dark, cold Pacific.

On the point were little houses of old Portuguese fishermen (who once doubled as prohibition rum-runners) and dairy people from the old days, along with the art- and driftwood-decorated cottages of painters, sculptors, poets, and college professors. The houses rested under fog-dripping gnarled, weathered cypresses and windswept pines. Giant bushes of flowering sawgrass framed entrances to well-kept gardens graced by stone Buddhas and tinkling wind chimes. The tiny streets that crisscrossed the steep hill were one-laners.

Muir Beach was an artists' colony, full of intrigue and cliques, but close-knit at the same time. Everyone knew everybody and who they were sleeping with; who had a drinking problem; who had pot. The little community was a dysfunctional extended family of sorts, but when there was a crisis, everyone pitched in together. There were, and still are, around two hundred houses in total.

The community has been grandfathered into the Golden Gate National Recreational Area. Very few new houses can be built in the GGNRA; most of the vast, beautiful, wild western part of the county is forever protected from development. Hallelujah. Inland from the beach runs a narrow valley aptly named Green Gulch. When I was young, Green Gulch was a breeding ranch for world-class Hereford bulls, but later it became the home of the Zen Center, so very appropriate for the setting. The center's organic gardens are just inland from the beach and the beach is just down the road from the redwood groves of Muir Woods National Monument. Mount Tamalpais rises above it. It's a stunning, peaceful place.

Back then, the only structures on the beach proper were nine funky one-bedroom cabins set in an L-shape around a gravel-and-mud parking lot and the tavern. The cabins, which must have been built in the thirties or forties, rented for fifty bucks a month and were occupied by a collection of hipsters, young and old. My brother Lew's childhood best friend, Peter G., had Cabin Five, right in the middle. It was action central, a safe place where we could get high and talk about the universe or play music until the sun came up. An older, bearded self-styled guru named Buddha lived with his *old lady* (what a term of endearment) in one of the other cabins. He was like an R. Crumb character: *ex-biker and small time hood, this cat has a beautiful head*!

The one-story, unpainted redwood Muir Beach Tavern dated back to Prohibition, when locals ran rum from their fishing boats into the sheltered cove. It had been a speakeasy and a restaurant and was currently mostly unused. It had a great big deck in front that overlooked a scraggly, unkempt patch of lawn and the wind-blown gray-sand beach beyond Redwood Creek. To the right of the creek's outlet to the ocean was Little Beach, which was a nude beach. Oh boy, naked hippies playing Frisbee in the fog.

I grew up with Muir Beach as my backyard. From Homestead Valley where I lived it was a three-hour hike. When I was eleven my buddies and I sometimes carried sleeping bags on the trails over the ridge and camped out on the beach. In those days, there was detritus from all over the world washed up on the sand: lots of tree trunks, bottles, dead sea-lions, jellyfish, fishing gear. It was a treasure trove. And there were no safety-minded tight-assed authorities to make it "safe" and therefore no fun. We ran on the tops of gigantic boulders washed by crashing waves at the foot of the towering cliffs. We climbed the cliffs, we ran out into the extremely cold ocean, we stalked steelhead and salmon up the creek. We built huge driftwood fires and melted down cans and bottles we found. We awoke in the fog-bound morning with cold, wet sand in our faces, but it was freedom.

Man, we had it good. Kids don't get that anymore. Fear was the Russkies incinerating us with H-bombs, not child-stalking killers. We all got the *don't talk to strangers* speech when we were young, but we still hitchhiked around and slept on the dark beach with the big waves pounding and clouds rolling off the mighty Pacific. Our parents weren't scared about it, and neither were we. A fire, a pack of hot dogs, and sometimes the wildly-illicit pilfered six-pack of god-awful beer. What a life! We didn't even drink the beer that much. It tasted like cans. I didn't know what adults saw in it. Sometimes we'd put one in the fire and stand back as it exploded from the heat.

But back to being hippies.

Clover and our other "family" band that opened for us a lot, the Flying Circus, were Muir Beach's home bands. The tavern was the scene of many wild days and nights of music and drugs, guitars, and girls. It was way off the map of straight-people-land in those days, a hippie *terra incognita*. There were a lot of jam sessions, day and night, in the tavern. We played and strangers wandered in and joined in. One afternoon Mitch and I played along with a weird, stoned guy who Johnny Ciambotti knew a little named Bummer Bob. He played catatonic guitar, eyes glazed over from god-knows-what coursing through his veins. We felt like little kids playing with a weirdo. Later, Bummer Bob killed the bagpipe player with a sword as part of Charles Manson's "family." But I digress: it was usually not anything like that kind of dark. There were often hippie picnics and cookouts on the beach. Not just hippies, straight families too. There were lots and lots of musicians and artists and Zen people. Eric Burdon of the Animals was frequently there, digging the peaceful vibe. Bob Mosley from Moby Grape, one of the great bass players of the day, hung out. Blue Cheer recorded an album outside on the deck of the tavern. I must say they were horrible, even from a half-mile away. Sorry guys.

Clover played all the time at the tavern, drawing kids from Tam High and hippie surfer dudes and dudettes from neighboring Stinson Beach and far-out Bolinas further up the coast. Bolinas, "BoBo" to us, is a place that keeps itself off the map to this day by cutting down any and all signs on Highway 1 that say "Bolinas." The state of California keeps putting them up; the inhabitants of Bobo keep cutting them down. Bolinas is on the west side of the San Andreas Fault. When I was out there, I always felt like the Big One was going to hit and I would be split off from the coast and washed away by a tsunami, but Bolinas was the coolest place outside of Muir Beach.

We knew a couple of guys who lived at an isolated group of old dairy buildings perched on the cliffs above the ocean between Stinson Beach and Muir Beach called Slide Ranch. They were patrons of the arts and maybe herb businessmen.

Hah! I never asked. Like hell. They took care of us band guys. We were like exotic pets they could show off to their cool friends. Slide Ranch was an ultra-cool place to hang, far from civilization. In fact, all of west Marin was open and free. We smoked pot and rambled all over the hills, running like madmen along the rocky shores. It was our own Wild West, unknown to the straight world. No one, even the dreaded authorities, *the heat, the pigs*, cared much about what was happening out there. I don't think there were more than three or four cops for the whole west county, hundreds of square miles of open lands. During one Muir Beach gig, we were all out in the darkness on the deck of the tavern between sets, passing around a pipe. I took a big hit and, still holding it in, handed the pipe to the next guy, who to my deep chagrin was a sheriff's deputy. He took the pipe and passed it along, no comment, no arrest. The good ole days.

The morning of the outdoor gig with Creedence, we got into a little speed and a gallon of Red Mountain. We might have had a reefer or two just to mellow us out. Good combo. We started playing, but for some unfathomable reason, we sounded like shit. During the second song, a funny little guy came up and requested some song that Ciambotti evidently didn't care for. He went after the guy with his bass, trying to ram it up his ass. This set us off, since we were a bit messed up, and we pulled a *Who*, kicking over our amps and knocking down the drums. We stomped off the stage, both pissed-off and self-amused after a song and a half—too out of it to play but kind of digging the fact.

It was a beyond-terrible performance, nothing we were too proud of because we thought of ourselves as a good band. But the Creedence guys, who are quite together as human beings and were respectfully watching from the lawn, somehow saw and heard enough in our song-and-a-half to recommend us to Saul Zaentz, owner of their label, Fantasy Records. From this highly unlikely audition we were signed to an album deal. The dream of every rock band. Go figure the process that got us there. We soon found out that the Creedence guys were great guys, though I still didn't like their crappy P.A. system or the Susie-Q voice.

Sol Zaentz's Fantasy Records was a company that had made its rather prestigious name by putting out jazz, classical, and comedy albums. Vince Guaraldi's enduring classic *Cast Your Fate to the Wind*, the eternal *Charlie Brown and Peanuts* sound track, was immortalized on Fantasy's distinctive clear red and green vinyl records. They operated out of a warehouse in an industrial area on the border of Oakland and Berkeley. There was a studio area in the building. Train tracks ran right alongside the thin-walled warehouse. You'd have to stop recording when the freights thundered by. The studio partitions were flimsy — just plexiglass, sheetrock, and chicken wire. Anyone in the building could watch us record. We watched them box up records for shipping. But it was a friendly, family place and we were super-jazzed to be recording for a major label. Mr. Zaentz was called Uncle Sol.

The tape machine was an eight-track, two-inch tape Scully, a very good machine in its day, which had by then passed, as twenty-four track machines were being used by all the major studios. Mixdown was handled with a bunch of hi-fi component parts; I don't recall there being a proper mixing console. It was a far cry from what studios would become in a couple of years, that's for sure. Classical violinist Ed Bogas, a skinny, nerdy Ichabod Crane intellectual with a prominent Adam's apple, big black-framed glasses, and a great sense of humor, gave it the old college try as record producer. Ed is great guy who is very talented. Making an album with an inexperienced, wild group of rockers must have been a daunting challenge for him. He was trying to figure it all out, and so were we.

McFee played brilliantly. Check out *Lizard Rock-n-Roll Band*, if you can find our first Fantasy album. You must hear the amazing riff John made up. He combined country chicken-pickin' with psychedelic-surf-guitar meets Jimi. Johnny Ciambotti, who'd started as an upright bass player with a bluegrass band in L.A., was solid as a rock: a rock with a little bottle of white port in his overalls, and wildly different alter egos. He could be as natty as a boutonnièred mafia lawyer in a thrift-store pinstripe suit or he could walk in with grease under his fingernails from replacing a broken water pump on our '52 Chevy. Mitch held up his end on drums and had a couple of truly hot tracks when the drugs were just right. I got through the sessions somehow with a series of ill-timed sore throats, half-pints of Christian Brothers brandy, and a few performances I'd never want to listen to again. The album was pretty funky and uneven and it didn't sell, but it wasn't Ed Bogas' fault.

The problem was that most of the songs I wrote were not complete songs. I knew how to write basic chord progressions and some of my melodies were good, but other parts sucked, and my lyrics suffered from the same affliction. On *Stealin*, I sang about getting out of prison and shooting somebody. And I complained that John Fogerty was trying sing black? *Al, get real*. I didn't know about any of that stuff. Last time I looked, I was a skinny white suburban kid with a goose-necked bicycle and a chickenshit inability to steal even a candy bar from the corner store.

We could've put our heads together and worked on the songs a lot more. That remained a Clover problem until the end. I was almost the only writer, though Ciambotti had two funny country songs called *Monopoly* and *No Vacancy*. Johnny had played with a legit bluegrass band called the Valley Boys with Steve Gillette in L.A., so he had a better handle on country songs than I did. We also recorded our non-traditional and chaotic versions of Junior Walker's *Shotgun* and the stand-by *Wade in the Water*. McFee and I did write a pretty song that might have gone somewhere called *Could You Call It Love*, but once again, my lyrics were so vague that the song didn't have much point to it. *Lizard Rock-n-roll Band's* incredible guitar riff was as brilliant as the words were dumb. It started as a song of mine called *Tell Me*, but once again the lyrics were too vague and we needed to come up with something else. I think Ed Bogas came up with *Lizard Rock-n-Roll Band*. It's about a guy driving through the desert who hears a band playing, and it turns out to be lizards with guitars and a sax man "playing his scales." *When I went to grab the leader of the band, his tail came off in my hand.* Embarrassing, but original. At least the guitar lick was brilliant and original.

For their part, Fantasy didn't do much to promote our record. John Fogerty worked there in the warehouse and learned to promote his own records. He filled the trunk of his car with copies of *Susie Q* and hit the mom-and-pop radio stations and record stores from Redding to Bakersfield. He worked with an infamous old small-time gig promoter who booked him into places like Lodi and Red Bluff, and a dozen other Central Valley and East Bay high schools, roadhouses, and bars. Fogerty made it happen. All the Creedence guys were hip to how it was done. Fantasy apparently expected us to do the same. The problem was that we didn't have a clue.

It was a home-grown album, for sure. There was even a silly cartoon I drew of the band on the back cover, along with photos from Brown's Hall gigs. The cover shot was taken in our living room at 96 Laverne in Mill Valley. There we were: long hair, mustaches, hand-sewn clothes, and cowboy shirts in front of an American flag that hung as a door to a room whose walls were made out of discarded lumber from a torn-down house. But at least we had a record out on a legit label. That was the first test.

Music is like professional baseball. You get signed to the Big Club and then work your way up through the minor leagues to make the majors. In those days, it was a rule of thumb that it might take three records to build up your name with audiences and at radio stations and to get to the good album that would sell. I think the contract called for us to make two guaranteed albums, with Fantasy having an option for a third, fourth, and if we got there, a fifth. So it wasn't a total kiss of death not to blow the doors off the commercial world with our first record. We were expected to go out and play a lot, which we did, and come back fairly soon and cut another, better record which would do better.

Ed Bogas brought us in to record jingles and other bits. We played a bunch of cues for the cult-classic flick "Payday," a great film in which Rip Torn plays an alcoholic country-western star on the skids. Johnny's song *No Vacancy* is on the radio in the scene in which Rip is sitting on the can.

We played a lot more gigs, and our audience grew by

quantum leaps. We already had a bit of a fan base happening before we made our record and then we started pulling in lots of high schoolers from around Marin. We still didn't have airtight arrangements for many of our songs, but we had raw energy and we were wild and uncalculated on stage. When the chemistry was right, that is. Sometimes one or more of us might be over the top on booze or speed or pot or all three. All of us except John McFee would take almost anything that was available. Then again, the audience was usually stoned out of its gourd as well.

We played one gig at the Marin Civic Center, a very plush modern concert hall designed by Frank Lloyd Wright. Our fans ripped up the seats and threw them on stage. The Civic Center banned future rock gigs. Someone in the local press called us the Kings of Marin, though truly, we were more like the Dukes of Muir Beach. We even blew off Steve Miller at a big place called Pepperland in front of a thousand of our high school fans. He humbled us a couple of days later by giving us a tour of his office in the city, with its big, push-pin-studded wall map showing the sites of his upcoming U.S. tour dates at college stadiums and famous halls. It was hard to ignore the huge collection of guitar cases in the entryway to his office: Fenders, Les Pauls, Guilds, Gretsches, Martins. I could only afford one guitar at a time. Over the years I tried them all: Strats, Teles, Gretches, Gibsons, solid-body, semi-acoustic, f-hole, three pickups, wiggle sticks. You name it: I've owned it. I kept trying to find the model that would make me a good player. It took me thirty years to figure out that I needed to play in open tunings to sound good. Steve tried to recruit McFee to join his band, but McFee stayed with Clover out of loyalty, though he did play on some of Steve's records.

Because of the album, we got a gig in Houston. We couldn't afford to fly, so we took the train there and back. We stayed in a house of willing groupie girls who treated us well. It was our first experience with wild girls like these. I liked their accents, too. The Hofheinz Pavilion was a way bigger venue than we were used to and we had trouble getting across to the big crowd out there in the darkness of the huge hall, until I winged a long, improvised version of Bobby Blue Bland's *Turn on your Love Light*, which sort of worked. That gig was with Mother Earth, whose singer, Tracy Nelson, was a great, bluesy singer and a very pretty hippie chick. I really liked watching and listening to her. I didn't meet her, though. I was too shy.

We were starting to get the feeling that we belonged in the bigger venues. In San Diego we played some big place with the Velvet Underground and the Electric Flag with the great Mike Bloomfield. We stayed in a huge, rambling Spanish-style house owned by the local Hell's Angels. They were so clamped down on by the police that they kept their shiny choppers in their rooms instead of on the street. At the gig, we played our all-time most embarrassing song, *Come*, during which we rumbled into a Latin breakdown thing with our road crew coming on stage to beat time on bottles and rip up cardboard boxes. The shit you think is funny when you're high. Afterwards, the other bands made us look silly with their professionalism. It was a lesson, though not one we necessarily got right away. I hooked up with a girl there that Ciambotti called Lizard Woman, something about her nose. She was hardly reptilian between the sheets, however. Or maybe I have some iguana blood.

One of the guys in our road crew had grandparents who lived outside of San Diego. Their place was a gorgeous, rambling hacienda, with patio fountains and a perimeter adobe wall twenty feet high, the gardens full of sinsemilla pot plants with buds eight feet long. It was astonishing. The grandparents were old-time musicians, big musician union supporters. They didn't smoke the stuff, they just grew it. Their crop was worth a fortune. The late '60s was the golden age of pot. At gigs the sweet smell of reefer wafted through the crowds. Joints were passed along from stranger to stranger.

Far out. Peace, love, and groovy, man.

Through the old-school, small-time booking agent who also booked Creedence, we got a gig playing a Homecoming Dance at Lodi High School, in the Central Valley town later made famous by John Fogerty: *Stuck in Lodi Again.* John must have played the same gig. I guess Lodi High had lost the football game because the crowd was drunk and ugly, and they didn't like us one bit. They should have had a toke or two. Here they were, hiding in the flat expanses of the Central Valley: my old friends, the hard guys. We were doing our country-rock thing, and they wanted hard rock. We found that a lot; audiences liked country in the city and hard rock in the country. The gig got worse as it progressed, with insults shouted at us, birds flipped. We got plenty pissed off in return and finished the last set with Cream's *Sunshine of Your Love*, a song we wouldn't normally play, in three or four different keys. In a reprise of our Muir Beach fiasco, we trashed the microphone stands and kicked over our amps, making insane loud noises while doing it. Mitch knocked his drums all over the stage. Ciambotti, never one to back down, exchanged mutual unpleasantries with several young tough guys. We hurriedly packed up our gear and prepared to make a run for it while an angry mob of drunken short-hair football players and their girlfriends gathered outside the gym doors. We made a break for our station wagon, a line of Lodi cops providing cover. We were lucky to escape without a group thrashing.

Oh Lord, stuck in Lodi again!

We did a live show on KSAN, one of the pioneering FM stations that helped liberate radio from Frankie Avalon and Neil Sedaka (who Ciambotti, who had funny names for everybody, called Neil Sedato.) You have to be old enough to remember how bad AM Top 40 radio was even in the swingin' sixties to understand what a happening revelation KSAN (and KMPX) were. They were the first stations to play Jimi Hendrix, Cream, and the Doors, and album cuts from everyone that was hip. They played *Sgt. Pepper* in its entirety the day before you could buy the record in the stores. Hats off to DJs Tom Donahue and Dusty Street (Lusty Treat.) They were true Heroes of the Revolution. The show was live-cast from the state-of-the-art Wally Heider Recording Studios in the city. We did our thing pretty well, I thought. But then Tower of Power came on. *Fuckin A!* Those East Bay bad boys showed us Marin country-rock dorks how to put it down so it stayed down. I felt humbled, but energized by it all. We simply had to get better in a world that had bands like Tower of Power in it.

Despite being occasionally humbled and chased out of town, as we headed toward our second album we were drawing good crowds and the general feeling was that we were on our way. We were going to make a better record and take our rightful place as a big band. Maybe someday we'd even make some money.

***

During this period we moved to a funky old house in the woods near the entrance to Muir Beach. There was a plywood camper shell up on blocks next to the creek that we covered with plastic tarps and used for a sweat-lodge. We built huge bonfires right in the dirt road and tossed on steel engine heads and fuel pumps, whatever was lying around from our perpetual automotive repair efforts. The steel parts got red-hot in the flames. We'd crowd naked into the camper, our feet tucked up on the narrow side benches. Six people fit, but it was tight. The last one in slid the glowing engine parts with a shovel onto a metal tray on the floor. We sprinkled water on them. The heat and humidity were stifling. Ciambotti invariably farted loudly and laughed. Everyone else went, "Fuck you!"

"Cheezus H. Kee-rist!"

"You tryin' to gas us?"

We sweated and sweated. This was supposedly healthy. We needed it to cleanse our blood of the cheap wine we drank. When we'd had enough steam and fart gas, we crawled out and jumped into the icy creek for a moment, then stood around naked and steaming in the bitter air. This wasn't southern California. It was cold at the beach.

The creek flooded periodically. One morning when it had broken its banks and spread all the way across the valley, Ciambotti was up salvaging guitars and stuff floating around his room. He wore nothing but a pair of knee-high rubber boots.

I took a tool shed behind the little house for my personal domicile. When I moved in I disturbed a large clan of fat, sleek rats who'd been living with impunity under a rotting chest of drawers. They actually challenged me, rearing up on their hind legs and growling and hissing at me! But I had a broom. Out you go, rats! We also had skunks that came into the house through holes in the walls and ate butter off the kitchen table. You gotta let skunks do their thing; they're armed. In my rat-liberated shed, I made a bed and a desk using logs cut from the surrounding woods and driftwood from the beach; an old door served as platform for my Goodwill mattress. The shed didn't have any insulation, so I got a little pot-bellied wood-burning stove from the surplus store. It made the shed cozy, if smoky. I ran an extension cord from the house for electricity. I loved that place. When you don't have much, it doesn't take much to feel like you have it all.

***

The government annexed Muir Beach in '69 as part of the Golden Gate National Recreation Area. The move was inevitable and not a bad one in the bigger scheme of things. The GGNRA protects hundreds of thousands of acres of coastline and adjacent lands from wanton, unbridled development. If the coast weren't preserved, there'd be a blanket of gazillion-dollar houses shrouding the steep hills of the shorelands of Marin and Sonoma as far as the Mercedes and Volvos could drive.

But it was the end of a brief, free era. The cabins were demolished, and the tavern was, too. On New Year's Eve 1969, a local grizzled ex-biker (and small- time hood) set fire to the debris pile of redwood decking and knocked-down walls. It made a magnificent, symbolic bonfire. Nobody bothered to put it out. It was a cold, wet winter night. By morning it was a smoldering ash pile, nothing standing except the stone footings and steps and a chimney to mark the great place where the rum-runners and hippies had had their days in the sun and nights in the fog. The tavern had been the unlocked building of my childhood.

In years to come the beach would still be a cool place; the last free-running dog beach on the coast, until that was ended by the Park Service and zealous, over-amped environmentalists. I lived there in the '90s, on top of the hill above the beach in a nice house with two Explorers and a Beamer in the driveway. Highway 1—the road where there used to be a car every once in a long while making its winding way around the hairpin turns above the three-hundred foot drop-offs—was bumper-to-bumper on weekends.

By the time everybody finds something really cool, it's gone. It's strange, but it seems that finding it is what makes it go away.

DROPPED

Hit the road Jack
And don't you come back
No more, no more, no more, no more…

RAY CHARLES

There was a note from my father in the mailbox at 96 Laverne early one July morning in 1969. It said: *Your mother died this morning.* He didn't knock on the door or call. I stood there holding it my hand. It wasn't like I didn't know it was coming, but I didn't know it would be so soon. My parents weren't in the business of leveling with us about life's big issues. It was always more like: If you don't know, then I'm not going to tell you. If you do know, then I don't need to tell you.

She'd been fighting cancer for eleven years and had finally passed away at home. I'd seen her just a few days before. I was on foot, carless as I was in those days. My sisters were driving her someplace. She was sitting in the back of the car, wearing a print dress which was bright and cheerful, but she was skin and bones. Her once-graceful arms looked like pipes draped with loose, gray skin. The car stopped and she rolled down the window and told me that her mother, my Grandma Nonie, had just died. I said, "Gee, I'm so sorry, mom." I felt a stab of guilt.

I never had anything helpful to say to her in her illness, and I felt equally ineffective at that moment as well. I didn't know that would be the last time I'd ever talk to her.

She'd been sick for so long, it seemed like she would just go on. I didn't think about her death being imminent. At least when my father died I got to tell him I loved him before he went. I have the memory of those last words to hold inside of me. But not with my mom. She hung on for only one more week; I think she willed herself to live until her mother was gone. I have now come to see the way she, and later my father, carried themselves as they approached death as having a lot of dignity, for which I am today grateful. It was an unspoken life lesson, teaching by example. That's the way of the parent, since kids, especially teenagers, don't listen to advice. But we absorb the way our parents handle themselves as human beings.

But right then, I didn't think about dignity. I was in shock. I quickly walked the mile across Homestead Valley to my parents' house. I was afraid her body would still be there, but they'd taken her away earlier. I couldn't even bear to look into her room. I was spooked. There was a floor-to-ceiling mirror right at the foot of her bed and I thought that if I looked in it, I might see her propped up on her pillows in the bed, the way she had been for almost two years. I was two months shy of my twenty-first birthday. My mother would have been fifty-two that November.

Though I'd been saying to my friends for some time that it would be better when her suffering ended, when it actually came to pass, I was hit harder than I could imagine. I learned in a dizzying moment that blood is thicker and deeper than intellect. Death is visceral and ethereal at the same time, but it's only peripherally intellectual. In the inscrutable, hard way that life works, her death pushed me into the beginning of my spiritual life-journey.

As I look back on my life, I know I've always been a seeker. Even as a child I looked up at the sky and wondered why I couldn't just spread my wings—in fact, where were my wings?—and leap through it into some glorious, pearly somewhere, free of all the crapola of life, the hard guys, cold girls, homework, and terror of H-bombs. LSD drop-kicked me sideways beyond the edge of reason and gave me a glimpse of great potential. But when I came down from that high, the vision would blur, even seem ridiculous and downright frightening. But my mom's death inexorably pulled me down the steep trail into that lonesome valley we must walk by ourselves. I didn't know that I was descending into that labyrinthine maze yet. I just knew that, while I got through most of the service and memorial all right, I felt suddenly more like an adult. And one-half orphan.

My older brother Lew came down from far northern California, where he'd stayed on after college, and we drove around together, even wearing sport coats and ties for the wake and funeral. We talked as equals for the first time. We'd been of almost separate generations in our house. He was a big kid and I was a little kid, because we were five years apart. It makes a difference when you're a kid. We little kids would be up at dawn on Christmas while the big kids annoyingly slept in until seven, no longer hungering for the wish-fulfilling BB gun or toy soldiers under the tree. We'd all been sent off to boarding schools during high school, in the tradition of my highly-educated dad and mom, so we sibs barely knew each other. I'd always looked up to Lew. He stood up to my father's blustery posturing at times, even having a bit of a slapping match with the old man in the TV room during dinner once when I was home from school on vacation. My poor dad, he didn't have the heart to be a disciplinarian, so he made a lousy, non-credible one. He failed at it in the same way he failed at many things.

Thank God, my mother's wake was anything but a dreary affair. There must have been over a hundred people at our house, drinking, laughing, reminiscing, and playing piano and singing, like a cast party for one of their light opera shows. It was a grand send-off. Mom would not have looked well on a dour, whiny event. In fact, there was one person there being maudlin and she was shown the door by one of my mom's friends. My parents were part of a lively crew, educated, funny, and talented, with a taste for life that has left a glamorous picture in my mind. I drank a pitcher of something with one of the grown-ups, a man who boozily confided that he'd been the only one who really understood my mother. I guess I didn't know much about her myself.

After the whirl of activity passed, I stopped and looked around. I was worn out. My life had changed in a subtle way. I hadn't lived at home since I was thirteen, but there'd always been a home with a mom and a dad. I didn't know what to think, how to feel. I wasn't seeing my reaction with any perspective and there wasn't anyone to guide me through it. My dad was emotionally unavailable and Lew was gone back north.

Mortality had never hit me before. People actually die. My mother was gone. I'd never see her again, peering over her reading glasses with that penetrating, suffer-no-fools look. One anchor chain had been severed, and the other didn't have much hold on me. After a few days, my dad started cleaning out the house, something my mom had begged him to do for years. He replaced the cat-peed drapes in the living room and threw out a bunch of junk. I suppose he was trying to clear out his mind. He had quit drinking when my mom got cancer. His life had been a hell of guilt and suffering too. But why did he wait to do the things she'd always wanted him to do? It made me kind of mad, also very sad and lonely. I had no girlfriend right then, in fact I was in a long drought. There was no one to hold me.

It wasn't long before a real San Francisco fog bank of depression enveloped me. I reached out for comfort and the first thing I got my hand on was a bottle of bourbon that I lifted from the wake. Booze had been in my life for awhile: taco pig-out and a bottle of Red Mountain or a quart of Brown Derby, but I'd been more into pot. I hadn't wanted to screw up good, creative marijuana highs with liquor. But that changed now. I'd still been in the throes of ripping myself away from my family, battling about not going to college, avoiding the draft, living like a hippie—full rebellion. Rebel without a clue. I'd walked out on Christmas six months before my mother's death. Teenage karma. I needed something to dull the guilt and pain, the pain I wasn't fully even conscious of as pain. I couldn't face my mother's death straight-up as an issue. So I told myself I was just drinking to relax, to be cool, to be confident, but it was more profound than that. Her death had cut away the floor beneath my feet. My childhood demons of fear and failure had risen from the depths and sunk their talons into my ankles. They were going to pull me down.

Somewhere deep in me—and believe me, I know I'm not alone in this one—is a drive toward self-annihilation; a blinding, hell-bent desire for personal obliteration; a sneaky intuition that there's no self worth keeping alive. My acid-born spiritual ideas came apart in a chain reaction like that room of ping-pong balls on mousetraps they showed on TV to illustrate the A-bomb reaction. Shit was flying everywhere in all directions in my head and guts.

Did I start drinking so I wouldn't have to face my feelings and lack of self worth? So I didn't have to face myself? I couldn't even conceive that idea. I just knew that when I drank, I found some respite, some relief. Maybe I'd be somebody I liked, that other people liked. I needed that drink, that bottle, that obliteration. Everyone saw the problem long before I did. Nah, that's not true. I knew it was there almost as soon as I started. My nickname wasn't Al'C'hol for nothing. Alcohol was going to dance me around for the rest of my life. It's not always been a fun dance, though it's had its moments. Ginger Rogers with an ice pick in her hand on your shoulder. Sometimes it was fun. But other times, I slid into oblivion of the dark variety.

One night I got drunk and played with a pistol, putting the barrel into my mouth, imagining that I would pull the trigger. It was a pointless, maudlin moment; I knew I wouldn't do it. I was just feeling sorry for myself and being self-dramatic. But it was an emotional place I would return to over and over again. *Bang. Just kill yourself, you fuckin' loser.* Instead, I wrote a song about it called *Sound of Thunder.*

I sit on the floor with my rum
I cannot pull my knife or use my gun.

Though Lew headed back north after a few days, from that

time until the end of our lives we would be real brothers, no more big kid–little kid, with many things in common through the years to come: good old alcoholism, spiritual seeking, and fly-fishing. Sometimes all three at the same time. Out of sadness comes opening.

***

Clover was going in to record our second record for Fantasy. This time we were at Coast Recorders, a full studio with a big console and grand piano and Hammond B-3. It was a big, cool jump for us and it was very exciting. We thought we had some songs ready. We'd been playing ever bigger, better gigs, becoming more polished, trying to gain entry into the legit upper echelon of bands in the Bay Area. We weren't one of the San Francisco "Psychedelic Era" bands. We were six or seven years younger than most of those guys, still doing some spur-earning. But the progression was going in the right direction. More and more people recognized us as up-and-coming. We opened more shows for name bands. We played the Avalon, though our name was so tiny it didn't look like we were on the poster. That's okay. I can't remember who we played with, but I think we outlasted them.

We had a ridiculous song called *Chickenbutt*. It was a group-write that had become a mainstay at gigs. It had an infectious bluegrassy riff: McFee virtuosity all the way with once-again abysmally dumb lyrics. My old drummer chum from VVS, Bruce Campbell, played banjo on it. I had a fast yodeling bit on the end which I'd be stuck with for years. Well, I am a fast yodeler. What a talent. I should have moved to Switzerland.

I might have been a huge hit with ex-Nazis. *Yah, yah, do the fast yodeling!*

I'd written a couple of songs for this album that were later recorded by Carlene Carter: *Mr. Moon* and *Love is Gone*. Mitch played the crap out of *Love is Gone*. It's a song that had a chance, perhaps, but the verse lyrics weren't up to the level of the chorus melody. *Mr. Moon* is from a piano riff I had. It's a dreamy tune about lust and the bottle.

Mr. Moon, he's a powerful man
Pulls the ocean on the land
Makes men tell their women lies
When he comes over the rise

Mr. Moon is the one song that seemed to take on a very minor, but long-lasting life. Nick Lowe and Ian Gomm and other British pub rockers got hold of our record somehow and actually played *Love is Gone* and *Mr. Moon*. Ian recorded both songs years later, and Nick produced them on Carlene's first album. Elvis Costello sang a bit of the refrain of *Mr. Moon* on the end of *Alison* at a concert I recently attended, and Bob Dylan played it on a series of songs about the moon for his radio show. So there you go. It should have been a single, maybe. But it wasn't.

Old Man Blues was a Merle Haggard-style song about a man who lost his son to the war. There were a lot of coffins coming home right then. You watched them being unloaded on TV every night. Fifty-eight thousand of our buddies died in Vietnam while the military lied about body counts and winning an unwinnable war. The song wasn't perfect, but it did get the message across. *Sound of Thunder* reflected my alcohol-fueled, impotent suicidal impulses. *Harvest* was a song with a cool riff, but no lyrics. There was some kind of written text lying around in a vocal booth from a documentary of some kind, a PBS-style thing that talked about the Chinese sailing to the West Coast in the fifteenth century. That sort of stuff appealed to the historian in me, so I took lyrics out of that and turned them into a song contrasting the settling of Virginia with the Chinese exploration of America. Far-out stuff, no? *Do the fast yodeling thing again!*

The Band was big right then and I was influenced by their songs inspired by history. Farmers, union men, *carnivals on the edge of town.* That was the coolest. Not too many singers had taken on history, my favorite subject, in a serious way. The Homer-and-Jethro *Battle of New Orleans* didn't count, though it was funny, and *Please Mr. Custer?* Where the fuck did that come from? *There's a redskin waiting out there fixin' to take my hair.* There were gunfighter ballads from the '50s and early '60s, *Liberty Valance, El Paso, Big Iron.* I almost hate to admit it, but I loved all those songs. I could sit down and play them from memory right now. Even *North to Alaska.* What can I tell you? That was a different age. Our song had no blood relationship to a gunfighter ballad, that's for sure—and it was way out there where no one but John McFee and I had any interest in it—but at least it was original. As original as a PBS script, that is.

As on the first record and other sessions, I didn't play much guitar. It was a tough situation for me because McFee was such a great player that it made sense for him to play my parts. Usually we started with me playing, but before long I'd hear

Ed Bogas' voice in my cans, "Al, can John borrow your pick?" That was the joke signal that I wasn't cutting it. I got nervous in the studio when the light went red. Afraid to make mistakes, I didn't play well. Since I knew that I probably wouldn't play anyway, I didn't work that hard at getting better. I played well enough to write on both guitar and piano, but I didn't develop a good playing style for many years. Even today, now that I play a variety of open tunings that serve me well for performing, I still don't feel that I'm a "real" guitar player. I'm just sliding around on the strings like when I was kid, still waiting for McFee to borrow my pick. But hey, it's my studio now, so I get to play the parts.

Much deeper fears affected my singing. I tended to come down with a sore throat when it was time to cut lead vocals. It took me learning to make my own records to get over that. In a way, recording vocals is a technical issue with me. I need to listen to every syllable and make it exactly the way I like it. A good lead vocal takes me about two hours of focused singing. Being put on the spot didn't help. *Time is money, hippie: Shit or get off the crapper.*

The second record was better than the first. The songs, though still incomplete, had a little vibe to them. Ed Bogas had a good engineer, Mike Fusaro, help with the technical end. We also did some of the recording with a producer named Roy Segal, a cool, older New Yorker who had engineered for Simon & Garfunkel and made a lot of big records. He regaled us with tales of legendary sessions and songwriters from New York. He tried to get us on board with the commercial program. He harangued us in his New Yawk accent, "Come down from Mount Tamalpais, hippies! Time to make a hit record!" Roy, you were the best.

Kevin Haapala, the lead guitarist from the Flying Circus, who was a really talented pen-and-ink artist, did hand-drawn, folksy, nouveau cover artwork. Mike Walter took album photos of us out at Slide Ranch fooling around with guns, a horse, and a burro. Our image was country-hippie-outlaw, I suppose. We called the album *Forty-Niner*, for the Gold Rush pioneers, not for the San Francisco football team. The Joe Montana era was still twelve years away.

When the second record came out, it didn't get played on the radio. Once again Fantasy didn't do much to support the album. We were getting beat by the big boys: hair bands from the U.K., Buffalo Springfield, The Band, Jackson Browne, Little Feat, Steely Dan. So although, like the first album, this record didn't do anything commercially, it earned us a few fans far away, across the pond in England. That would prove to be interesting much further down the canyon.

There was some real high quality music being put out there. Ours seemed a bit rinky-dink compared to that stuff, because it was. Nonetheless, we couldn't begin to get on the radio if there was no record company promotion. Fantasy had now built a state-of-the-art building in the East Bay with high-tech studios: The house that Creedence built. We figured they could spend some money on promoting us.

But there were some better gigs showing up from time to time. The Fillmore West, Playland at the Beach, Pepperland in San Rafael, gigs at colleges and ski resorts in Tahoe. It was not quite the big time yet, but we were slowly getting more established. And we became one of the best known bands in Marin County. We settled into a long-running Monday night gig at the Lion's Share on the old Miracle Mile in San

Anselmo. The Miracle Mile. How many towns had a Miracle Mile? What was a Miracle Mile? It was a miracle of shopping? Malls were futuristic visions at that time. *Popular Science*: In the future, high-speed railways will deliver modern shoppers to domed shopping arenas in which the air will always be seventy-two degrees. Children won't ever cry and women will find the exact smart shoes they're looking for, from anywhere in the world. Dog farts won't smell. The world of the future awaits! You supposedly went to the Miracle Mile for all your high-end shopping. There was an early McDonald's: *Over 800,000 served.*

But on one end of that less-than-a-Miracle Mile was the Lion's Share, a pub in a run-down building that became a real rock hangout. It hosted great nights of memorable shows: the Sons of Champlin, new Marin resident Van Morrison, Tower of Power, "Cast Your Fate to the Wind" Vince Guaraldi, and Sly Stone's band, Graham Central Station. Everybody played there. Touring acts came through and the stars of the city scene came and jammed. Jimmy Buffet drove up in his rental car and played one night on his way to Margaritaville. We held down Monday nights, something that would be a Clover tradition for the next few years in one club or another.

We sure packed 'em in. The place was full of cute high school and junior college girls who took advantage of purposefully lax, lust-filled door guys to sneak in and drink, dance, and make eyes at the boys in the band. The place reeked of pot, pints of Jack Daniels were passed around, and the backstage bathroom was always full of partiers sniffing up the new drug, cocaine, which was suddenly the next big thing. The '60s had slid sideways into the '70s: *Totally different head, man.*

The backstage was just as crowded as the main room of the club itself. Stoned-out, liquored-up, coked-up bands—that being us and everybody else that played there—went on forty-five minutes after their sets were supposed to start. Nobody cared. The owner liked it because he sold endless pitchers of the most watered-down beer in the history of alcohol. The girls didn't care; they had more time to flirt with the band guys, and the band guys were having a blast. At last, a semi-harried Mike Walter came and dragged us away from the distractions to the stage. Like herding drunken cats.

One night Andre Pessis got a hold of a tank of helium and sang the blues to us back-stagers. He was like Donald Duck on acid, beyond hilarious. It was hard to leave and go out there and play, but out we poured onto the stage. The club was packed with the backstage crowd spewing into the club. The girls lined up along the bar, which faced the stage. I spotted a curvy redhead one night and flirted with her between sets. I managed to make out with her the second time she snuck in. *She was just seventeen, you know what I mean.* Her name was Dede.

For fun, we formed a loose aggregation of fellow country and swing musicians from Marin into a big acoustic band that played on the street below Ghiardelli Square near Fisherman's Wharf in the city. There were twelve players, more or less: Danny Morrison and the Hereford HeartStringers with Phil Richardson and John Casey and a couple of other guys and girls, one being the police chief's daughter Janice Orr, called Kitty Queen from her band Kitty Queen and the Beaver Boys, plus Johnny Ciambotti, John McFee, and me. The HeartStringers' bass player, Sean Hopper, played double string bass with Ciambotti. Hopper played bass, but his main instrument was keyboards. He was really quite talented. He could play two pianos facing each other, one hand on each keyboard. Amazing.

Huey Cregg, another guy we knew, came and played harmonica. I'd known Huey or at least who he was since Little League, where he was the star pitcher in the Strawberry league. I was last alternate all-star in the Mill Valley American League. I don't think he knew of me back then, but it's a funny thing, because I distinctly remember being in eighth grade, looking at his picture in the middle school yearbook, and thinking: I know that guy, don't I? Huey had a natural foods delivery company and was a very cool guy, a long-haired former preppie with a doctor-dad and artist-mom, Magda, who had been part of the true Beat generation. Magda's friends ran from Alan Ginsburg to Gary Snyder to Albert Saijo and other Beat poets, philosophers, and intellectual alcoholics.

We wore Hawaiian shirts and berets, and called ourselves the Aloha Street Band. We did all the funny non-rock music that we liked to listen to, everything from Bob Wills to the Mills Brothers, to old fifties songs like *Mountain of Love*. We did four-part horn section parts—modeled on the old Mills Brothers' records from the thirties—with kazoos. Somewhere, we found kazoos that looked like tiny trumpets and saxes. We were pretty good at that. Check out the oldest Mills Brothers recordings, if you can find them, for a lesson on singing horn parts and solos.

It wasn't always warm on a San Francisco night, but we got some nice crowds from time to time as the evening went along. It didn't matter: we were having so much fun playing the songs. Everyone could sing, so it was fairly grand. We should have recorded it, but that was long before hand-held cassette recorders. All proceeds that ended up in the guitar case placed on the sidewalk (usually, a couple hundred bucks in two hours or so) went to pay for rounds of Irish coffee at the good old Buena Vista Café bar down the street near the Cannery. We had a fun run with the band, but had to quit when there were a series of random drive-by shootings in the city. It only takes a couple of jerks to spoil the party.

Huey and Sean wound up playing alone at the Lion Share gigs after a while. We were open to it. Our record was going nowhere fast. The fresh energy was good and Huey had ideas about putting on more of a stage show. Huey showed up from his daytime yogurt-pushing gig with a big wad of keys on his belt loop and a harmonica or two in his pocket: a working guy to the hilt. But he was just playing at that; he had bigger things in mind, like being a rock star.

While we headlined in our little scene, we weren't selling many records and we got pissed off about Fantasy's lack of promotion. In the manner of all young bands that haven't figured out which side of the toast the caviar sticks to, we figured we could get signed by Columbia or Warner Brothers. They'd know how to promote us. This ludicrous-but-inevitable internal band-meeting babble soon leaked out beyond our inner circle and got back to Fantasy in the form of "how we'd like to get dropped" so we could find a better label. I don't think it helped that Johnny Ciambotti, in a classic maneuver that would've been a great sitcom bit, jumped across a desk in an attempt to strangle Ralph J. Gleason, a legendary music critic who was then a Fantasy Records executive. That's how to keep your deal alive!

As the situation deteriorated, there were vague threats from each side and a couple of "conciliatory" meetings that turned confrontational. In a classic drama of misunderstanding, we heard that we'd been dropped and went over to Fantasy's brand new palazzoffice and angrily cleared out our personalized coffee cups. Sol Zaentz, the company president, expected us to apologize for talking about leaving, but we didn't get that. So we actually *did* get dropped!

In our righteous how-dare-they, they'll-be-sorry-indignation, we were sure we'd get signed by another label right away. Various manager-types told us this kind of nonsense.

There were some minor overtures from a couple of labels, but they soon faded away and as weeks drifted into months, we realized that we weren't such a hot commodity after all. Record companies didn't hear hits in our demos. They liked the guitar player; that was about it. It turned out we were up shit creek without a canoe, forget a paddle. We hadn't yet had a radio hit and despite our local popularity, no one was going to take a chance on us.

We were in denial—a famously deep and wide river—and it took a long time for this truth to percolate down into our pea-brains. We were still drawing crowds of cute chickies and doing good gigs, and we were still one of the hotter bands around. Someone would sign us.

***

I followed my inner voice, playing the music that came out of my hands and head. But was it good enough? I listened to Steely Dan, Taj Mahal, The Band. Their music was so grown-up, so cool. How could I get to that depth? I kept sliding my hands around the guitar neck; I kept playing chords on the piano. I was moved by the notes and sounds I found, but in my lack of confidence, and lack of critical feedback from the band, I got caught up in trying to sound like other bands. Sometimes I was a lame version of Stevie Wonder, sometimes a crappy version of The Band.

The worst thing I found myself doing turned out to be a life-long bad habit: Poorly imitating songs I hated. Now, that's a real recipe for bad results. If I heard something that everyone liked, I subconsciously copied it in some half-ass way. The best way to avoid that was to not listen to rock music. So I spun Merle Haggard, Jim and Jesse, Bob Wills, and listened to Huey's R&B albums: Donny Hathaway, James Brown. Thank God for all of them. My doing Zeppelin would have been cringe-worthy in the extreme. But I was getting lost. And I was avoiding the music I needed to respect, the music of people who came from the same background, like Jackson Browne and Dan Fogelberg. I thought I didn't like Zeppelin or any number of other artists. Bullshit. I was intimidated by guys who were more on their game, more dedicated than me. I told myself that they were sell-outs, but I hadn't even bought a ticket to the dance.

My spiritual slide was accelerating too. Andre Pessis gave me an interesting book, Gurdjieff's *Meetings with Remarkable Men*. I instantly gravitated to the romance of the "seekers of truth," and the meditating holy men in their monasteries and walled-up caves in the deep recesses of exotic inaccessible mountain ranges. I read more about Sufism, seeking the essence. I felt drawn to it, but wholly inadequate in my ability to get there. I knew I was doomed. I became somewhat obsessed with an amorphous idea of immortality. Yet this was all so unconscious, because I hadn't looked at consciousness yet, and I wouldn't for a long time. My mother's death and this far-off, unattainable mysticism drove me into paralyzing despair and depression. I suffered and my creativity suffered. The band suffered.

An older, experienced A&R man came to listen to us rehearse. He told us to do our best five songs. Afterward, he told McFee that he was great, but advised me to lock myself in a room and not come out until I had figured out who I was, who I really was as an artist.

He was right. When I was first singing in the band in high school, I had such passion for my idealistic beliefs that my wish was to have a microphone that would enable me to reach the whole world so I could change the way people acted, the way they treated each other. In a sense, that microphone was right in front of me now, but I couldn't figure out what I wanted to say or how to say it. I was so easily blown this way and that by the stuff I heard, even by people's subjective opinions and tossed-off comments. My insecurities hounded me, drove me like a wounded animal deep into a depression in which I couldn't function. So I faked it. And I drank. And drank some more.

Naked Girls and
Lost Planet Airmen

Son, you're gonna drive me to drinkin'
If you don't stop drivin' that hot rod Lincoln...

As recorded by Commander Cody

Though the afternoon fogbank was pushing through the eucalyptus trees waving in the sea winds at the top of the ridge, naked girls were still lounging in the last of the summer day's rays by the pool. Naked guys, too. Everybody was naked! I'm not sure today whether it was our generation or whether all early-twenty-somethings go around naked as much as possible. I certainly am not privy to such cultural displays these days, but then, there's an age for covering up. *Turn, turn, turn.* The older nudies out at Little Beach, tossing Frisbees with their various less-than-firm body parts flapping were not the most attractive emissaries of middle age. *You got to know when to fold 'em.*

But these were liberated times, 1972. Ciambotti, Huey, and I were living at my dad's house for a few months. With its fenced-in backyard with the pool, it was pretty much our clubhouse. On any sunny day there might've been twenty naked girls hanging around languidly at the edge of the pool. Some were a bit underage, but old enough. Judy, Linda, Debbie, Jeannie, Terry, Pam, Olivia, Susan, Dede, Tracy. If you've got it, let it out in the sun.

It wasn't really a sexual thing; it's just that we were young and carefree and thin. I was twenty-three, Huey was twenty-one, and Johnny was twenty-eight. My dad, a fiftyish widower, was off traveling somewhere: the Galapagos, Europe, or South America. He liked trains and was riding as many of the remaining steam-powered railways as he could before they and he disappeared, I guess. You could have slapped one of those bumper stickers on his suitcase: *Spending my kid's inheritance!* So we held forth at my childhood home, enjoying our version of endless summer.

Huey was a full member of Clover now, as was Sean Hopper. We hadn't gotten that shiny new record deal yet, but we were riding on a crest of local popularity. There was a new gig, Whitey Litchfield's place in San Rafael. Whitey, who must have been in his sixties, was a real character. He was short, wiry, and tough; a film-noir pug-faced gangster with a heart of gold. Huey and Ciambotti hit it off with the Saturday-Night-Special-in-his-briefcase kind of guy, though I had no idea how to relate to a character like him at the time.

The Bermuda Palms, Whitey's place—complete with a grove of blinking neon palm trees above the marquee—was both a "ballroom" and a motel. The ballroom was a cool venue. It had been a happening nightclub in the early fifties or so, and had that movie-theater big-band deco vibe. You could picture men in tuxes and gals in cocktail dresses with corsages drinking Manhattans and listening to Duke Ellington, the parking lot full of sleek, shiny convertibles and fat sedans, the chromebumpered emblems of a booming post-war golden age. Perhaps that is the movie version of what the Bermuda Palms had been while it was probably closer to the post-war tough-guy culture, with pints of booze, plenty of fist fights, and loose broads letting it hang out in the back seats of '38 Fords. No doubt the motel, from the fifties, was more legit before Highway 101 became a six-lane freeway and left that part of San Rafael on the wrong side of the road, but it was always attached to a rowdy night club with a long bar. By the time Whitey's old culture had died off and he scraped up the idea of booking long-hair bands in the Palms, it was a welfare motel, with outlandish transvestites, hookers, and heroin dealers living in rows of dilapidated pink stucco rooms.

In other words, it was a perfect rock-n-roll venue.

There were some hot new bands on the scene that matched up well with Clover: Commander Cody and His Lost Planet Airmen, Asleep at the Wheel, Norton Buffalo, and the Tubes. Commander Cody, immigrants from the University of Michigan, made a big splash with their gonzo rockabilly. *Hot Rod Lincoln*. They quickly became darlings of the Bay Area. We had a lot of fun playing with them because they kicked our asses into higher gear with their energy and sense of humor. They were beer-swilling, pot-smoking, coke-snorting, faux-country fools same as we were: Bill Kirchen, Andy Stein, Bobby Black, Billy C. Farlowe, Lance Dickerson, and the great showman, George Frayne.

Kind of their companion band at first, Asleep at the Wheel was a mind-blowing recreation of the Bob Wills and the Texas Playboys sound that we loved. Ray Benson, a self-described "Philadelphia Jewboy with size thirteen sneakers," led a cast of very talented players including Lucky Oceans and Floyd Domino. Great names. They were musically outstanding. Ray played that Western Swing hand all the way to a Hall of Fame career. He's still going strong. They've probably played more gigs than Willie Nelson has over the years. *I Been Everywhere, Man.*

Norton Buffalo was a fantastically talented local harmonica player. He was also a good songwriter and an engaging showman. He dressed in nouveau-Roy-Rogers meets voodoo-hippie-zoot-suit chic, if that makes any sense. It seemed right at the time. He and McFee hooked up musically and personally, a pair of detail-oriented virtuosos.

Then there was an amazing band from Phoenix called the Beans, who inexplicably changed their name to the Tubes. They were insanely, but very purposefully, hilarious with their *sexaphones* with obscene painted Styrofoam tongues lolling out of the bells and with their wax-paper Elvis hairpieces. "Snowy Ramirez," who came to the U.S in a plastic bag from Peru, was one of their stage personae, as was "Ben Dover, Jr." You never knew what they were going to come up with next in their set, or show to show. They were awesome players as well.

So it was a second wave of Bay Area-based bands which had resonance with Clover. We played whatever we felt like playing, from funk to swing to country rock. We were so eclectic that we were capable of going from James Brown's *Hot Pants* to Merle Haggard's *Okie from Muskogee* in the same set. There was no coherent theme to what we did; each song was its own thing.

We often split the bill with Commander Cody, the Wheel, or the Tubes at the Bermuda Palms. The gigs were always packed with several hundred patrons. It was a fun thing, more "showtime" than the Lion's Share had been. But it got a little out of hand sometimes, like the night a group of Hells Angels mixed it up with some black guys from Marin City. Someone fired a pistol and there was panic in the hall. I can still see the audience moving like wheat being blown by a gust of wind, people pushing and running, trying to get to safety. The hippie love-in was way over, baby. The Kingdom of the Stoned Groovers had been invaded by drunken cokeheads.

With all this fresh musical blood in the scene, we had to step it up. Huey and Sean had brought something new to our music and our show. Long-haired Huey and his very New-York-Jewish partner Gilbert had a yogurt delivery business, Natural Foods Express, going pretty well. They employed a handful of our gang—the guys we played softball with—to supply hippie groceries with organic dairy products. They distributed Nancy's Yogurt from Ken Kesey's Springfield Creamery in Oregon. It's ironic that Kesey, the merriest of Pranksters, promoted a yogurt that was proudly advertised as *acidophilus*, since that sounded to me like *acid awful is*. NFE had warehouse space in industrial San Rafael with walk-in freezers and a wild assortment of stoned-out guys driving trucks. They were slogging it out, racing their aptly named reefer trucks to edge out their competition. You could go over there and get high as well. The young filmmaker George Lucas, quietly making a "Star Wars" movie up the street, sent some guys over to record the sound of Huey and Gilbert's walk-in refrigerator doors being slammed and locked. They were reverbed out and used as door-closing sounds on imperial battle cruisers.

Huey had a natural bent for organization. He was always

analyzing whatever situation he found himself in, figuring out a plan, and bringing it to fruition. At our regular rehearsals, he would *run it down* in his own style. When Huey explains something, he usually starts by sitting, talking calmly. As he gets going on his subject of the moment, he stands up and takes over, walking up and down the room, making points with hand gestures. He talks like a politician; I mean a good, smart politician á la Bill Clinton. Huey is a thorough thinker. He has a logical mind that can see a problem from top to bottom and from various perspectives. He was an engineering major at Cornell. So he can lead a process to a conclusion. He's also a natural-born charismatic leader. He was a star baseball player in his prep school. He soon assumed a leadership role in Clover, along with the ever-vocal and opinionated Ciambotti and the quiet yet logical and calmly assertive John McFee.

This is not to say we always took Huey seriously. He was not the only smart cookie on the plate. And he was the rookie. We felt that we were more experienced at the rock-n-roll game. Huey wasn't singing that much in the band at that point; he mostly played harp and sang a few blues songs, like *Peaches Tree, Barefootin'*, and *Checkin' Up on My Baby*. Sometimes *Barefootin'* turned into *Barenaked*:

> *She takes off her top and away she goes*
> *She's doing a dance without any clothes!*
> *She's Barenaked,*
> *Yeah!*

We gave Huey a nickname that came both from his partly-Polish ancestry (his mother was from a well-known Polish family of artists and intellectuals) and from his penchant for trying to talk us through the brick wall of the moment. We started calling him the Polish Bulldozer: Loud, Confident, and Wrong! The name undoubtedly came from the mind of Johnny Ciambotti, the nickname master. Johnny was the first to call me Al'C'hol.

But Huey became *our* bulldozer, and we tried many of his ideas, even if they seemed silly. For a while we wore white Levis and green t-shirts and grew goatees, a particularly embarrassing period. Over the next three years we tried this, that, and the other without much success. Ultimately, Huey would find a formula that would be highly successful. It just wasn't with Clover.

One thing that Huey added to the band is sex appeal. Not to say we didn't have some to begin with; our audiences were always predominantly female. But the guy was and is a major chick magnet, no doubt. Women just loved the guy. One day, an attractive, though culturally way different, door-to-door cosmetic sales gal, looking for the lady of the house, came by the place that Huey and I shared in Mill Valley. An hour later, after Huey had gone somewhere, she was back, looking for him. "Is your roommate around?" At our Squaw Valley ski-lodge gigs, it seemed like he always had two snow bunnies. Those of us who struck out were left with cases of snow-balls.

Huey was good-looking and charismatic, but that's well known, isn't it? He was also a thoughtful guy who was a good friend to many people. And because of his upbringing and schooling and street smarts, he could hang out with everyone from bar jocks and 2AM Club dicey ghetto cats to label heads and investment bankers.

Sean Hopper added a whole new dimension to our sound with his keyboard playing. A gear-head, he got a Hammond B-3 with a Leslie speaker and an electric piano. He picked up a van just for his gear. Sean was a smart guy, like Huey a doctor's son, who was always up on the current thing. He was the authority on which kind of speakers, or racing bikes, or rare wines, were au courant. He then went out and procured them. He was a good practicer and also a well-educated, funny guy with an infectious laugh. During the Clover era, he wasn't a big instigator; he usually managed to keep his cool when we were all flipping out in one direction or another.

The two of them gave us a bigger sound. Both Sean and Huey come from a more R&B background, so there were new influences creeping in. Hence: *Hot Pants*. Alex Call wouldn't dare take on a James Brown song, or even conceive of it. Give me a country-influenced song or a ballad. *Uh-Huh, Good Gawd!* In terms of set-up, Huey had the better deal. He just had a couple of harmonicas in his pocket, while Hopper not only bought an extra-long van but also wore a back brace to haul his huge pile of heavy gear to gigs.

Another important guy in our crew was Frank Martinet, our New York-raised road manger. Dark, ultra-cool, Latin-lover Frank was as good looking as Huey and was hit-man street-wise. He handled the money and drove the band van. He artfully and coolly steered us through many a sticky situation.

With Huey and Sean onboard, we tightened up our beginnings and endings and transitions. We now had five singers, so we worked out even bigger vocals. Huey and McFee started playing kind of horn-section lines with harmonica and pedal steel. Sounds crazy, but it worked to a certain degree. Okay, so it was weird. But it was our weird. We also had some new songs. They reflected the influences of the new guys. It was a long and wandering growth phase. There were tentative forays into styles we hadn't done before. Not all the songs were successful. We were evolving, and it wasn't clear what species we were mutating into yet.

Since I tended to be influenced by whatever I was hearing, my writing picked up more of a soul and R&B feel. I probably should have listened more to guys like me: Jackson Browne and other singer-songwriters. In many ways, I hadn't found out who I was yet. I needed to lock myself in a room, just as the A&R guy had said. Part of my trouble was immaturity. I wasn't having the kind of real romantic and personal relationships and responsibilities that I could write about. And I hadn't learned to give myself credit for the things I did feel. So I copied other people's music, and did it in a half-ass way. Deep down, I wanted to make a difference in the world, to sing into that big microphone. But I was so unsure of myself, I couldn't get there.

I loved Donny Hathaway, Stevie Wonder, and Johnny Guitar Watson. But could I write the way they do? I'm a white kid from the 'burbs. Huey and I had parties at our house in Mill Valley. Huey would go abalone diving and bring back a bunch of abs. We'd have an "ab" feed and dance party. The old house shook from people dancing in every room. I picked up progressions from all the soul records we were listening to. I grew up listening to R&B, but I could only do so much. Since I was an unschooled musician I didn't understand the sophisticated voicings that guys like Wonder and Hathaway used in their music. They were hyper-talented. I was still the kid with the two-string guitar. I see now that my lack of self-confidence kept me from writing directly from the heart. It took me going off on my own to start to get to that. But Stevie Wonder was a hell of a good influence, and I did slowly learn a lot of cool stuff.

We played a lot, often with Asleep at the Wheel, at a club in Berkeley called the New Orleans House. At first, these were great gigs but as time went by we began to have less than full houses. There might have been a passel of naked girls by the pool, but there was also a disturbing trend setting in.

It had been a while since we had any interest from record labels. Audiences in the Bay Area had seen us a bunch; you can't get your friends out to hear the same thing over and over. There was a slow decline of crowds everywhere we played. We still had some good gigs, but the direction was obvious. Without a record deal, we were going down.

I slid into one of my nose-dive funks. I tended to take everything personally, so I thought, no, *I knew*, that we lost our deal because I wasn't good enough. Maybe it was time for me to go do something else. There was great loyalty in our band. We had a large extended "family" that stuck together through crisis after crisis. In fact, we tended to protect each other's weaknesses and gloss them over, not work on them as hard as we needed. Essential things went unsaid for long periods of time. We never discussed the lyrics of our songs. What a big mistake. I needed help with lyrics back then, and we had incredible musical minds in Clover.

Despite having the new energy of Huey and Sean, there was no forward motion for Clover. I was drinking more, putting on weight, getting sloppy. I became pessimistic about our future. I went to junior college to take music classes, but I couldn't be bothered to attend after a few weeks. I went to bars instead. My relationship with Dede was on and off. I dated other girls in the off periods. It was becoming a nothing phase for both me and the band, though there was enough action to keep vague hope alive: A great gig or new producer or label would appear to put us back into the machinery of the Big Show.

The boozing got worse. After a gig at Chico State University in the Central Valley, I woke up extremely hung-over with a fishing rod propped on a chair in my motel room. What the fuck? It turned out that the night before, after the gig, I'd harangued some guy about how I wanted to go fishing the next day, and he loaned me his spinning gear. I didn't remember it at all. I felt like shit; so stupid and low. My stupid goatee floated on my now-bloated face. But rather than make the logical decision to clean up my sodden act, I decided I'd better give myself a drinking name. I came up with "Maurice Alexander." If I was going to act like an idiot, then I wouldn't sully the good Call family name. The guys on our softball team instantly took up Maurice and then started calling me Moe. Huey and Danny still do.

I wasn't the only problem drinker in the band. Ciambotti was famous for his wild booze raves. He was a different kind of drunk than I am. I'm a sloppy, maudlin drunk. I get *faced* and dumb; my features slipped and sloshed around like they'd broken loose from their moorings. *Hey baby, d'ya think I'm good-lookin'?* But Johnny was a wild man, a Dr. Jekyll and Mr. Hyde.

One night we were driving back on the freeway in my dad's Volkswagen bus from the Oakland Coliseum, where we'd watched the Warriors play the Lakers. Johnny had gotten psycho on booze. While I was driving, he took my glasses off my face and put them on his. I was blind without my glasses, especially at night. I screamed at him, "Shit, Ciambotti. I can't fuckin' see!" Johnny, with my coke-bottle glasses on his nose, said, laughing, "That's funny. Neither can I." I somehow squinted my way off the freeway into a parking lot, where I slammed on the brakes and Johnny crashed forward against the back of the front seat. Danny grabbed my glasses off his face.

Because the night was still young, maybe midnight, we headed for the 2AM Club, aka the Deuce, a classic corner boozer down the street from my dad's house in Mill Valley. Huey was there shooting pool with a guy we didn't know. Ciambotti started in with rude comments to Huey's pool partner, who was even shorter than Johnny. Huey, who wasn't particularly drunk, came to the defense of his new buddy. Ciambotti provoked a fight, trying to sucker punch Huey while holding a steel shuffleboard puck in his hand. Huey shoved Johnny over the shuffleboard table, trying to get him to cool it. We were all trying to hold Ciambotti down. But Johnny, who was laughing maniacally, broke a glass like he was in a Marlon Brando flick and came after Huey with that.

There was no stopping Ciambotti when he was lit up like this. His drunk alter ego found this kind of stuff highly amusing. It's not like he was letting out some dark, pent-up side, it was more like his idea of a good—if psycho—joke. The problem was that the rest of the world didn't find his antics so funny. The two combatants fought on out into the street. Finally, there was a break and they stood on opposite sides of the street, under the glow of the streetlight. Ciambotti held his arms out in a conciliatory way: *Hey, brother. I love you!* Huey rolled his eyes and very reluctantly went to meet him halfway in the street for a brotherly, it's-cool-man hug. At the last second, Johnny dropped and tackled Huey at the knees. The fight was back on. Danny and I stood on the sidewalk, cracking up. Then two cops screeched up sideways in their squad cars and jumped out, cracking their shotguns and shouting for the fighters to "Stop right now!" Johnny and Huey got off the street and made like they were getting into it for fun, no biggie. The cops told us all to go home, which was my dad's house right up the street. Huey had a bag of weed sticking up out of his shirt pocket; fortunately it went unnoticed.

Back at the house, things settled down. Or so we thought. Huey, Danny, and I were watching TV in the front room when suddenly a large carving knife came flying end-over-end out of the kitchen and stuck, quivering, in the hardwood floor by the heater. Next thing, Ciambotti, now wearing nothing but a t-shirt, was out in the front room. The fight was back on yet again. This time, Ciambotti got his ass branded with the crosshatch marks of the very hot floor heater. Huey was rightfully pissed and disgusted at the whole thing, which he didn't start at all. Danny and I certainly got a few good laughs out of the evening.

Johnny was a complicated person. (Aren't we all?) On one hand, he was a very open, compassionate guy who was an instant hit with almost everyone he met. He was handsome, outgoing, and street-wise. He had a great sense of humor and he was quite well-educated. He could move in any level of society with fluid ease. He could be, and often was, a wise, caring mentor and personal confidant in times of darkness.

But he was also capable of being cutting and derisive, unreachable and crude. He had a way of berating and belittling me which triggered and deepened my lack of self-confidence. He called me "Silver Spoon" because he had this mythology in his head that I came from an aristocratic family, because my dad went to Harvard and my great-grandfather was the "father of the electric stove" and founder of Hughes Electric, though the money didn't reach my generation. And I was interested in ancient history and other arcane subjects. I was raised in Mill Valley and went to a private high school (as did Huey) while Johnny grew up on the streets of East L.A. But truly, he's the one whose parents had some real dough. He went to UCLA.

I must have driven him crazy with my self-doubt. He couldn't understand why I wasn't more like him. He constantly said to me, "You've got to take your balls in your own two hands and lead yourself through this world," which was a funny image. But his mentorship was too harsh for me. It was an endless put-down without the positive feedback and encouragement that might well have made a big difference. I looked up to him. He was older, he was strong-willed. But he bullied me, and I took it like the same chickenshit I'd been in middle school.

Mitch, my childhood buddy, was getting into dangerous drugs. He'd been doing "business" for a while, so he had access to blow and heroin all the time. It was becoming a problem for the band. Most of us liked the occasional toot now and then, not that we could afford it, but heroin was different. I tried snorting a bit once and didn't dig it, and I dug *everything*. It was an obviously messed-up trip, one that was becoming increasingly popular in our scene. One of the most beautiful girls we knew got it into it because the sleazy coke and smack dealers turned the good-looking chicks on. She nearly OD'd; it was close. But it didn't serve as a wake-up call. People kept doing smack.

Mitch was not playing drums as well as he once did, and he wasn't participating fully in the band. He was slipping into a dark world that would get a hold of him for long time, though he finally got out later in life. Poor guy, coming from his abusive upbringing in his frequently-missing, alcoholic mother's cat-shit-filled house, he had a couple strikes against him from the beginning. The band offered him at least an outside chance at a better life, as had his close association with my family when he was younger, but he chose to pass on those models in favor of coke and smack. He was getting busted over and over, for dealing small amounts. Eventually we had to fire him. Huey did the dirty deed, but Mitch seemed okay with the few hundred bucks we offered in settlement.

It was sad. Mitch was my best friend from age five. I still remember the day my parents drove me over to meet "Mitchie." We were just a couple of little boys who played war and then baseball and then music. At the end, we barely spoke. At one point, he was on the lam from the law. I believe he did some time. After much travail, he's doing much better now.

We were still a good band, technically better than before, but slowly, something was slipping away: our innocent vibe. Having left our wild, untamed youth, our new course had to take us to a place we hadn't yet been: a higher level of professionalism. We were going to have to take it all apart and put it back together. How were we to find this new direction? I sometimes felt like I wasn't part of the band anymore. I wasn't writing as much, and what we were coming up with as a band—disco-oriented and dance-stepping things—were less than inspiring to me.

I started getting into fly-fishing and the American West. Huey, Frank, Bruce Campbell, and several other guys and I took a life-changing road trip to Montana in the spring of '72. We drove out there in my '57 Chevy pickup and a couple of other old junkers. It was our own fear-and-loathing trip: We were modern-day Kerouacs without the literary skills. We had blow for the drive, bags of pot, cases of beer, pints of bourbon, sleeping bags, guitars, flyrods, and even a couple of dogs. We started by driving up to Reno in the late afternoon and hitting the casinos for a few drink-filled hours and then driving all night—snorting coke and drinking beer—to Weiser, Idaho, the home of an old-time fiddler's convention and bluegrass festival.

Driving near the Oregon–Nevada state line at four a.m., I saw huge, black Carlos Castaneda monsters charging out of the sagebrush at the truck. I outraced them all. We finally got into a whitewash-sky Idaho at dawn and crashed amidst camping bluegrassers, most of whom came in RVs and camper-shells on pickups. We were way out of our normal, long-haired scene. The pickers mostly wore Stetsons and nice boots. Some couples had matching fringed outfits. There were folding chairs and tailgate parties and pavilion tents and crafts, very straight middle-America stuff. I don't think those folks had seen many long-hairs. Frank woke up on the lawn camping area in his sleeping bag at noon. He was surrounded by circles of guys in white straw rancher hats strumming, picking, and fiddling. He squinted into the bright Idaho sun and croaked, "When does it fuckin' start?"

We moseyed out of Weiser after a day or so and crossed over the Lolo Pass into Montana, and for the next three weeks we camped out on free-running rivers under the Big Sky. We fished, and beat the friendly local short-hairs in softball games, and drank and played music in the legendary old cowpoke and gambler bars in Virginia City, Montana, where Danny Morrison and other Marin expats were tending bar and playing Cowboys and Indians. Some of our buddies were up there hiding from the draft, sneaking in and out of Canada, working on no-questions-asked mining, timbering, and ranching jobs under assumed names.

Virginia City—VC, as it's called—was a real *drunkard's dream if you ever did see one*. It was a Wild West town, a one-street affair with hundred-year-old false-front red and tan brick buildings with step-sided roof lines and arched brickwork windows, and a handful of authentic saloons (way more than the tiny population should require) including the Bale of Hay, where Wild Bill Hickok once played cards. You could see the original log houses and half-dugouts, with their tiny windows and bend-down-as-you-enter doors, built by the first cowboys and miners that came there after the Civil War. Our buddies were living in them. The original Boot Hill overlooked the town. Rustlers and other outlaws were hanged up there. We went up and cracked a six-pack and lay on their graves. It was still an outlaw town. There were long-haired wannabe artists, some of them with real talent for western art, bloodshot early morning drunks, and lean, sun-baked miners and wranglers tossing back a shot and a cold one in the bars at noon. The local sheriff was in the bar as well. He had a stick-on light that he put on the roof of his car when he made an arrest. Guys had names like Knot-Hole, Buckshot, and Red. It was the kind of place where you might invent for yourself whatever character you wanted to be. It was a good place to avoid the draft, for sure.

The Vietnam War had made guys make radical moves. None of us thought that fighting and killing our little yellow brothers was a good idea. It's funny, because I grew up playing army and good guys and bad guys and all that, but when it came to the real thing: Forget it. There was no way in hell I was going to go get killed or kill someone. Not for some trumped-up bullshit like the Commie threat. As Mohammed Ali said, "I ain't got nothin' against no Congs." One man's Commie is another man's freedom fighter. A few years later, we were buddy-buddy with the people of that land of killing fields.

We all evaded the draft in different ways. Some fled to Canada, some dropped out in Montana, some painted bulls-eyes on their asses and got deferred. I was called up, but I found the ultimate way out, by using the Selective Service's own bureaucracy. The first time, I went to the induction center in grimy downtown Oakland. There were two hundred draftees in the cold, old government building trying to get into the army and four of us trying to get out. I refused a blood test on the grounds that needles scared me and was told by a gentle psychologist to go home.

Two years later, I was called up again. This time there were two hundred guys trying to get out, including the guy with the painted bull's-eye on his ass (and the guy with the dead lizard tied to his privates with a leather thong—most inventive—don't think it worked for him, though), and four young bucks trying to get in. I passed that pre-induction physical and was told that at the next one in a few weeks I should bring my toothbrush because I'd be leaving directly from there for boot camp! *Sorry, but no way, Jose.* I waited until two days after the induction physical and typed a letter on my mom's old Olivetti stating that I'd be out of town on that date and would they please reschedule me for the next one? The next time I heard from them, Nixon had resigned and our troops were being pulled off the embassy roof in Saigon.

Fifty-eight thousand of our guys died. Countless Vietnamese were killed and maimed by napalm. Thousands of vets came back broken, and they still are. You can't raise a generation on "Leave it to Beaver" and then ask them to slaughter women and children. It was way too schizophrenic. America's egomaniacal leaders conducted a proxy war with the Soviets and the Chinese, and used our schoolmates, our buddies, as machine-gun fodder. It was as obvious then as it is now. A shameful waste. *All we are saying is give peace a chance.*

That Montana trip made quite an impression on me. I'd always pictured it as a bit of Shangri-la. My dad was born there and summered at ranches when he was a teenager and regaled us with tales of tough cowpokes, quarter-horses, cattle drives, and starry nights around the campfire. He tried to recreate that for us in the Sierras during our California childhood and succeeded to a pretty high degree. Some of that old Montana was still there in '72. We camped up in the Pioneer Mountains and caught cutthroat trout and cooked them in bacon grease in a skillet over an open pine fire and washed them down with iced Budweiser and pints of bourbon. We drove on gravel roads over high ridges—where snowfields lay back in the aspen and graced creases of the bare peaks—and through wildflower-starred meadows. We saw the lonely old log cabins out on the open slopes, falling back into the earth log by log. "One more payment and it's all ours, honey," read the postcards. The state wasn't much touched by tourism yet, though that would change in time. The roadside bars and mercantiles still had jackalopes and elk heads above the bar and wagon wheels on the wooden sidewalks not because of tourists, but because it was Montana, dammit! We came up against some tough, hard-working men with short hair and sun-and-wind-burned leathery faces who turned out to be good guys, once you bought 'em a beer and talked some fishing.

The day we drove down out of Idaho through the Lolo Pass into the Bitterroot Valley of western Montana, my beat-up grey '57 Chevy pickup, the one with the Appaloosa Horses logo on the driver's door, broke down. Frank wrenched on a new distributor under a funky corrugated metal awning next to a gas station/auto parts store where the Lolo Pass road met the then two-lane Highway 93, the north–south main artery of the Bitterroot Valley. Towering black-bottomed thunderclouds were rolling up the valley from the south. Snow-capped peaks rose into the sky to the west. A warm wind blew through the lodgepole pines and cottonwoods. The country was big! It was beyond words. My heart said to me: This is the place, this is where you belong.

Someday I'd be back. For a while, anyway.

THE SCOREBOARD

Aahh, ahh, ahh, ahh
Stayin' alive, stayin' alive...

THE BEEGEES

After being in Montana, returning to the Bay Area was a real letdown. The Bermuda Palms was history. Whitey had given up the ghost and the mean-streets people took over his motel for good. It hadn't been but a couple of years since the San Francisco second wave of Commander Cody, the Tubes, the Wheel, and the rest, but things were radically changing. We still had a few good gigs, notably at the Keystone Berkeley, but it was so plainly slipping away from us. We'd lost the old Clover wild boys thing and hadn't come out on the other side of that ol' lonesome valley. Our new sound didn't mean anything, yet. We were finding it hard to get it up for our regular rehearsals; there was nothing to look forward to. Still, we were Clover; we'd made two records. A producer came up from L.A. to check us out. We were so lackluster in our rehearsal showcase that he never bothered calling back. We started getting desperate for gigs.

There was a new club in San Rafael, the Scoreboard. It was

just what the name implied: a sports bar with a swinging-singles vibe. The name had just been changed from DiscoWrecks. The chromed-up front end of a Chevy Impala stuck out of the wall, like it'd come through from a high-sped impact and was now hanging out over the bar. The Scoreboard was a place where *wild and crazy kind'a guys* went to score. There was no scent of patchouli oil about the place, no incense, not a hippie thing at all.

The hippie era had died. Guys had mustaches and wore burgundy polyester suits and platform shoes. Women were into heavy makeup and pouffy perms. Sequins were in, as well as wide, drippy collars on men's shirts. Long hair—slightly long, insurance-salesman long—had become the mark of the sleazy guy: a smile on the face, cocaine in the pocket, a stab in the back.

The Scoreboard was run by a short, oily fellow whose oversized blonde wife had tits that very much resembled footballs in shape and size. This odd couple was from the East Coast somewhere, perhaps Miami. They gave off a porn background vibe. The wife's daughter was a pretty good looking girl. One night she hit on Huey, who was intrigued. She seemed a nice girl with all the attributes that the average superficial dude found attractive, but she was wasn't hitting on him for herself, but for her mom. She said to him, "Do you have any idea what kind of pleasure a woman like that can give?"

But Clover needed a gig. Any gig. The owner liked us, especially Johnny and Huey. Those guys could hang out with anyone. The owner might as well have been from Porno Mars as far as I was concerned. I had nothing to say to him on any level, besides, "How many drink tickets do we get?" It was a three-set gig, something we'd wanted never to do again. But, hey, it was a gig. We couldn't get by on one or two college gigs a month.

The little sleazeball wanted us to wear band outfits, so he bought us these fucking off-white disgusting made-from-old-motel-curtains leisure-suit type things which we wore over flop-collar rayon shirts so stretchy that they couldn't have been torn apart by two sumo wrestlers pulling on the sleeves. We looked like disco guys. It was horrible and demeaning, but we didn't have anything else going on, so we went along with it. Huey was in his goatee phase. Leisure suits and goatees. What next? Sequined jeans? It's amazing what you buy into when you're not happening.

We also played a funky roadhouse spot, way out past Sebastopol in Sonoma County, called Uncle Sam's. It was a biker bar. On a good night, a huge hairy guy got you in a meth-fueled love-fest headlock and drooled on you while he exhaled stale beer fumes in your face and said, "I fuckin' love you, man!" *Sure pal, me too.* Once, after a particularly rousing night with bikers and their unfortunate women (who came in two types: large in the rear from riding hogs and bikers, or the skinniest, zit-pocked speed-freaks you ever met) Danny Morrison and I drove the fifty miles back from Uncle Sam's to Mill Valley with a case of Bud longnecks in my MGB. We tossed the empties out on the road as we finished them. We got pulled over a block from my house. I irately slurred that "I fuckin' live right around the god-damn corner, ocifer! I fuckin' grew up here, man!" There must have been fifteen beer bottles behind the seat. Amazingly, he let us go. That would cost my license and freedom in this day and age. It was not my finest moment.

Oh my God, how the world had changed in such a short time. Instead of free-form dancing under strobe lights, everybody was doing the hustle. It was urban line-dancing. I suppose it was fun. Our girlfriends all liked it. I was no good at it—I'm a free-form dancer—but Huey and Sean were both good hustlers. They'd get off the stage and go out on the floor and lead the group. This evolved into a dance bit that Huey and Sean began doing on stage: the *Chickenfunk*, a child of the hustle. We'd play *Hot Pants* or some other funk groove, and they'd do this dance.

Funk grooves weren't my thing. Not that I didn't appreciate them, but we were doing a very poor imitation of great black music. Sonny Boy Williamson was great, but white middle-class blues bands, of which there were three on every corner, sounded boring and pointless. That's what you did with your musical opportunity? The small audiences seemed to like our clownish dancing and half-ass funk grooves, but we hardly had much of a Clover audience, it was just whomever happened to walk into whatever dive we were playing that night, like the polyester creepazoids who showed up at the Scoreboard, looking for perm girls who'd give them blow jobs in the parking lot for a couple of toots. We played another small dive on Union Street in the city, as well. The stage there was behind a waist-high railing, so when Huey and Sean did their *Chickenfunk* thing, you could only see them from the waist up. You couldn't even see their fancy footwork. Watch them turn to the right; turn to the left, no, back to the right again. *Whee!*

This was very depressing. I was struggling with alcohol. I'd quit for a while and then start again. These gigs didn't help. It was so dead-end, plus the music wasn't ours anymore. One night at the club on Union Street, Johnny had a crazy vodka night, going psycho in the kitchen of the club. I was dry for the moment. It could just as easily have been me being fuckin' out of it. I looked at McFee and wondered what the fuck we were doing. I didn't know why John stuck around, aside from his deep sense of loyalty. He'd been offered other gigs. He could have been playing with Steve Miller, Van Morrison, or the Doobie Brothers.

I can't remember writing much during the Scoreboard stint, though I guess I did a little. The soul influences weren't helping me. I was trying to write things that sounded like the Jackson Five and Earth, Wind, and Fire, for Chrissake. It was disco fever time and we were "hustling" into it in our John Travolta suits. Clover goes disco. No wonder I didn't think "Spinal Tap" was funny the first time I saw it. It seemed like a real, very depressing documentary.

Disco sound had taken over to the point where our main criterion for a drummer was that he could play the offbeat hi-hat disco beat. Since we'd canned Mitch (who could do this beat), we'd been through a few drummers. They were all good guys. "Madman" Kirk Harwood had the gig for a while. His thing was to do a long solo during which he went out into the audience and beat on tables, on people's drinks, on the dance floor. Like I say, he was a cool guy, but this kind of thing was completely cringe-worthy. We finally found a decent drummer in Mickey Shine, a New York transplant who could do the offbeat hat and keep good time.

I was gaining weight around my Budweiser consumption. I'd always been a skinny guy, but with my non-stop drinking, my weight ballooned from 160 pounds to 220 pounds over the course of eighteen months. I kept thinking I'd skip lunch and lose the weight, or I'd quit drinking. But I wasn't doing it.

During this time, as we played the Scoreboard and other dumps, we had a succession of managers who kept trying to bring labels to gigs. At Keystone Berkeley one night, some top execs from Warner Brothers came to hear us. We played pretty well, and they hung out in the dressing room while we poured down pitchers of that famous weak Keystone Berkeley beer. But they passed on the band. Later, I heard from a girl who knew one of them that the reason they passed was because they saw a drinking problem. I didn't pass her insight along to anyone in the band.

Because I knew I was the problem.

Hotpants, lookin fine, walkin', feelin' mellow.
Give me the fever, like any other fellow.

The world seemed to have been taken over by a sleazoid disco army wearing platform shoes and leisure suits. Where was the Country and Western music? Where had Bob Dylan gone? The Band? I wasn't even wearing black anymore. Now it was blue rayon stretchy shirts with enormous collars and pants with a line of sequins down the side. My depression and my drinking had overwhelmed me and I had morphed into a bloated, fucking mess.

One day as I walked into Jolly King Liquors in Mill Valley to buy even more beer, my old junior-high nemesis Allan Acree—hard-guy hair still greased up—was sitting on the sidewalk. Alan wasn't king of the hill anymore, he'd fallen on drug-induced hard times. He'd peaked in junior high and everyone knew it. It had been fifteen years, and I didn't think he'd even remember me, but he squinted up into the sunlight and said, "Hey Alex, you're really putting on some weight." Holy shit! Even Allan Acree thought I looked like crap. I knew then I had to change myself. I couldn't go on like this.

I decided to shave off my god-damn fucking goatee.

THE ROAD BACK

Get back, get back,
Get back to where you once belonged...

THE BEATLES

Despite my personal doldrums and the nowhere clubs we found ourselves playing in, we were still a good band. We rehearsed without fail at a studio in San Rafael and we were tight. We did things no other bands did; some *a cappella* stuff, like Sam Cooke's *Chain Gang* and the old Coasters' song, *Keep On Rollin'*. As weird as they might have been conceptually, the harp and pedal steel "horn" lines were unique. We could still blow people away when the gig was good and the audience had some savvy. That's why the Palomino was a good spot for us.

The Palomino Club in North Hollywood was a place that should have been preserved forever, turned into a Museum for a Time That Never Was, though it unfortunately died a club's death after a few years. It was a Country and Western nightclub out in the San Fernando Valley, far enough off the Sunset Strip–Beverly Hills power grid to seem like it was in Bakersfield. There wasn't much around it, just industrial sites, power lines, and porn-shop-graced billboard-lined dirty streets that stretched off into the smoggy night. The Pal was a holdover from an earlier era, the age of yodeling cowboys or something like that. I don't know if that time ever existed outside of MGM lots or the western reaches of the pre-tract-house San Fernando Valley, where they must have filmed those old, cheapo B-cowpoke flicks.

The Palomino was a good place for music people to go and drink and pretend they were in the sticks, while still doing the biz. The waitresses were gorgeous and ever-so-friendly. They called you "sweetheart" and "baby," like Southern girls. There were always a lot of well-known pickers hanging out. It was the only club in that part of L.A. where real country acts played. One night we opened for Roy Rogers. Yes, that Roy Rogers and his wife, Dale Evans. Merle Travis was backstage, telling us the tale of writing *Sixteen Tons*, about working at the mine and trying to pay off the company store. He had a bolo tie made with a token that he was paid with for working at that famous mine. Merle had a star's face: it seemed just a little bigger than normal folk's, like it was from a cartoon on a restaurant wall, tiny body, big ol' head. He held court in the band room. Hailing one of the sweethearts of the bar, he ordered a double Bloody Mary, "vodka in one glass, Mary in the other." When the pretty waitress brought it, he downed the vodka in one gulp. With a twinkle in his eye, he said, "I hate the taste of this shit, but I love what it does!"

This gig was more like it. There was a top sound system and real stage lights. The stage was angled in the corner, facing both the tables and the curved bar. The patrons were attentive, knowledgeable, and appreciative. Though it was a small place, it was Big League, and it was where we wanted to be, even if that night's pairing with Roy Rogers was a bit odd. We played a more country set than usual. Huey and Sean canned the Funky Chicken. We sounded good, tight. I was momentarily off the sauce and therefore present. McFee played brilliantly. Huey was busy both accommodating and fending off busty waitresses. The only problem was that I was wearing a yellow-and-green "Fuckin' A's" t-shirt beneath my thrift-store sport coat, in honor of the rowdy, long-haired, mustachioed Oakland Athletics. There I was in the back room, talking to Dale Evans, who was so straight she made Nancy Reagan seem like a wild groupie, with the word "Fuck" in big green letters showing between the lapels of my coat. Ah well, I guess she knew the word, anyway. But I'd grown up watching Roy and Dale and Roy's palomino Trigger and Bullet the wonder dog on our old, tiny black-and-white TV. I should've worn another shirt.

I had finally had enough alcohol before New Year's Eve, 1975. I'd announced that I was going to stop at New Year's, but made myself sick of it all by Christmas and just quit. No more hangovers. No more blackouts. I started playing basketball two hours a day and eating almost nothing. By April, I'd lost more than sixty pounds. I was now ready to rock. I wasn't going to be the reason Clover wasn't successful.

My transformation was just one part of Clover's resurgence. Our rotating drummer position had been filled by Mickey Shine. We'd stopped playing the Scoreboard, though the court ordered us to pay back the owner for the leisure suits he bought for us. And our new sound was at last beginning to form into something viable.

There were a couple of new gigs: a place in Marin called River City that was hip and a club in Fresno called the Wild

Blue Yonder, which we played as we went down to L.A. to play the Palomino and another big club in big Hermosa Beach. The leisure suits were ungracefully relegated to a landfill, where they'll be slowly unraveling for the next ten thousand years. We were back to California hip: football jerseys, tank tops, tight jeans, stuff we wore day-to-day. We wouldn't look or sound out of place opening for Jackson Browne or the Doobie Brothers. That's what we set our sights on.

What a relief it was for me to look in the mirror and see myself again. In fact, I looked better than I ever had. Now I was in my glory days. I was twenty-six and skinny. My hair was long and I ditched my old wire-rimmed glasses and got contacts. That horrible, facing-stealing goatee was gone, shaved off and washed down the drain. That was the best shave I ever had. At least I could look at myself and know that my sloppy drinking and beer-gut weren't the problem anymore.

People started liking Clover again. There was some interest from L.A. labels and there were managers. A guy named Joe Gottfried, who Ciambotti dubbed "Joe Gottbucks," financed a studio stint with Keith Olsen, who'd just produced Fleetwood Mac. Jeff Pocaro, soon to be in Toto, played drums on some cuts. It turned out well, though we felt a little like field workers compared to the rich cool guys, who seemed to be in on a private joke they weren't interested in sharing with us. Personally, I had a hard time getting into the new yacht Keith was buying. Maybe that's because I was still making fifty bucks a week, on a good week.

One interesting character we met was a songwriter from Nashville, John Hurley. He wrote *Son of a Preacher Man* and a bunch of other big hits. He became an advisor, a mentor, to us.

He was a hopeless alcoholic—on a different level from me in terms of the sauce—but when he wasn't disappeared on a deep bender, he filled our ears with tales of how it was done.

One night in L.A., we were invited to a party at some studio. There were ten-foot lines of coke on a counter. Literally. There was flowing booze, hot girls, and guys with overly-stylish L.A. haircuts and expensive sunglasses. B.J. Thomas was there. He'd had a string of big hits, including *Raindrops Keep Falling on My Head*. Hurley told us to watch him pitch a song to B.J.

The party had been going on for some time. B.J. was holding court on a couch in an office, surrounded by a circle of coked-up sycophants. He wanted to hear John's new song. Hurley kept telling him, "Hang on. Not yet." B.J. seemed irritated at having to wait. Finally, John finessed B.J. down a hallway full of women with luscious, alluring fake boobs into the studio's crowded control room with its big monitors. He said, "You've got to hear this, man, I wrote it for you."

B.J. gave him a sure-you-did look.

The song came on. It was a good song, quite commercial. People were nodding their heads.

"Is it cool?"

"I think it's cool."

It was cool, but not great. B.J. listened with his head down, intent, giving it his best attention. When the song was done, he turned his head slowly to John and said, "Hey, don't fuckin' shit me, Hurley."

Hurley laughed. "Okay. I'll stop fuckin' with you, brother."

Then Hurley started the machine again. The next song was a pure smash, a ballad called *Give Them One More I Love You*. It was a great song, a whole different mountaintop of song, a Grammy song.

B. J. grinned. Hurley grinned. Yeah, it was a great song. Hurley had scored by stringing him out, by playing a not-so-great song first, making the moment dramatic, and then hitting him with a real hit. It was a fun dance to watch, and a big lesson. The problem was that we didn't have that kind of song. Hurley was smart enough not to pitch his great songs to us: We didn't have a record deal.

We played the Palomino frequently. It was a blast to be out on the road again, playing good gigs, and the bright lights and neck-snapping girls of L.A. were calling to us. One night an English drummer, Pete Thomas, who we knew from John Stewart's band up in Marin, brought a couple of chums down to hear us. Pete was originally from the British pub champs Chili Willi. He later ended up as Elvis Costello's drummer in the Attractions, and he's still holding down the drum fort for Elvis.

He had with him a chap named Nick Lowe and a singer, Paul Carrack. We knew of Paul, the lead singer of the British rock band Ace, who had a big hit with the great *How Long*. We were fans. Nick wasn't yet known to us. He was the former bass player for the Brinsley Schwartz Band, heroes of the pub rock scene in London. Nick was as outgoing and loquacious as Paul was reserved and soft-spoken. Nick told us the Brinsleys really dug the old Clover records. They alluded to us in one of their songs, and actually played my song *Love is Gone* for a couple of years. He was there with one of his managers, Andrew Jakeman. We hung out. It was very gratifying to know that these hip English musos liked those Clover fantasy records, the ones I thought should be melted down and turned into Frisbees.

Meeting and hanging out with Nick and Jake led to us going to hear a British band, Dr. Feelgood, at Winterland.

The Feelgoods were a hard-slogging cockney blues band. Lee Brilleaux was their singer and harmonica player and their guitarist was simply named Wilko. They came to Marin and we showed them around. It was a whole new world for us, these guys with their thrift-store suits and skinny ties and short hair. They were so pasty white they looked like they'd never seen the sun, so I guess it was a new world for them, too. We brought them along to a private party in Palo Alto, where they sat in. Lee, who was quiet off-stage, got up and sang on the old blues standard *Checkin' Up on My Baby*, which was usually Huey's song. From the opening note, Lee was transformed from a mild-mannered working-class Brit to a spazzy wildman, blowing on the harp and lurching around the little stage. The people went crazy. We dug it, too. We'd never had anyone turn to the drummer and scream, "GIVE IT SOME FUCKING STICK!" before.

I guess the Feelgoods and Nick talked us up a bit back home. Apparently, Wilko raved about McFee. Why wouldn't he? Andrew Jakeman had the notion that we could come to England and do what the Eagles had just done. The Eagles recorded their first album there and had a hit with *Witchy Woman*. Our five-part harmonies were in the same vein as theirs. We had the same California sound, rock with a bit of country. Jakeman thought the time might be right. He and his partner Dave Robinson went to Phonogram U.K. and made the pitch. Once we knew someone was coming to hear us, we set up an ambush back at home.

We decided that we'd stage a show in a warehouse in Marin: full stage with lights, free bar, place packed with the best-looking girls we could find. Then the gents from Phonogram would fly in and we'd do a killer show for them and hopefully set the hook.

It worked perfectly. The Phonogram executive, Nigel Grainge, and his associates were ultra-London-hip and our age, anyway. Mickey Shine had the bright idea to call local FM stations and tell everyone to come on down to the warehouse, which was soon jammed with awesome California girls. We played a tight, well-rehearsed set while the girls, some of whom were our girlfriends, fawned over the charming and charmed British men. Nigel seemed to have a very good time. Within days, Jakeman sent back word that Phonogram might sign us, though they'd want to hear new material. Jakeman and Robinson decided to chance it and bring us to London to make it work. Nick Lowe would oversee preproduction and we needed to come up with enough songs for a record. We'd be winging off to London within weeks. It was sudden and unanticipated, but it was a rebirth for Clover. We jumped at the chance. London!

I stared at a map of England. There were so many famous place names on it: London, Dover, Liverpool, Bath, Canterbury, and York. I'd always been a history buff: Stonehenge, Romans, Druids, Vikings, Normans, Plantagenets, Queen Victoria, Lawrence of Arabia, Churchill. I went to England with my family when I was ten. At our dinner table we had a required after-dinner game in which we kids had to name the kings and queens of England back to Ethelred the Unready. I remembered a lot from the childhood trip because I'd been just the right age for castles and history. Nowadays, London meant the Beatles and Stones, the Who, Led Zeppelin, mods and rockers and all that. Was there destiny at work here? It's the unexpected events, both good and bad, that shape our lives. This was certainly unexpected. Out of the proverbial fuckin' blue, as Ciambotti might say.

We said goodbye to our friends and girlfriends and flew off into that blue on August twenty-third, 1976. There was a magnificent lightning storm out at sea overnight before we left. Around midnight, there were brilliant flashes of light across the sky. It was so strange that Dede and I got up and drove all the way to the top of the ridge overlooking the ocean. There must have been hundreds of lightning strikes. I couldn't recall ever witnessing a similar event. Huge thunderstorms are so rare in San Francisco that I took it as an omen of good things to come.

LONDON CALLING

I'm leaving on a jet plane
Don't know when I'll be back again...

JOHN DENVER
(How the heck did he get in here?)

Gray clouds scudded across the wind-blown fall sky, mirroring the gray buildings of the low London skyline. We piled into a couple of the ubiquitous black cabs and excitedly craned our necks to see the sights as we drove through the chaos of the unfamiliar streets. Every once in a while we'd glimpse a landmark: the Thames, Harrods, Speaker's Corner.

We'd nearly been turned back at the airport. We didn't have work permits and claimed we were just tourists, though we looked like an unlikely group of Buckingham Palace gawkers in our rock duds. And we reeked of high-octane transcontinental flight hangovers. But we had blagged our way through the brightly-lit passport checkpoint manned by stern and suspicious customs officers and we were in London, baby. It was hard to believe that we were actually there and that it looked like we were finally going to make another record after five years. After all our hard times, we'd clawed our way back up to the edge of the big time.

We all felt a sense of vindication. But perhaps Johnny Ciambotti, John McFee, and I felt it a bit more. We were the ones who'd had a record deal and lost it. We never stopped believing that we'd make it back. Maybe we'd just been too dumb to admit defeat.

Being in London was a bit like being kids in a candy shop, for sure. London fucking England, man. It certainly wasn't like being in Lodi. Our management, Dave Robinson and Andrew Jakeman, put us in a tourist hotel on the north side of Hyde Park, near their office off Queensway. It was typical little cheap tourist hotel, a former townhouse carved into tiny, multiple-bed rooms, but with balconies overlooking the streets of a nice neighborhood. There were a few trees and a few shops, lots of hustle and bustle. Nottinghill Gate was not too far, nor was Portobello Road, home of the famous mod flea market. As we wandered there, we imagined John, Paul, George, Ringo, Mick, and Jimi hanging out, buying hip threads. London was so exotic, even to cosmopolitan San Franciscans. There were stylish men in suits, older women in print dresses and warm coats, girls with too much eye makeup, and the dark-blue-black-clad Bobbies (who the cockney Feelgoods called "the filth," pronounced "filf"), everyone carrying brollies against the frequent splattering of passing rain showers.

There were bookstalls, chemist's shops, tiny, untidy markets that seemed to sell mostly hard candies, black London cabs, Tube stations, fish-and-chips places, open-air Middle-Eastern doner kebab joints (where they sliced the ground mystery meat off a huge, slowly-turning spit, pushing past a few flies to get at it, and dropped it and some vinegar-soaked lettuce and onions into half a pita bread), and lots of neighborhood pubs:

the Queen's Head and Thistle, the Bunch of Grapes, Churchill Arms, the Stanhope Arms, the King's Arms, the King's Head, the Cock and Bottle, the Hope and Anchor (called by our new friends "the Hopeless Wanker.")

Hyde Park was right down the street, across Bayswater Road. Chelsea, Knightsbridge, and Kensington were across the park. We were within walking distance of Embassy Row, Kensington Palace, and further to the east was Speaker's Corner. For me, London was full of history both ancient and recent and it was very glamorous. I could picture Henry V, Queen Victoria, Sir Richard Burton, and Winston Churchill passing by on horseback or in carriages or sitting in the back of graceful, long-fendered black Bentleys on the streets where we now walked. I looked at the skies and imagined Nazi Stukas dropping screaming bombs through bursts of flak from the anti-aircraft batteries.

Nick Lowe acted as our liaison and guide, a job for which he was well suited, as our tour seemed largely to consist of going to pubs. He took us to the Churchill Arms, near the Kensington Palace at the west end of Hyde Park, where we met Dave Edmunds, Billy Bremner, and other rockers. We quickly learned British pub etiquette: each one buys a round and passes his smokes around the table and then it's the next guy's turn. That's the way it's done. It made for a good communal evening around the table or at the bar. Tobacco was seemingly unavoidable; there was no pot to be found, a serious blow to us California hippie potheads. Hashish, more easily smuggled past the notoriously tough customs officials than pot, was heated with a match and crumbled into spliffs filled with tobacco, preferably from strong Senior Service brand smokes.

Hash was highly illegal; Her Majesty's government had harsh penalties for possession. So we were very discreet. We were foreigners and phony tourists; we could quite easily be expelled from the country.

Nick, in any case, was a gent who seemed to prefer a pint to a puff. The pub was a natural home for a talented raconteur like Nick. Pub life was different from our home bar culture. It was more about discussion and storytelling than about mindless staring at football on TV, though football matches—boring soccer to me—were up in a few places. Pub life seemed to be passionate rather than passive. Nick regaled us with fabulous stories of his rock life. He'd been on the road with the Brinsleys and had opened for Paul McCartney and Wings and had Elton John open for him. He'd played all over the U.K. He mixed his tales with wonderful humorous bits and insights into the personalities of those household names. Until Nick told us, we didn't know McCartney could hold it all the way from Glasgow to London while drinking beer on the bus with the band. If he got off at a roadside stop to pee, he'd get mobbed. This seemed like very glamorous, valuable, inside information.

We were booked into a modest recording room called Eden Studio with Nick producing to work up our material for the record. Nick had a unique style, one that earned him the nickname "Basher." When recording, he didn't like to get too worked up about getting a perfect take. He just wanted to get the basic shape, just bash it up on the speakers and see how it was working, then refine it. It was about energy and form, not the finer points. This was a technique that would suit me well later, in my home studio. Basher Two: The Sequel. (But I'm not as literate as Nick.)

Our schedule was to get to the studio around ten or ten-thirty, half-ten in British parlance, get some sounds up, listen to yesterday's stuff, and get the juices flowing. Right at half-eleven, Nick would look at his wrist as if he were wearing a watch, and say, "Sun's a bit over the yardarm, lads!" He meant that the pubs had just opened for the day and it was time to get that prime-the-pump pint or two in before settling down to anything serious. So off we went to the local for a couple of lagers and a pork-pie until one o'clock, when it was closing time again. Not like the Montanan cowboy bars, or even Mill Valley's Two AM Club, where there were serious patrons in at seven in the morning, getting limbered up for grueling day ahead. The public house was a bit more civilized, but then again, one had to pound the pints before the bell rang.

Now we were ready to make some noise, which we did, with occasional breaks for trays of tea with milk. One shouldn't be fooled into thinking that the Brit tea tradition is some sort of pinky-off-the-cup sissy thing: there are English teas so highly caffeinated that they make your heart beat funny. This was the stimulant that enabled the Brits to conquer the world and withstand the Nazi Blitz. The daily tea ceremony was a lovely high-voltage pick-me-up-until-the-pub-opens-again tradition.

We were cutting basic tracks, overdubbing guitars ("Al, can I borrow your pick?"), doing vocals, experimenting. We needed the sound of rain for *Raining in My Heart*, so we stuck a mic in the studio's shower and ran the water. We stuck a mic out the front door as well, since it seemed to rain about every twenty minutes or so. We also tried singing in the bath for the tile room effect. We were having fun, and it wasn't too serious yet. We were still trying to figure out how to create a marketable sound out of our diverse elements—the old Chickenfunk/bad-white-boy Earth, Wind, and Fire sound vs. Al's vague message songs. Was the ground-breaking new album coming together? Not quite, but there wasn't any panic. Yet.

Robbo (Dave Robinson) and Jake (or "Jacko," aka Andrew Jakeman) had come up with a project to help pay the bills until we started generating some income. We were going to be the studio band for the famous swingin' sixties model Twiggy, who'd been signed to Phonogram and was going to make a record in Hilversum, Holland. The label wanted her to sing one of my songs, a ballad called *I Lie Awake and Dream of You*. It would be my first cut by a signed artist. It seemed like a bit of a joke. Twiggy? What we knew of her was the old image of ten years earlier, with a little boy haircut and oversized black eyelashes, the ultimate sixties androgynous look. It wasn't like Aretha was cutting my song, but what the heck.

We met Twiggy at the Phonogram studios. Her real name was Leslie and she was no longer so twiggy. She was quite pleasantly curvy and had long blonde hair, her famous bright eyes, and a quick, funny smile. She was quite at ease with who she was. She could play the supermodel diva, or get down with the band and apply the humorous needle in a cockney, street-smart way. I don't know if you'd say she had a legendary voice, but she could carry a tune. Rehearsals went smoothly. We flew off to fabled, wild Amsterdam. We got the VIP treatment at Heathrow and boarded the plane first because of Twiggy's star status.

This was a whirl for all of us. I was trying to roll with it. I'm a nervous guy, and this stuff was heady. Being in London, making a record with Twiggy, getting my first cut as a writer, and hanging out with Nick and the Feelgoods was a big, new experience. I'd begun to drink a little again, but I was trying to keep it down to a dull roar. The allure of the pubs was undeniable, especially when combined with the unspoken pressure of the situation. It was apparent that this was do or die. If we delivered, the world was our oyster. If we didn't, we'd be out on our asses and most likely done as a band. So I tried to hold it together and not get too "legless," or "pissed as a newt," as Nick might say. The so-called room-temperature beer (it's cold) they drink is a lot stronger than the watered-down horse piss we call beer in this country. You know what would crack an Englishman up? The concept of "lite" beer. Each pub had an affiliation with a brewery and most had stronger ales and porters, like modern local breweries of today. Three pints seems harmless until you stand up and find yourself falling into a wall or peeing in the street because you can't find any other logical place to go.

So far, there wasn't any heat from the band to not drink. Johnny was drinking and cutting up for all of us. I loved Johnny, but he could get into an unreachable, psychotic space when he'd gotten into hard stuff, as he was wont to do on occasion. His antics frequently started out funny, but his sense of humor was edgy, and might verge into dangerous in a hurry. One afternoon we were at the hotel. McFee and Frank and I were in our room when we heard Ciambotti yelling out on the balcony of the next room over. He was calling out to some Arab guys in the street, saying something to the effect that if they didn't give him some hashish, he'd cut their throats with the knife he was waving around. Johnny always seemed to have some big pocketknife or other. I think his actual threat was, "I promise not to stick this knife in your throat if you give me some hashish." Nice, diplomatic language, to be sure. The Arab dudes were pissed off. They threatened to come up and get him. Of course, we in the adjoining room tried to cajole Johnny to stop, but he wouldn't listen. Eventually, the guys in the street wandered off, but that could have been trouble.

It was strange, but Johnny engaged in erratic behavior like that and got away with it. Nick and Jake and everyone we met just loved and respected the guy. He certainly radiated an air of legitimacy, and there was no questioning his brains, education, and musical talent. But it was sometimes hard for me to reconcile the various aspects of his personality with the treatment he got. If I got blotto and stupid, everyone came down on me. But when Johnny went psycho, which happened fairly frequently, we all just rolled our eyes, laughed, and said, "That's Ciambotti!" Maybe it's because I didn't have the confidence that he did. Maybe the band came down on me because I was a lousy, sloppy drunk, tending towards maudlin and with a face that would slip sideways when loosened with a wee drop. *Faced*. And, I was the fuckin' lead singer. They'd seen me in action for years and knew where I was capable of going, so they were counting on me to not blow it this time. It was their lives on the line. So for now I was walking on thin ice, the stuff they make the cubes out of for life on the rocks.

Off to Holland. Amsterdam was a gas. We were staying at a very classy hotel on the Prinsengracht, one the main thoroughfares, on Twiggy's tab. She was recording in Phonogram's state-of-the-art studio in Hilversum, a few miles away. We walked the lovely streets of the old city, which had been spared the bombings of World War II, its canals lined with fantastic three-and four-story buildings topped with dormer windows and gables, neat shops, elegant bridges, and herds of bicycles.

The contrast with London was striking. Much of London had a kind of gritty feel to it. Many of the buildings were well past their glory days, reflecting the fall of empire. English shops tended to be small and poorly-lit and laid out in haphazard fashion. English plumbing seemed to often be an afterthought— showers and even a good supply of hot water were not a given.

Amsterdam, on the other hand, was a combination of beautifully-preserved old and ultra-hip modern. The Dutch have a way with design. The stylish neon signs, the orderly shops, and the hanging flower baskets everywhere gave the city a delightful, sophisticated air. Even the famous red-light district was well laid out, as it were, on clean cobbled streets. The exotic hookers, from every corner of the globe, of every skin color and size and shape, and reflecting every taste of the sexual world, sat in the windows in their lingerie. One simply shopped the windows until you found what you wanted. We only window-shopped. I had no money for hookers, and was too shy to visit one in any case, though it would have been fascinating to hear their stories. The truth was probably far less glamorous than the showy fronts of the red-light district, I suppose.

The food everywhere was spectacular. After eating fish and chips and doner kebabs, the broodjies and frites were a real treat. Then there were drugs. The Dutch were famous for their enlightened approach to the issue. Drugs were available and cheap (and regulated by the government.) You could easily get hash. At nightclubs, dealers had their goods laid out on tables for inspection. The whole country felt cosmopolitan, comfortable, and culturally wealthy. We felt quite at home, though I was struck by the relative paucity and crassness of our culture compared to the history and sophistication of the Dutch. It was a bit intimidating to realize that most people there spoke five or six languages. Many Americans can barely speak English. Physically, it also seemed that most Nederlanders were taller and fitter than us Californians. There were gorgeous, tall women everywhere, open, alluring, and goddess-like.

The record was going smoothly. Veteran Tony Ayers was producing. I wasn't doing that much. McFee was borrowing my pick as usual. Twigs, as she was called, cut my song. I'm afraid it might have been a stretch for her vocally. It had a melody that called for some long, high notes and was really quite demanding. The label guys and the producer had been calling it a possible first single, but as the album came together I could see that slipping away. That was all right. It was still on the album, still my first cut as a writer.

On my birthday, we had a dinner to celebrate the completion of the album. We went to a nice restaurant near the hotel. Dinner was on the label, so we ordered good wines and cognacs. Twiggy's husband had flown in. He was an American, an actor, a very impressive guy at first take. He was a big, handsome guy who had that Robert Mitchum thing that many actors that we met across the pond affected: the tough, sophisticated, hard-hitting, scotch-drinker pose. The problem was that he wasn't a very good drinker.

The dinner started well, with him telling us highly-entertaining tales of movies and actors and, oh yes, doing his de rigueur Mitchum impersonation. But as the evening went on and the booze flowed, he became quiet and morose. Perhaps he wasn't comfortable with each of us wanting the spotlight nearly as much as he did. We felt the tension brewing as he sat red-eyed and sullen at the table. As dinner was winding down, he broke out into anger over something Twiggy said and cleared the table in front of him with a sweep of his burly forearm, knocking wineglasses and plates onto the floor, causing a scene and a mess. We beat a hasty retreat from the restaurant, giggling and shooting each other raised-eyebrows. Whoa, dude, like, hold your booze! I felt a bit sorry for our new pal Twigs.

London and Amsterdam. Hyde Park, Chelsea, the Tower, the tube, Twiggy, pubs, Harrods. It was a far cry from Chico and Fresno. Definitely a much bigger road trip. We'd pulled up stakes so fast it was like a dream. One day we were playing softball and smoking pot on the beach in Marin, the next day we were in the U.K. and Europe. We had to figure out our sound in the studio somehow, but surely that would fall into place. We'd been on a solid ride for a while; we felt unbeatable. Meanwhile, we listened to Nick go on about the Beatles and Elton. Cut the album with Twiggy. Checked out cultures that had serious histories. Got treated with some respect for a change. It was a marvelous shift of scenery. The reality of the high stakes we were playing for hadn't yet hit home. For the time being we were just gaga-eyed Yanks far from home. Clover in Wonderland.

Thin Lizzy and
Scottish Roadies

The boys are back in town...

Thin Lizzy

Dave and Jake had exciting news for us. We were going to be opening for Thin Lizzy for thirty dates. We knew Thin Lizzy from their big hit, *The Boys Are Back in Town*. Wild. I remembered hearing that song the summer before and thinking how cool it was. It had been one of those prescient moments we all experience: I knew there was something about that song and that band. Funny how that works sometimes. We'd be starting in Oxford.

We'd just done a mini-tour with a black jazz-soul singer named Linda Lewis. We'd opened in Aberystwyth, Wales and played a handful of small college dates, very tame and polite. Nick Lowe rode in the van with us, helping us to navigate both the confusing roads and the frequently awkward world of English bed and breakfast accommodations. Since we didn't have any money the band was split up in pairs and put up in tiny B&Bs. These weren't tricked-out tourist places but families which rented out a room or two in their house, with few amenities or nods to the tourist trade. No bottles of water or fancy soaps on your pillow. There might be a small TV in the living room, on which you watched sheep dog trials with the family. (Those dogs are awesome!) Breakfast was a piece of undercooked, thick bacon with a bit of bone in it, a triangle of fried bread, and two invariably bubbly fried eggs, eaten with the mister and missus of the house. It was a bit hard to face the folks in the morning when one was hung-over, like finding yourself in a movie dream sequence featuring elderly gnomes. But we were rolling on the cheap. We prided ourselves that we were doing it the way the old bands did, the Beatles and the Stones, back when they too were nobodies.

We weren't earning any money yet. Opening acts, called simply *Support* weren't paid anything. We, the proud members of that ubiquitous poster-fame band *Support*, were driving in a mini-van, eating pork-pies or fish and chips, lucky to have fifty pence in our pockets. It was a shoestring operation, and would be for a while. We were game. We were happy to be there, getting a shot. I loved seeing the rolling countryside of England and the hills of Wales, with ruined castles, Bronze Age hill forts and Neolithic standing stones, tidy little villages and big, ugly industrial midland cities. I drank it all in.

Between the Linda Lewis and Lizzy tours, we got a night at the Roundhouse, in London Camden Town. It was an old railroad roundhouse that had been converted to a rock venue, a very happening place right then. It wasn't as prestigious as the Hammersmith Odeon or the Rainbow, but it was a gig that would draw a good crowd, a lot of punters, and media attention, which is what the U.K. is all about. It's been redone over the years and is an important venue once again. McCartney recently did a TV special there.

Fans in the U.K. were called "punters," which I gathered was an old horse racetrack term. British slang was a whole new language. One wasn't drunk, one was "pissed" or "legless." You didn't pick up chicks, you "pulled" them, and they weren't chicks, they were "boilers." You didn't pee, you "had a slash." Male homosexuals were "poofters." Assholes were "cunts." This took a self-proclaimed women's libber like me a bit of getting used to (like, five minutes), but I managed somehow. "You fucking cunt!" Some of my favorite slang was terms for masturbation: "wanking" (which gives rise to the useful term, applied to those despised or envied for real or imaginary reasons, "wankers"), "doing a blue vein solo," with or without the prepositional "on your beef bayonet," or my personal fave, "galloping your maggot." Jeez, them Brits have some language skills, don't they?

Then there was the whole world of rhyming cockney slang. Bristol City = titty ("nice set of Bristols on that one"); skyrocket = pocket; wicks = dicks, etc. I couldn't possibly follow it all, though Huey was good at picking it up. Huey is a whiz at learning complicated slang systems and also at remembering people's names. It's part of his orderly mind, I guess. He can meet someone at two in the morning after having six scotches and remember him three years later. Amazing. I was often left nodding and saying "uh huh, uh huh," when talking to a real cockney, who might have been speaking Swahili for all I comprehended.

The Roundhouse was packed with new-wavers, punk-rockers, hard-rockers, and old pomped-haired mods in their long leather coats, because the bill was a mixed bag of different kinds of bands. It was our official coming out party for London, and for the music press.

The rock press was vital. It's a small island. Everyone read the weekly music rags: the *New Musical Express* (NME), *Sounds*, and the *Melody Maker*. A good review could make your band; a bad one could sink it. Jake and Dave were masters of this press game, as time would show. They'd been hyping us a bit, but not over the top, setting us up as eventual headliners without portraying us as the second coming.

Jake powered into the dressing room rubbing his hands and grinning. He was a very intense, brilliant, dark-haired guy, a former boxer, who is a genius of promotion and a great lover of competition. His eyes kind of bugged out, either from the pressure of the moment, which he usually created, or from the stimulants he'd probably taken to stay on top of his game. Or both. He and Dave both got a twinkle in their eye and a wide grin on their face at the prospect of winning. It's what it's all about.

I'd picked up a black leather, tasseled, gunslinger-style vest from the trendy Kensington Market, where you could get real rock leather stuff. We were all crowded in the back room, holding our guitars—nervous, psyched—waiting to go on.

Jake said to me, "You look like a gambler in that. I want you to go out there and gamble tonight."

I answered, "We're going to be dynamite."

He said, "You're very fucking expensive dynamite, you'd fucking better go off!"

He was laughing, but he was wide-eyed manic and dead serious. They'd put their own money on the table and gone out on a limb with Phonogram and the press for us.

Come down from the mountain, California hippies! Time to go off.

The gig went okay, not too bad. After a high-energy entrance, we failed to really take the punters to a higher level, to capture them and make them go nuts. But still, it was a fairly good set. There was encouraging talk backstage afterwards—"nice one, lads"—but no one said we hit the jackpot. We got decent notices in the press, but it could've been the honeymoon effect. Or perhaps Dave and Jake had the writers in their pocket, calling in a favor to be returned later, that sort of thing.

We had a two-fold problem. First, our material was still too scattered. Some of it was kind of rock, but it was light, compared to what the Brits were used to. We also had the lame R&B element, which showed, frankly, a writing side of me that was influenced by current stateside stuff like Earth, Wind, and Fire. It's hard to believe I wrote the crap, which was no reflection on EW&F's music, because their stuff was great, but in my hands, it was pure crapola. The pedal steel and harmonica horn lines, which kicked ass back in Fresno, were light in the loafers for the London crowd. "A little smooth around the front," as Nick might say. Have horn lines? Get a fucking horn section. Give a couple of sax guys pork-pie hats and shades and have 'em do steps. That'd be cool. Pedal steel and harmonica? Wankers aweigh!

The other problem, unfortunately, was much deeper. I was the lead singer, but I was still struggling as a frontman. It wasn't that I didn't have a good voice. It's pretty pure compared to a lot of rock singers. Part of it was the country influence; part of it is that my voice is just like that. But that wasn't the problem. I found it hard to relax into the role of ringleader. I found myself over-thinking, internalizing events as they happened. I'd be singing while also wondering if I was good-looking enough, if

I was cool enough. *Am I rich enough, am I hard enough?* My deep-seated insecurities tripped me up, big time. Remember the old cartoon, where Elmer Fudd has a little angel-Elmer on one shoulder saying, "You can do it!" and a little devil-Elmer on the other saying, "Forget it, you'll never win!" It was like that for me on stage. Instead of reaching out and connecting to the audience, I was running internal dialogues. I had a hard time sustaining eye contact with the punters. That old self-conscious chickenshit side of me was saying, "You can't cut it. They don't want to look at you, you're a fucking loser."

But there was no admitting that to anyone, not even the band guys. I had to act as if everything was groovy. I had to hope and believe that next time it was going to be different. I kept thinking that if I only had that perfect song, it would all be right. Every song I wrote seemed it might be the one, but then someone would criticize it and I'd be back in my doubter's corner. But I was the fucking lead singer, and we had our label deal now, and the show had to go on. It wasn't terminal at this stage. People liked us. We had a big vocal sound, unlike most bands. Huey was also singing more now. But as great a singer and frontman as he would become, he was still learning. It was up to me.

There are unspoken contracts in a band. We'd operated with the status quo for years, and to speak of changing it—or to admit that it might not be working—would break the deal by which we functioned. It's like a family. Dad may be an alcoholic and mom bipolar, but it was our family, by God, and that's the way it was. Then the kids grew up and moved on. That's what happens to a lot of bands, especially if they don't quite make it. No one would come right out and say I was an inadequate singer. We weren't anywhere near that yet. The band guys tried their best to keep me from going under. I had to succeed. The stakes get higher the closer you get to the big time. Like I said, it's do or die out there.

In any case, the Thin Lizzy tour was starting. They'd come and checked us out and determined that we didn't pose a threat to their twin-guitar hard-rock sound. Rock-n-roll is about competition. We're all best buddies at the bar after the gig, but when it comes to being on stage, winning over that audience at the expense of the other band is the game. Thin Lizzy had won an audience through years of hard roadwork and they weren't going to jeopardize their position by having an opening band that would challenge them. Our light country-rock sound wasn't a problem. We'd only make them sound that much more bad-ass powerful. They'd see to it that their status was not challenged.

The gig posters and marquees went up, with *THIN LIZZY* in huge letters, and *Support* in tiny letters. We were getting used to our new no-name. But the *Support* bit went further. Even after we'd become tight buds with Phil Lynott and the rest of the lads, including their crew and management, we'd still find that while the monitors were perfect during sound check, they'd have been moved and the volume balances changed when showtime came. When we'd hit the stage, we'd find that the microphones were taped to the stage just out of the fixed spotlight zones. It wasn't a mistake. No one is going to set themselves up to be blown off the stage by another band. That's part of what makes rock-n-roll so fun. Today's *Support* is tomorrow's headliner. If you want to win, you have to find a way. The good ones do it, the lesser ones don't.

We opened in Oxford, just down the street from the storied university. Despite Oxford's illustrious reputation, much of the town is working class. I didn't see many dons in the audience; the punters were mostly fifteen-year-old males who wore heavy clod-hopper boots and drab coats. They didn't like us. That was something we'd get used to. To be *Support* was to be booed, especially when the audience was teenage males. They had their heroes and we weren't them. Besides, booing is fun: it's you and your buddies giving a strange band a hard time. We were Yank wankers to boot. We played, we survived. Barely. Okay, we got fuckin' booed, some. That's okay, it was the first night. Not too bad. After toweling off, we watched the Lizzys in action.

Thin Lizzy was truly great. Phil Lynott. Did you ever see the man? He was a tall, thin blade of a bass player with a Dublin Irish mother and black American merchant marine father. His skin was somewhat dark, but he had unmistakable Irish looks as well. It was a deadly combination, part randy rake, part bluesman, part Irish sea-dog-poet. He had an afro, but it wasn't the standard-issue 1976 American job, it was a little wild and unkempt, not a puffy blow-dried pomp. And it kind of sluiced off to the side, like a living beret. He wore a gold earring and a gambler's pencil mustache. He was a fighter and a lover. Just like in Nick Lowe's song, *All Men are Liars. He's grown a mustache, the sneaky little brute.*

Phillip was completely cocky confident on the stage. He owned it, like you're supposed to. His swaggering smile told the punters that they were his lads, they were his boys. And the boys were back in town. The band was Brian Robertson from Glasgow and Scott Gorham from California on twin lead guitars, plus Brian Downey on drums. Brian Robertson, their "Robbo" (ours was our Irish manager, Dave Robinson), was a wild child, maybe twenty years old, who occasionally got a little deep into the auld whiskey, but he played great, without inhibition yet with control on the twin-lead stuff they did. Scott Gorham was a handsome Southern California guy with long hair who had a distinctive move: He did a sort-of skip-step and then flipped his dark mane forward and back. Strangely, John McFee, who also had very long hair, developed a similar move right after the tour (and kept it for years, just as Huey kept a bit of an English accent forever). Phillip Lynott played a black Fender Precision bass with a mirror pick-guard that he used to redirect the spotlight onto individual faces in the crowd, which brought victorious fist-pumps and cheers. The punters were his boys. Phillip was the Man.

There was nothing all that innovative about their sound. They had harmonizing twin leads, but it was basic U.K. hard rock. They were great at "throwing shapes," which is something we learned from them. In a big venue, you must use body language to get your point across, so movements are exaggerated. You strike a pose and hold it. *Air Guitar 101: Throwing Shapes.* They had some good songs: *The Boys are Back in Town, Suicide, Johnny the Fox.* They employed minor pyrotechnics, smoke bombs and fog. It was good fun is what it was, and it was all about being one of the lads. There were hardly any women in the hall most nights.

As Phillip put it in his low Manchester–Dublin drawl, "Youse gotta do something fer the kids, man!"

The Lizzys were personally great to us. Phil and the boys and Frank Murray, their road manager, went out of their way to make us feel part of the tour, though it was clear we were going to get our asses kicked from Bristol to Glasgow and back again. And we did. We played the grimy cities of the Midlands, the industrial heart of England: Birmingham, Leeds, Sheffield, Leicester, and Phillip's home town of Manchester. We went up to Scotland and played Glasgow and Edinburgh, rough Newcastle in Geordie land, and so on. Most of the towns were depressed and depressing. England's economy was in a long slump. Truly, many places hadn't fully recovered from the war. In Glasgow, we saw areas that were still bombed-out ruins, thirty years after the war had ended. Lizzy's crowds were mostly young, tough kids who liked a drink and a fight. The reaction we got varied from non-responsive to semi-hostile to actively hostile.

I was standing on stage between songs in Leicester Town Hall, enduring one of those terminally endless, indifferent, forty-five-second silences between songs that afflict *Support* so frequently. My hand was on the guitar neck holding an E chord when from out of the darkness of the hall, I saw a wadded-up beer cup flying towards me in a long arc. Before I had time to react, it brushed across my strings, striking them perfectly. Nice shot. Thank goodness glass beer bottles had been banned the year before across Europe, as a response to stage-destroying showers of angrily-hurled empties.

We played Liverpool Town Hall, where the Beatles had once played. We went to the site of the old Cavern Club, where they got their start. It had been turned into a clothing shop. I bought a kelly green satin baseball-style warm-up jacket that caught my eye. Liverpool had a serious reputation for crime and even the Town Hall was no exception. The Liverpool police couldn't guarantee our stuff wouldn't be pilfered out of the dressing room, so we took our wallets and cheap watches and the rest of our meager possessions on stage with us. Well, it might have been a tough town, but what a thrill to stand on the same stage that the Beatles had stood on only a few years before. Take that, Lodi! I was taking a shower in the dressing room when Ciambotti ripped back the curtain and took my picture. I'd have to deal with that later.

When we drove a few days later into Glasgow to play the famous Apollo Theatre, I was wearing my new cool green jacket, my arm out the window of the van. We drove past the soccer stadium where Rangers and Celtic United, the two rival Glaswegian football clubs, had just played. There were sullen looks from the partisans, evidently Rangers supporters, as green is a Celtic United color. I slipped off the jacket and laid it on the floor.

If Liverpool was tough, Glasgow was war. It was said that street gangs fought it out there with claymores (Scottish swords) and war clubs. Real *Braveheart* shit. The stage at the 5,000-capacity Apollo Theatre was fifteen feet off the floor, to prevent rowdies from getting at bands they didn't care for.

Leave it to me to commit an enormous faux pas while on stage. Introducing a song I'd just written called *Streets of London*, I addressed the hostile, dark cavern full of young, drunk males and said, "Here's a song that we wrote since coming to England."

Oh shit.

"England" was the wrong thing to say in Scotland, and especially at the Apollo.

Boo! Hiss!

Thank God for the altitude of the stage.

So we took some lumps. As they say, what doesn't kill you makes you stronger. Or wears you out. We weren't ready to throw in the bar-towel quite yet. We were learning that we must get up to speed if we wanted to compete. We always worked on stuff as we drove in our van, and tried it out at sound check. McFee came up with some twin-guitar stuff. Of course, it was torturous for me, the parts were so fast and complicated. For once I wanted McFee to borrow my pick, but he insisted I learn the parts and play them well. Fair enough. I was supposed to be able to play. I found I could cover most of the riffs. Huey visualized new stage moves. We threw some shapes, more every night. We didn't always get booed heavily. Part of the audience always liked us: We were a pretty good-looking crew, so we got the girls. But we were up against a largely male hard-rock crowd and most nights I looked out across the lights onto a sea of dull, sullen faces.

We made a new friend and companion and major partner in crime in John Burnham. JB was a singular character who stayed around us for years to come, following us to the States to work for Huey. He was then at Phonogram as artist liaison. His official job was to shepherd us through radio interviews and other appearances and to generally act as our guide and interpreter as we toured. His unofficial job was to teach us how to party and get laid in a foreign country.

JB was from Glasgow, but he'd studied and worked his way out of that hard town and seemed more sophisticated Londoner than street-fighting Scot. He was extremely witty and charming, tall, and dressed corporate, in slacks, sweaters, and penny loafers. His dark hair was company-man short and he had Roy

Orbison glasses. He could make upper-class tea chatter with a prim Duchess or get wildly randy with a nymphomaniac waitress from Hull. He disarmed the most potentially tight situations with his outrageous sense of humor. He might meet a stuffed-suit corporate chap in a social setting and while proffering his hand, say in an upper-crust Surrey accent with just a wee Scottish twinge, "How lovely to meet you, sir. Tell me, are you firm?" He'd follow that with a loud guffaw that brought everyone in on the joke, including the stuffed suit. His social approaches almost always worked.

He was a thorough crack-up. In Glasgow, he led us to a fancy hotel far above the status of the cheap dive we were staying in. We went into the bar area and lounged around and had a bevvy or two, posing as guests. Every few minutes JB—or one of us, at his bidding—went and requested that someone be paged, like Hugh Jorgan, or Phil Jerpanties. It was juvenile, but entertaining. We finally got eighty-sixed and went somewhere else to party until late. JB knew girls of all types in every town as well, like the one in Manchester he called "Suspenders" for her garter-belts, and he met the ones he didn't yet know and then introduced them to us. He was always up for the moment, whatever form that moment might take. He was a valuable resource and a good, soulful pal. And he wasn't much of a Glaswegian street fighter, as I'd find out later.

After our gig in Manchester, we piled in the van and went to Phil Lynott's mom's after-hours club. She had a place in a house that opened after the pubs closed at eleven. Most of England just shuts down after nine, really. Nothing is open except the odd Italian or Indian restaurant. Phil's mother had been around in Manchester. I'm not sure of the details of her history, but it's clear she had a working relationship with many principal figures in Manchester's political and organized crime scenes. There were people of influence there, drinking and hanging out with desirable young ladies who might not have been their wives, until dawn. It was an interesting hang, though the snooty girls were above our economic station.

It was difficult to meet women just to talk to, actually. You couldn't pull girls from the gig because they were out front and we were backstage. Barmaids were sometimes available, but somewhat risky, for obvious reasons. There were the girls who worked for the label, but we'd been warned off them by Jake and Dave. "They're going to love you, but keep your hands off them!" That didn't stop things from happening in the hinterlands away from Phonogram's London office, though. Sometimes one just wanted to talk to someone who wasn't snoring on your shoulder in the van every day, smelling like last night's scotch.

Indian restaurants, usually the last open businesses of the otherwise dead British night, were post-gig favorites. Clover was broke. We almost never had even fifty pence apiece. So if JB wanted to pull out the corporate card, we were ready. The Lizzys, our Phonogram label-mates, were ready as well. We often had a large crew, maybe twelve or fifteen rowdy dudes around a bunch of tables pushed together. Since there was booze backstage after the gigs and wine at the restaurant, it wasn't long before the onion bhajis began to fly. Ciambotti, naturally, was a great instigator. He'd surreptitiously hit an unsuspecting member of the party with a food item and it was game on. Food fight! JB was quick with a curry-loaded spoon. The embattled but persistent Indian families who worked hard to run the restaurants were patient with their wild late night customers. There was a big cleanup. But JB didn't skimp on the tip, either.

It was a way of letting off steam. The pressure of performing, the boredom of waiting through sound check, of driving all day, and getting only cat-naps took its toll. Nobody was over thirty, so who was going to be the adult? It was also a way to bond with the Lizzys. It wasn't all food fights anyway, it was mostly conversation. Until Ciambotti catapulted the first bhaji across the table, that is.

Hotels were another setting for our youthful high jinks. That's where we hooked up with the roadies, who'd worked far beyond the Indian meal hour. Come two A.M., they were ready to party.

There was, and presumably still is, I hope, a sub-species of humanity known as the Scottish roadie. Of course, they're not all Scots. We had one Englishman, Michael Sinclair, our sound mixer, known to us as "Sinque," from the SLA leader, and two Americans, Mark Melanson and Steve Liebert, Danny Morrison's younger brother. Sinque and Mark were big guys who later acquired the monikers "Super-Slab" and "Massive Roggie" after we'd been exposed to CB lingo on our American tour. Young Steve was "Lybo." All three were definitely honorary Scottish roadies.

The day in the life of a roadie is long and only vaguely rewarding. They started early, frequently leaving for the next town immediately after taking down the gear from the gig. They drove hundreds of miles a day, which in the U.K. was more complicated than in the States. Roads there are often indirect, being a hodge-podge of ancient foot-trails and wagon ruts, Viking invasion routes, fairy circles, and Roman roads, overlaid with modern motorways whose chief feature was the roadside stop with the worst food in the known world: canned peas, soggy fish, soggier chips, and bagged biscuits, which were called cookies. Maps were bewildering. Plus, for Americans, you had to drive on the wrong side of the road, which is tiring in itself. Did you ever see the Monty Python skit where Hitler and his staff are at a B&B in Brighton, trying to figure out the best invasion route from road maps? John Cleese tries to help with all kinds of insane short cuts: "You take the A13 right 'round Dandruff-on-the-Lapelle, catch the B29 to Henweigh, back on the A13 again to Dingbatt, 'round the roundabout in Toodle, and right up the M4 to Foote-on-Pedal." Funny, because it's true.

Once the crew arrived at the venue, they unloaded the heavy gear, often in cramped alleys with no loading docks, with maybe a flight of stairs or two to go up. Not many of the old venues in England were designed as rock venues; they were originally theatres. It was always cold and rainy. The gear got super-filthy, giving rise to the joke that a musician washes his hands *after* he pees, the roadie *before*. They set up the gear and worked hard though sound check, when they invariably had to solve one equipment dilemma or another. Amps, keyboards, and drums were set up. Endless miles of cables were hooked up, for every single piece of gear. Sinque did the sound mixing during sound check and at the gig. Monitors fed back; a mic didn't work; the lights were wrong. Hopefully, there'd be a chance to eat something at the venue between sound check and the performance. Then they set up the band room and tuned the guitars. We acquired a string endorsement deal with Rotosound, so the roadies had to change our strings endlessly, which was really unnecessary, but, hey, we had an endorsement. We certainly couldn't be bothered to change our own strings!

Gig time approached. There was an eternal checking of things, solving of crises. We had an electric current converter that reduced the native U.K. voltage from 220 to American 110, so we could run our American amps. The black, sizzling thing, with multiple hot wires sticking out like oily porcupine dreadlocks sat in a milk crate looking like something salvaged off a U-boat. It heated up to about 200 degrees as we played. You could smell it across the stage. Sparks flew, the converter smoldered. The band was led on to the stage: we obviously couldn't find it ourselves. Every set was like live fire. Something always broke: an amp went out or a mic died or the monitor changed and soon enough, Mickey Shine was complaining that he couldn't hear.

Then we were done. We went back to the dressing room and had a beer, changed our clothes, and got ready to pull boilers. The roadies scrambled to hustle our gear off the stage so the Lizzys could go on. When the gig was over, the bands went off for Indian food while the roadies stayed and packed up, then hit the road again. We should have paid them more, I suppose, but then we weren't getting paid ourselves.

Nowadays, when I meet some twenty-eight-year-old music publisher or A&R person who took some classes in college to learn about the music business, I often think to myself, *Shouldn't there be a requirement that they go on the road and haul amps for a couple of years?* It might give them a better perspective on the industry.

The Scottish roadies had a secret helper in their war with the impossible: it was called "sulfate." Methamphetamine sulfate is the drug that beat the Nazis. It was straight speed, meth. The Germans came up with it to power the Wehrmacht during World War II, but soon it was adopted by the RAF and the U.S. Air Force as a way to keep pilots awake and alive on fourteen-hour bombing runs over Europe. Jacko, on the way to New York to talk contracts over a long weekend, was busted at Heathrow with a packet of white powder. He made an impassioned case to the customs officers that it was sulfate, just like their daddies took to defeat the Jerrys, not that dread evil of all evils, cocaine (which it was.) He further argued that he was going over the pond to bring back business and money to England. They confiscated it, but let him go. They understood. Their fathers had fought that war for real.

The roadies didn't have much choice. No one could do all that work for all those hours, day after night, on the natch. It became a problem only when it was time to wind down. Whiskey and beer were the tools of disengagement. The combination of sulfate and alcohol was predictably crazy sometimes. We wouldn't touch the stuff. Mostly.

Hotels are the playground of road people. Everyone is away from home, so anything goes. In the case of the Scottish roadie anything goes out the window. Rockers were famous for ripping things off the walls, bowling with TV sets, and laughing hysterically while running naked down the halls at three in the morning. The Scottish roadies took this as a starting point. There was a perverse desire to make life as miserable as possible for the poor, undeserving-of this-treatment hotel staff and management, who, after all, were working stiffs like everybody else. There was an inverse proportion between destructive desire and class of hotel: the better the establishment, the worse the mayhem. A favorite trick was to take a twin bed into the elevator and lean it up against the closing doors and then send it to the lobby, where it would fall out—ta-da!—when the doors slid open. Or, one might send the hotel's wall-hanging artwork to the lobby. Walls might be painted a new color with wine, ketchup, or urine. And cheap shower stalls come right down with just a gentle tug or, if necessary, a good, hard pull.

The Lizzy tour ended with a concert at the famous Hammersmith Odeon, one of London's most prestigious venues. Naturally, Ciambotti's bass amp died on the second song and we were sunk. Par for the course. But afterward, there was a big swanky-danky label-funded soiree at a fancy London hotel. Nice suits, low-cut dresses, wine in glasses, champagne in hand-held bottles for convenient personal consumption, a spread of easily-airborne pates and cheeses under an ice sculpture of a swan. And crystal chandeliers, high-brow London accents, drunken rockers, and sulfate-sniffing roadies. Elton John was there, pinching guys on the butt. I was introduced to Rod Stewart. I'll never forget the words he said to me: "Cheers, mate," as he turned away. A couple of roadies took fully-clothed belly flops in the floating-lily-garlanded indoor pool, and pushed in a few unsuspecting guests as well.

It had been a great tour.

We'd been out and seen it now and we wanted to rock out, like the Lizzys. We'd gotten creamed by tough crowds. I was fired up to write some faster, harder material, stuff that would work in the larger venues. Simpler, more direct is the key. We weren't ever going to be heavy metal or even hard rock, but we needed to get up to speed. We were dressing like real rockers now, on and off stage. McFee and I were wearing these cool shorty silk-rayon kimonos you could get in London. Huey had long hair and a motorcycle jacket. Phillip Lynott named him "Bluesy Huey Louie" and had him playing harp during their encores. Ciambotti had his own style: He wore Panama hats and red suspenders. Whatever he wore, he carried it off with swaggering personal style. We all had long hair, as long as it would grow. We were so thin that if we turned sideways you couldn't see us. Our sun-deprived faces were as pale as brie on a saltine.

All we needed now were some smash rock hits. That was still my job. It was time go make a hit record.

Mutt Lange

He's a magic man...

HEART

At last the roadies dried off, the red wine stains and smears of pate had been washed from Ciambotti's red suspenders, and our Phonogram deal was finalized. The songs were mostly chosen. And the label had chosen a producer for us, a young South African named Mutt Lange. Nick Lowe wasn't mainstream enough for Phonogram. They had slick, corporate offices. Their employees were more wine bar than pub, with suits, fancy leather coats, and '70s blow-dry accountant hair. Not all of them, mind you, there were A&R guys like Nigel Grainge who were as hip as the next dude, but Nick was the Jesus of Cool, and much like the regular Jesus, wasn't the right fit for a major label at that point.

Robert John "Mutt" Lange is now a household name in the music business, a producer extraordinaire and the writer of stacks of multi-platinum records. While he is publicity-shy and doesn't like to be seen in the world of the glitterati, he's been the creative hand and ears behind AC/DC, Def Leppard,

Foreigner, many of the number one hits of the last thirty years, including his country-star creation and now ex-wife Shania Twain. He's certainly one of the top producers and songwriters of the era. When we met him, he'd recently emigrated from South Africa, where he and his first wife, Stevie van Lange, an incredible singer in her own right, had dominated the charts and the jingles market for years. He'd wanted a bigger pond in which to swim, so he made the logical jump to England. He looked like a surfer, with longish, curly blonde hair. He was of Boer descent and had that ruddy Dutch complexion.

Mutt wanted to do the album at Rockfield Studios in Monmouthshire. He liked to work out there, a converted farm a few miles to the west of the medieval walled town of Monmouth, in the Welsh border hills, far away from the distractions of London. (It was his home base for cutting tracks, though he mixed at Trident Studios in London.) What a picturesque location. Monmouth sits on a hill around which curls the River Mon. The western entry to the town is over an arched tower bridge that dates back eight hundred years. The old cobbled streets were narrow and winding, obeying the ancient layout of the town, which must go back at least a couple of thousand years, if not more. It is a strategic place, a hill overlooking a river valley. There was a rather ugly statue of Plantagenet native son Henry V in one tiny square. My literate-minded mother always called him Hank *Cinque* ("The Fifth," in French, which came out "Hank Sank.") I knew the eternally-young Hank from Sir Laurence Olivier's magnificent fifties movie of the Shakespeare play, "Henry V."

There was a tourist element to the town, but Monmouth was mostly a regional farming and shopping center. The surrounding countryside was rolling grassy hills several hundred feet high, with sheep on the heights and dairy farms in the narrow, stream-bottomed valleys. Low stone walls separated the fields. The farm houses were one- or two-storied and boxy, with thick walls and small windows. The winters are cold in Wales. On a cloudy winter's day, cold and windy, thin ribbons of blue smoke from the farmhouse chimneys trailed across the frosted fields.

There was a feeling of another, ancient time out in the hills. Here and there a Norman church with a stone bell-tower rose above centuries-old gravestones. But the churches were Johnny-come-lately interlopers, like little fortresses that sought to keep the older, more primal forces of nature and ancient spirits of dale and hillock at bay. The country was a place for long, wistful Dylan Thomas walks, walks through time, time twisting like smoke in the gravestones, the stones growing mold and stained with the tears of the women who wailed on the day our blessed Savior died, as the whiskey-song of our ancestors had it. Since I have Welsh blood, I imagined that I was back in my birth country. I loved the openness, it was very much like my native west Marin. London was a fantastic place, but cities drive me crazy after a short while. I get claustrophobic. The dark-watered River Wye wandered past Rockfield. I bought some local flies—one that looked a bit like our "renegade" from Montana that was called a "coch-y-bandu" here—and caught trout and dace and a few strong, twisty, slimy, disgusting eels that fought hard but disappointed me by their non-troutness when brought to hand.

The studio compound looked like any other farm at first glance. There was a quadrangle of one- or two-story, older whitewashed buildings and barns with a coating of many cold seasons' grey mud splatters working up from the wet ground, as if the Earth was determined to eventually claim the buildings from the ground up and return them to the dirt from which they had been fashioned. The quadrangle enclosed a large working farm yard, complete with a funky tractor and a few semi-rusted harrowing tools or whatever they were. There were a couple of scattered out-buildings and cottages as well. All looked worn and organic, like it had grown out of the ground, just another sheep farm, muddy and unkempt in a nice, workaday way.

But the sheep farm was a clever disguise, a funky façade, inside it was another matter. The interiors had been redone in bright knotty pine and gleaming white sheetrock: ski-chalet modern, Scandinavian in feel. Everything was bright and spotless, open and airy. After the rat holes we'd been staying in, it was like going to a Nordic resort. Most of the tourist hotels we'd been put in had limited plumbing and no kitchen facilities. A good bath was three inches of lukewarm greenish water in a cold, drafty bathroom down the hall. As Americans, we were spoiled, plumbing and otherwise. So with its hot showers and modern kitchen, Rockfield was a very welcome oasis.

The studios themselves were fully state-of-the-art, with Trident mixing consoles and all the up-to-date gear. There were four or five studios scattered throughout the complex. We were in one of the larger ones.

Mutt was a classic studio rat. He started work around ten in the morning and went until two or three the next morning. There was a second engineer, but Mutt was hands-on with the board. He was already highly accomplished, but as it turned out he was putting the last pieces of his own talent arsenal together. Soon, he would be among the best there ever was.

We rehearsed for a week or so, as I recall, and then started cutting, one or two basic tracks a day. There were false starts and many takes that needed to be just a little faster or slower, a bit tighter, or maybe the energy wasn't quite right. This was still before midi, before digital. We were on recording two-inch tape, twenty-four tracks. You had to get it right, because there was no going back and making digital edits like there is now.

Mutt was a perfectionist. That's an understatement. Mutt was an ultra perfectionist, a man truly dedicated to getting each phrase, each breath, each picked note, exactly right. I got sick of the word "baby," and vowed to never use it in a song again, because on *Baby, Just Take Another Look* (a pseudo-soul song I hated anyway) Mutt had me sing the damn word thirty different ways. It was exasperating. His approach to lead vocals was new to me. He wanted me to sing in an extremely breathy fashion, almost whispering. I was used to singing full out, going for the high notes by belting. I thought harder and louder was the way. He was right, of course. I would come to see it his way, though it would take me years to develop the technique for properly delivering a recorded vocal. But by then I wouldn't be making albums for major labels.

He loved to double-, triple-, or even- quadruple-track background vocals, mix those all down to one track, and repeat the process, then do it again and again. On some songs there were thirty-two vocal tracks. That produced a smooth, wide vocal sound that receded in the mix. It was the sound the Eagles were scoring with. It meant a lot of work for us. We were forced to take our singing to a new level. There was no letting a poor take pass, it had to be spot-on every time. Since we had five singers and complicated vocal arrangements, it could be infuriating, especially when it was someone else screwing up the takes. But the results were awesome.

Mutt and McFee made a good team. Mutt appreciated John's virtuosity. Who wouldn't? McFee is a producer's dream, a player with ultimate skill who is also a perfectionist by nature. Sean Hopper was a keen studio student who spent much of his time at Mutt's side, learning the board. In between cutting the basic tracks and doing the vocal sessions, there was a lot of time spent trying various guitar and steel overdubs. McFee did some amazing stuff. For the rest of us, it was tedious. It was fun to finally be in the studio, but recording an album is a trying thing. It's exciting, anxiety-producing, and, ironically, extremely boring, with a lot of personal down time. There was ping-pong or trips to town if Frank was at Rockfield with the van, though he found an endless string of reasons to stay in London, chasing women. I took my Dylan Thomas walks and went fishing.

The music had to be the best it could be. There were questions about the material. It was still that mish-mash of R&B and pop-rock. The chief hope lay in a couple of mid-tempo songs, *Love, Love* and *Streets of London*. We had that horrible imitation Jackson Five kind of song, *Baby* (I hate that word!) *Take Another Look*, which featured an *a cappella* bit. Oh man, it wasn't Thin Lizzy and it sure wasn't the Eagles. There was a Brit slang word that summed it up succinctly: cringe-worthy. All we could do was make it sound as good as possible, then wait and see what happened. Also in the mix was my song, the one that Twiggy had recorded, *I Lie Awake and Dream of You*, which Mutt said would have been a number one song in South Africa. Unfortunately, we weren't in South Africa, we were in

England with our eyes on America. We wanted the album to be more rock than it was, but we—or should I say, I—didn't know how to do that. We were stuck with the songs. There was no time to write more.

But we weren't freaking out at this stage. We were having fun. Mutt was a serious guy who lived to work, but he also had a patient, yet razor-sharp, sense of studio humor. There are two kinds of studio humor: Headphone banter and practical jokes. Their common feature is that the laughs of the many come at the expense of the one. Headphone banter is a way of letting off nervous energy, often by picking up on someone's clam (a bad note) or bad take. It's spontaneous and quick. But a good practical joke needs a little planning, timing, an inspired set-up, and an aware, quick mind like Mutt's.

We had one riff that didn't have lyrics. It was a little more rock than the others—and rock was what we lacked—so we needed to finish it. We worked up some words and it became *The Storm*, a God-awful piece of nonsense if I ever heard (or wrote) one, which I unfortunately did. Mutt had Huey do a bunch of harmonica overdubs on it. Huey also sang some low vocal bits. *The storm won't last, the storm won't last forever.* Everyone today is used to hearing Huey sing way up there in the register, but at that time he was down in bluesy frog-tone land, Howlin' Wolf territory. He was also grunting quite a bit in between breaths on the harp, something some of us—including yours truly—do unconsciously. In the headphones, Huey heard the music, not himself making those porcine noises. But in the control room, Mutt had Huey soloed on the big speakers, drenched in a cavernous reverb. He sounded like a giant turtle having an orgasm at the bottom of a hidden submarine base. We were literally rolling on the floor, peeing on ourselves.

Mutt kept encouraging Huey to do more, more, more, "just one more take, mate!" Then, once Mutt had a good sequence of grunts lined up, he said into the talkback mic (sounding pleased), "Great, Huey, come on in and have a listen." Huey came in out of the booth and stood in front of the big speakers. The turtle that roared. We tried, but couldn't hold our laughter in, and the poor guy realized that he'd been had.

In addition to being a tone, reverb, and vocal parts meister, Mutt was a great cut-and-paster. That is, he could take various sections of songs and rearrange them in different sequences very quickly. Let's say we had a four-line verse, a two-line b-section, and a four-line chorus, plus an intro riff. He'd have us try a full verse, b-section and chorus, then cut it into a two-line verse, one-line b-section and the last two lines of the chorus, then an intro riff, the b-section. No, wait. Let's try a two-line verse, two-line b-section, four-line chorus, intro riff, then a two-line verse, right into the first and fourth lines of the chorus. Etcetera. You get the picture. Cut-and-paste is how arranging and producing is done. It's fast and intuitive, and Mutt was the best.

He was also adept at taking bits of songs and sticking them together. Perhaps these bits were reminiscent of other people's songs. No matter, we all copy bits from our peers. There's really not much in music that's fully original. Elvis copied Muddy Waters and Big Mama Thornton, Roy Orbison took from country and R&B, the Beatles took from Elvis and Roy Orbison, the Stones took from Chuck Berry and old blues guys. Led Zeppelin took from the Stones and added some speed. Jimi took R&B and LSD, man. The most important thing is to be entertaining, and only steal the best bits. After all, artists making records are playing in the world of commercial music, and what's the real purpose of commercial music? To attract listeners to radio, where they are sold products through advertising. So we steal from each other in order to better sell acne products. Inspirational, isn't it? So much for saving the world, Superboy.

The album took a few weeks to do. The fact that we had some real dog songs was glossed over by Mutt's great engineering and arranging work, and by our sense of accomplishment. Hey, maybe it wasn't that bad. I liked a couple of the songs, like *Streets of London*. Whatever it was, it was over, and we headed back to London to eat more doner kebabs and take more lukewarm baths. Mutt took the tapes to Trident studio in London to mix. We went over there to listen. It was mind-boggling to hear what he and the engineer had done with the recordings. His mixing prowess was obvious. There were heaven-like reverbs. The stereo imaging was fantastic.

Unfortunately, his mixes were better than most of the songs. My songs.

Alex is Superman, age five 1953

Alex - Mill Valley Tigers

*Huey, Alex, & Jim Beam
1968*

Alex 1968

Clover - Muir Beach 1969
Alex, John McFee,
Johnny Ciambotti & Mitch Howie

Clover 1969

Early Clover promo shot
Muir Beach 1969

*Ciambotti, Alex, Andre Pessis in
background - Muir Woods 1969*

*Clover at Lion's Share with new faces
Huey and Sean Hopper 1972*

*Clover with
Nick Lowe, right*

Clover 1976

*Clover sings naked
at Rockfield 1977*

*Clover at Rockfield
Phongram promo shot 1977*

Clover & Phillip Lynott
Hammersmith Odeon 1977

Alex, John McFee and Huey Lewis
on stage 1977

Huey and Alex - Headley Grange 1977

John McFee with tools of the trade
Rockfield Studios 1977

Clover 1968

Alex in the shower backstage
Liverpool Town Hall 1977

Huey dances while a dapper Ciambotti,
Frank Martinet, and Dave Robison hang
outside Stiff Records - London 1976

Alex and John McFee
in Headley Grange living room

McFee and Alex 1977

Huey the harpslinger - London 1977

*Huey, Sean, Alex and John McFee
Record Plant 1982*

*Alex in a "If it Ain't Stiff T-Shirt"
King's College London, 1978*

*Alex Call 1988
Livin' in a Perfect World*

Alex 1986

If It Ain't Stiff

If it ain't Stiff, it ain't worth a fuck!

STIFF RECORDS, *motto*

And so it goes, and so it goes, and so it goes, and so it goes
But where it's going, no one knows...

NICK LOWE

Dave and Jake found us a place to live because we couldn't stay in tourist hotels forever. It was an old manor house out in the country, in Hampshire. It was a nice little stroll down a couple of leafy, country lanes from the quaint village of Headley, near Haslemere and Liphook. If you know where that is, you're from there. It's an hour south of London by train or car.

The house had a serious rock-n-roll pedigree. Led Zeppelin recorded parts of their albums there, and Genesis, Fleetwood Mac, Bad Company, Peter Frampton, and others had used it as woodshed for upcoming records. It was said that Robert Plant wrote the lyrics of *Stairway to Heaven* at Headley Grange. Woodshedding was the main motivation for our going there. The great old high-ceilinged living room there was a perfect place to rehearse and refine our sound. It had tall windows that let in welcome, church-like light. And because it was home, we could work on our material in our robes, jammies, and slippers.

Headley was built in 1795 and served in the early nineteenth century as a poorhouse, where paupers, orphans, and the "infirm" worked off their debt to their lords by forced field labor. They slept many to a room, sitting up on benches, slumped forward on ropes strung from wall to wall through big eye-hooks. In the morning, the ropes were loosened, and the miserable sleepers fell forward. Ah, the good old days of the British Empire, those storied and fabulous times, when Britannia ruled the waves and people were held in debtor's servitude. There was a riot there in 1830, of which it was said, "This was the storming of the Bastille for the poor." But the house went on as a poorhouse. I was glad the walls couldn't talk—or that I was bad listener—since I was told that my room was one of those used for miserable dorm purposes. It was a small room, maybe ten by twelve, but an old caretaker said twenty people used to sleep in it. Headley Grange was converted in 1870 to a manor house, but the old stories, and also presumably ghosts, remained.

The spirits of the departed notwithstanding, we Yankee rockers were not the only current inhabitants. Legions of rats ran blithely on the exposed pipes and electric wires. (Let's face it, they lived there, we were merely passing through.) We called the pipes the Rat M1, after the big motorway. As far as ghosts went, there was at least one seriously haunted room, the big bedroom Johnny and his girlfriend Susan slept in. The room must have been the grandest of the old rooms, the master bedroom perhaps, with a big fireplace and tall windows. It retained a nineteenth century feel. There were definite unnaturally-cold spots that you felt sometimes, though it was often so damned cold in general in that house that who could tell the difference?

The house was creepy, to be sure, dark and foreboding. There was a great, dark-stained wooden staircase that wound up three stories around a central hall, with wings of bedrooms and storage areas off it. The house made creaky, foot-steppy noises at night, and there were long, dark hallways I purposely didn't look down when I snuck out of my attic room to use the bathroom at night. Jimmy Page has been quoted as saying the house was definitely haunted. I've never seen a ghost in my life, but in Headley Grange at night I didn't look too hard.

It was a cold house, and it's decidedly chilly in England in the winter. It's quite far north, really. London is just a few degrees of latitude south of Juneau, Alaska. Only the relatively warm waters of the Gulf Stream keep the British Isles from being arctic. It's plenty cold, more the reason for nice warm pubs. The sun crawls through a dank, leaden haze along the southern horizon for a few hours on a winter's day. It took a lot of heating oil to keep Headley Grange anything like warm. Unfortunately, Clover was broke, and we often ran out of money for heating oil. We tried to make do with little deadly 220 volt electric space heaters. I accidentally left my beloved leather bomber jacket too close to one and the sleeve burned off.

The sole shower at Headley was another huge health risk. There was an electric coil around the exposed shower pipe. See, plumbing and electricity hadn't been invented when they built the house, so modernity was simply out in the open along the walls. And the 220 current packs more punch than our puny little 110 in the States, trust me. I expected to be electrocuted every time I stepped into the fricking shower. It emitted a few needle-like jets of momentarily scalding water, enveloped in a halo of freezing drizzle. The scalding stingers would quickly fade to lukewarm, so it was: pray, step in, lather, Sweet Mother of God, I'm not usually religious but right now I *beg of you to intercede with this hell-fire and frozen demon of a shower*, and rinse. Shaking with fear and chill, I'd scrub my hair and get out before I got fried. It was the price one paid for being a spoiled rotten, clean-haired American.

Dave and Jake laughed at our prissiness. The English are far tougher than we would ever be. It came with the harsh living conditions and their history of war. When you looked around at the Brits, Scots, and Irish you saw a lot of small, wiry people. In your mind's eye, they fit easily in those old Tommy helmets, slogging through the shit- and blood- and mud-filled trenches of Europe, sharing their last cigarette, fighting the Bosch. They sailed around the world and conquered vast continents on grit, determination, and balls of brass. But master-race specimens they are not.

Nick Lowe had a great description of his people: "Pure Anglo-Saxon, just a dash of Viking, teeth like a burned-out fort."

In any case, we were living in this freezing, rat-infested haunted house and we were out of money. On Christmas Eve, we sat around the big table in the crypt-like kitchen with its ancient walk-in fireplace, now barren and cold, wearing parkas and scarves and wool hats, our frozen hands jammed in our armpits. Our girlfriends from home were visiting. We didn't have a quid between us. We shared hunger and cold for our Christmas supper. We were a long way from Marin.

But there were some nice things about Headley Grange. It sat on beautiful grounds, what was left of the former manor acreage, with a huge lawn in front with a gravel drive, framed by tall old trees that also lined the country lane that led past the village common garden to the village. Headley was a wonderfully-typical small English town. There was no tourism, just a greengrocer, butcher, pub, church, post office, and small bank. It was just a few streets. We went to the pub and listened to the locals tell tales about World War II. RAF Spitfires and Luftwaffe Messerschmitts had dogfights in the skies above the town. Imagine that. Huey and I beat a few of the locals at darts now and then. That didn't go down too well. One of the townies had a crush on Susan, Johnny's attractive girlfriend. He came around to the house and made a drunken a nuisance of himself a couple of times. We weren't integrated into the community, we were another silly rock band, a curiosity lodged at the Grange house. And damn Yanks, to boot.

I loved the green, gentle countryside. It reminded me of the Shire from *Lord of the Rings*, complete with its hobbit-like local inhabitants. I had a split-cane fly rod I'd picked up in London. A couple of miles down the narrow lanes toward Liphook was a beautiful little chalk-bottom trout stream, the Wey River. It wound around through thick woods and under small bridges. I couldn't find out from the tight-lipped locals how to get a fishing license, or when the season ran, so when it turned into spring, I slipped my taken-down fly rod up in the sleeve of my big Mexican sweater, walked the two miles or so to a lonely stretch away from farmhouses, and snuck through the woods until I reached the stream.

It was wonderfully peaceful there under the trees, out of sight of anyone. I discovered a three-arch stone bridge. One of its arches had collapsed and fallen into the river in an age long past. It wasn't wide enough for anything more than cart or foot traffic, only about five feet across. There was no discernible road leading to it, so the bridge certainly predated the existing roads. This was Hampshire, where the roads are so old they're worn down sometimes six feet deeper than the fields, like wide ruts in the earth. I imagined in my romantic historian's mind that the bridge was Roman or at least early Norman. It had some age on it, for sure.

I've always been taken with history. From my earliest childhood I had read tales of knights and Romans, Vikings, and Druids. My interest hadn't waned with the years and I'd become better informed than I was in my childhood. England is alive with history. Every town we drove into had a castle somewhere. There were prehistoric standing stones in the middle of farm fields, ancient earthworks on the bald hill tops, Roman walls, and ruined abbeys. I knew that Hampshire was in the heart of prehistoric and Roman Britain, and was part of the first kingdom of the Norman conquerors of the Anglo-Saxons.

I was also the band navigator because of my interest in maps. So I was more aware than most of my compatriots of the historical attractions around us, though John McFee shared this interest as well. We didn't usually get anyone to go along with us to visit places not having to do with business. It was a pity. One afternoon Huey, Steve Liebert, and I finally got the van and went out to Winchester, Salisbury, and Stonehenge. It was only about forty miles from Headley, as the crow flies. I'd been to these places as a ten-year-old, on my family's great camping adventure to Europe in 1958. When we got to Stonehenge— now much more organized than it was in '58 when it was just jumble of stones in a pasture that you could just park and walk up to—we pulled into the new parking area and I paid the fifty pence to walk under the road to see the enigmatic Sarsen trilithons and bluestones. Huey and Steve stayed in the car-park, spending their 50P on pork pies from a refreshment cart. I guess if you've seen one stone, you've seen them all.

Dave Robinson came down to hear our new material. Dave is from Dublin. He was a few years older than we were, maybe thirty-five, thin, dark-haired, of medium height. He had that smiling Mick face that belies the tough guy beneath. He and Jacko were both indefatigable workers. Dave would arrive in his Volkswagen Golf sedan with its improvised pitching-wedge radio antenna, sit in an overstuffed chair, and listen as we rehearsed. We'd look to him for comments. Sometimes he'd fallen asleep. He always worked until he dropped.

Dave took me seriously and challenged me to be a leader. Both he and Jake did, but Dave to a greater degree. I was the lead singer and if I was a star, I should assume some leadership. I think Jake sussed me out before Dave did, or perhaps Dave just wanted to give me a chance to assert myself. Ciambotti and Huey were much more outgoing and vocal than I was. McFee was brilliant, but kept his opinion to himself unless asked. I tended to go along with the group thought of the moment. But in Dave's way of thinking, that was ass-backward. I should take the reins. If I couldn't do that, then I was a wanker.

Andrew Jakeman, Jacko, or "Jake Riviera," as he now called himself, was more volatile and charismatic than Dave. He had the high energy one expected of a former boxer. Shit, I wouldn't have wanted to box him. He'd have grinned as he tore you up with merciless jabs and below-the-belt shots, because that's how he was as a manager. He was outspoken, brash, and cunning. He could size up a situation—like he was sussing out a boxing opponent—in a flash. He always cut to the quick.

He was a great judge of talent and an artful manipulator of the British music press. He was the brilliance of the collective creative mind that made up Stiff Records, in partnership with Dave's solid toughness and heart.

Dave and Jake started Stiff Records in 1976. They were filling a need for a label that would put out records by innovative bands that wouldn't be signed by the stodgy corporate giants, and they wanted to have some fun by having successful artists who did things their own way. The Brits, Scots, and Irish have tremendous drive and ingenuity. Look how well British, Scottish, and Irish bands have done in the U.S. They know how to create a buzz that sounds much louder than the bug that makes it. It's all about attitude, showmanship, and those big brass bollocks.

Attitude central. One night we were at a house concert where Dr. Feelgood was supposed to play. A couple of bands had already been on. The packed house was going crazy, literally on the verge of doing damage to the place. The whole house, three stories, was shaking with clomping feet and soccer-stadium-style communal shouting, that soccer fan singing-in-unison *You'll Never Walk Alone* way. Maybe like Celts readying for battle with Roman Legions, fierce and strong. Wilko, the big-eyed, pasty-complexioned, bowl-haircut guitarist of the Feelgoods, sat in an overstuffed chair in an upstairs room and murmured, "I'm not fucking going on." He was dead serious. No one could make him budge, not Lee Brilleaux, not their manager. It was that attitude, that *stick* thing. It added to Wilko's and the Feelgood's mystique. English, Irish, and Scottish bands all had it. "No fucking encores till Berlin. That's bloody final, mate!"

There was an element of that iconoclastic, I'll-spit-in-your-face-and-you'll-fuckin'-like-it attitude behind Stiff Records. They were bucking the trend and they loved it.

Stiff's first premier artist and head guru-in-residence (frequently holding court at the pub next door) was Nick Lowe, who Jake had managed for some time. He and Nick stuck together for years to come. They also signed the adroitly-named Richard Hell, the Damned, and a host of other pub and punk worthies. Stiff's office in Nottinghill Gate was the antithesis of a corporate office. It looked like a packrat's house. There were Stiff '45 singles and record sleeves everywhere; photos, handouts, crumpled packs of Senior Service cigarettes, half-empty cups of tea, and an empty cider bottle or two left from late-night body-destroying brainstorming.

It was an in-house record label and assembly line, a beehive of activity. Various musos and artists came by and hung out, phones were ringing, guys with purple hair were stuffing '45 record sleeves, and somebody was thrashing a guitar on the narrow stairs. They came up with all kinds of innovative marketing tools. One I especially liked was a rubber hand stamp that read: *Artistic breakthrough—Double "B" sided single.* Jake was always on the phone, badgering or cajoling a club owner or a member of the press into seeing things Stiff's way. Dave was listening to Wreckless Eric or Ian Dury or one of us complain about something. At the nearby local, where the Stiff crowd had lunch and a pint, there was a buzzing vibe of adventure and a sense of great fun. Their official slogan was: *If it ain't Stiff, it ain't worth a fuck!*

The Damned were nice boys who were also straight-ahead, gobbing punks: Dave Vanian, Captain Sensible, and Rat

Scabies. Nick, who was house producer, had done their album. Ian Dury was a witty, smart fellow. He was partially disabled, and walked with the aid of crutches. But he wrote and sang a major anthem in the classic, *Sex and Drugs and Rock-n-Roll*. Why didn't I think of that title? Wreckless Eric was another one of the stable. Later Dave Robinson launched the video cult-fave ska band Madness. It seemed like successful acts were walking in off the street. Everyone was a punk star.

The punk scene was rocketing off. The Sex Pistols were all the rage in the *NME* and *Melody Maker*. There were punk bands and spray-painted band graffiti all over London. *Sex Pistols Rule, OK?* One Sunday afternoon I went to the Roundhouse in London's Chalk Farm to hear some Stiff band or other. There was a band on early called the Clash. We'd met a couple of them, Joe Strummer and Mick Jones. There were only a handful of punters on the floor. The Clash came on and bashed through what I would call a really lousy set: They were loud and way out of tune, it hardly seemed that they could play their instruments, and their lyrics were unintelligible.They gobbed on the audience and got gobbed on in return. At one point, Strummer, who seemed to be the sanest of the outfit, went over and tuned the bass while the bass player kept wanging away, not even noticing. It wasn't good, but there was something happening there, Mr. Jones. I had a sinking feeling in my gut. *They're terrible. But, you know what? I think we're fucked.* I knew this was going to be the next big thing. And I was right, as it turned out. At a gig at Dingwalls I heard Nigel Grainge and some other exec talking about the hard-ons they'd gotten when they heard the Clash. *Oh shit.*

There was a seemingly mild-mannered songwriter-type with

thick-frame glasses hanging out at Stiff, named Dec Costello. Costello was his stage name. It was hard to tell, since everyone had stage-punk-persona names. He seemed quite mousy and deferential. I guess Nick had told him we were hot stuff, or maybe he'd heard the old Clover discs. He was very respectful of us. He seemed like a very nice, intelligent guy, too nice to be a winner in the cutthroat horserace of mainstream commercial rock. We didn't know anything about his music, only that Jacko and Nick really dug him. He was Jacko's discovery.

The whole punk thing was unnerving. The way the press was on about it, it was clear that it was a major new movement, not a fad. Short punked-out hair, skinny ties, and thrift-store suit coats were *de rigueur*. This left Clover in a bind. We'd just been infected with the Thin Lizzy bug and had long hair, tight jeans, leather motorcycle jackets, and pointy lizard-skin Beatle boots. I'd spent a small fortune getting a pair of blue suede two-inch heel lace-ups at Kensington Market. They were suddenly passé? McFee and I had been wearing short silk Japanese kimonos on stage. We looked like genuine rockers. Now that was out of style? One could smell rotting dinosaur flesh over the aroma of the doner kebabs roasting down the street.

Jacko wanted Clover to back Dec Costello—who Jacko had renamed Elvis, of all things—in the studio. Nick would produce. They didn't need the whole band, so Huey and I were off that day. I went fishing down my lovely little river and Huey took off to London with his girlfriend. McFee, Ciambotti, Hopper, and Shine went to a tiny eight-track studio called Pathways to record four songs. The place was barely big enough to hold five musicians.

McFee brought a tape back to Headley and played it for me

on a crank-handled Wollensack tape recorder with a little built-in speaker. What I heard was astonishing: *Alison, The Angels Want To Wear My Red Shoes, Welcome to the Workin Week,* and maybe *Mystery Dance.* Four of the best songs I'd ever heard. Elvis's style was reminiscent of our management and record label stable-mates Graham Parker and the Rumour, but Elvis was better. Nick had mixed it all extremely dry, in your face, stark, beautifully under-produced, really. The melodies and lyrics were unbelievable. I instantly felt like quitting. This mild-mannered Clark Kent of the Jazzmaster was truly a Superman of another planet, talent-wise.

We all listened to his songs and wondered if Elvis might not be disregarded by the sometimes vicious music press as a clone of Graham Parker, who was riding a hot streak right then. We all agreed Elvis was a genius. The U.K. and later the world would concur.

When we came back from a U.S. swing, Elvis had been anointed King. *Sounds,* the *MM* and the *NME* had run multiple huge articles about him. His soon-to-be famous bespectacled face was plastered all over the magazine covers. In the U.K., the press can make you in a week if they choose. He was selling fifty thousand copies of *My Aim Is True* a week and was number one in the charts. So much for being dissed, instead he was the darling of the press. His intellectual lyrics and cutting music were right up their alley. Besides, rock critics are nerds. They love other nerds, artists that strike a meaningful pose. A normal rocker might be adept at his craft and enjoyable to see and he might sell millions of records, but he'll never get good notices from critics. Huey had this problem later on. Critics loved to slam him even while he was going octuple platinum, because Huey is in no way a nerd. He's from the cool guys' end of the playground, not the scorned, uncool corner where nerds plot their revenge. This is not to say that Elvis Costello didn't deserve the attention he got. Au contraire: he did and still does. And Elvis was King again, King Elvis the Second of the U.K. and the World.

Meanwhile, despite the rock world being stood on its head by spiky-haired, brazen punks, we were down at Headley putting together some harder-edged songs for a second album that we'd record the next fall. We needed to be better prepared to take on U.K. audiences. We rehearsed in the big hall of the drawing room, the same room Led Zeppelin recorded in. Dave Robinson would wake up in his chair, look at his watch and say, "Very well, lads, sounds good. Don't be afraid to give it some stick!"

Then he was off into the long English night in his VW Golf to London to find us a new tour.

LYNYRD SKYNYRD

If I leave here tomorrow
Would you still remember me?

LYNYRD SKYNYRD

Dave and Jacko managed to grab us a live one, another big tour, this time with Lynyrd Skynyrd. Skynyrd had been in the U.K. the year before, and had famously blown off the Stones at the huge Knebworth festival. Their big hits *Sweet Home Alabama* and *Freebird* were already classic rock anthems. This was humongous.

Our woodshedding down at Headley resulted in our adding more rockish material and we'd worked up some dual-guitar stuff that sounded authentic, though it was excruciating for me to play harmonies to McFee's leads. After all the years of not really playing, suddenly I had to match John Fuckin' McFee note for note way up the neck! Not only that, but they were harmony parts, which were sometimes conceptually strange. Not to worry, I found I could pull much of it off. We'd been working on throwing shapes as well. Huey was quite good at this stuff. The *Chickenfunk* meets classic British rock. There were now a lot of coordinated moves around the stage. Huey was jumping with his legs split off the drum riser, a move that he'd use for the next thirty years. One night he made the move and split his tight black jeans from stem to stern. Luckily (or not, depending on your view) he was wearing underpants. There might have been a riot. It might have made us famous. At another show, he jumped down into the audience, and then tried to hoist himself back onstage, but couldn't because it was too high and his pants were too tight. The roadies helped lift him back up, not exactly the rock moment he was looking for. *Hey, it's only rock and roll, but I like it.* It makes me laugh my ass off when I'm not busy cryin'.

We played many of the same venues with Skynyrd that we'd played with the Lizzys. These old theaters were lovely places, really. They were generally in the one- to two-thousand seat range, with some bigger, like the Glasgow Apollo, which had more like five thousand seats. The backstages were old, funky, and small, but charming. You could sense the vibes of the early days of rock. I often thought about the bands that had played before us on those stages: the Beatles, the Stones, the Who, Them, Eric Clapton, Jimi Hendrix, Traffic, the Animals, the Kinks.

On opening night of the tour we went out and were terrible, just terrible. The punters, once again mostly young males, really didn't like us, and that night, we all agreed with them. We sucked. It was just one of those nights. We all have them. You can be ready, even too ready, and then get out there and be flat, lifeless, with no way to revive the corpse. In the dressing room, we were disheartened. We'd rehearsed like crazy, and we hoped and expected to play well. We were embarrassed and wondered what Skynyrd thought of us.

The door opened and in came this skinny, wiry guy with a wild beard and a twinkle in his eye. He moved to the center of the little dressing room and put out his hands, inviting us to clasp them, which we did, like a basketball team. He looked at us circled around him and said earnestly to each of us in turn, looking straight in our eyes, "Man. Oh, man, man!! Oh, brother. Oh, man! Man. Brother! Ohh!! Man!!!" Then he broke off the handclasp and nodding repeatedly, muttering more emphatic "Oh, mans," backed out of the room. We all looked at each other and cracked up! It was Artimus Pyle, Skynyrd's drummer. He'd just come in and pumped us up without making any clear statement about how we'd stunk it up out there. No "You'll get 'em next time," or, "It's tough to open on the road," or anything like that. Just "Man. Oh, Man!!" That was way too cool. Like I said, laugh to keep from cryin'.

All the gigs were not as bad as that one. Some were worse.

It's not that we were playing badly. We just had another struggle as *Support* on our hands and some very hostile audiences, for sure. The Skynyrd punters made the Lizzy crowd seem like tea-quaffing twits from Eton. These were Brit wannabe rednecks, complete with big Confederate flags, Lord love 'em. Where the fuck they'd come from? At the University of Leeds—at which the entrance to the stage is at the back of the stage, behind all the gear—we picked our way through the jumbled lines of drum sets, wires, mic stands, and amplifiers in our tight pants and high-heeled rock boots, carrying our guitars to take the stage. A long-haired pseudo-redneck hippie stood up in the jam-packed but dead-silent hall and yelled, "I saw you with Lizzy and you're still shyte!" Thanks, we're happy to see you, too. And, if you want to be an American redneck, it's "shit," or "shee-yit," not "shyte." Get your vernacular straight!

Were there any two tougher acts to open for than Thin Lizzy and Lynyrd Skynyrd? That's what trial by fire is, baby: Swim or sink. We did both. The Skynyrd guys were good to us, but they had their own scene going on. They were on another level of partying from us. Every morning they each had a bottle of Moët & Chandon and a pot of tea with a chunk of hash in it. These were Southern guys, used to doing heavy hitting of substances. I was on the natch for this tour, having had my booze cut off by the band. I played a lot better that way, plus I was in a better position to watch all the crazy shit go down.

Like a night in Liverpool at the Holiday Inn. It was our second go-round for this hotel, one of the better ones in which we stayed. We got there in the afternoon and drifted into the bar to hang out. There was a cosmetics salesgirls' convention happening, which was somewhat promising, if a bit straight. The dolled-up, made-up ladies, both young and middle-aged, were chattering away in the lounge, having a bevvy or two. We were there checking it all out. John Burnham arrived with a box full of our Phonogram single *Chickenfunk*. Ciambotti, warming up for an epic night, took a 45 out of its sleeve and fired it like a Frisbee across the bar. It sailed and cut through the crowded room, miraculously just missing several pretty gals at high speed, and shattered against the far wall. It was an expression of contempt for Phonogram's product. I didn't like having a single of *Chickenfunk* either. I didn't write it, and felt left out of the whole process. Plus, the song stunk. *Ain't no bunk, the Chickenfunk.* But forget the song, the main event was just beginning, the night was very young. Somehow Johnny corralled an oddly out-of-place wooden Indian from the reception area and sat it next to him on a bar stool, where he proceeded to pour drinks on it. Eventually, he was asked to leave the bar by the management. He tried to take the Indian with him in the elevator. And off he went.

We all had a day off, so the roadies were rested and ready to have some fun. Ciambotti hooked up with them, a frequent *modus operandi* for wild nights, and for the next several hours, beds flopped out of elevators into the lobby, loud noises emanated from various rooms, and overgrown boys in varying states of inebriation and nakedness ran up and down hallways, laughing hysterically, well past their and everyone else's bedtimes. Complaints to the Holiday Inn's management led the hotel staff to investigate. When Ciambotti and his wild cohorts, including Steve Liebert, or Lybo, as we called him, proved to be too hard to catch for the harried hotel security, which consisted of a couple of zit-faced night clerks, the Bobbies were called in to take part in what became a merry chase. It finally ended at three in the morning, when Liverpool's Finest caught Johnny with his pants down, having a slash in an elevator. The coppers took him outside and let him know in no uncertain terms that any more of these activities would result in rather unpleasant consequences. As it turned out, we had a fairly early departure in our van the next morning. Ciambotti was a bit green. *It's been a hard day's night.*

We plowed through the Midlands again, getting little respect from the punters. If anything, it was rougher than it was with Thin Lizzy. Skynyrd fans were hard-core. They didn't want to listen to any sissy Californians singing in harmony. *We wanna rock!* We did our best, throwing shapes and flipping hair and playing twin leads. We were still having fun, playing pretty well, but it was frustrating to not make much of an inroad with the fans. As we played our way north, the band tried to shield me from an anticipated review in *NME* in which the reviewer called me a "journeyman singer, at best." When I saw it, I was cut to my heart. And pissed off. I overcompensated by going over the top at the next gig, over-singing and over-shaping, trying to convince the audience and myself that the review was wrong. It didn't work on either score.

I wasn't being allowed to drink, so I wasn't taking part in some of the fun that was going down. There was a lot of booze and drugs around Skynyrd and our crew. Things had gotten wild on a number of nights while I got my sleep. J. B. was out with us once again, leading the charge into the night. Skynyrd had three attractive young ladies singing with them. One afternoon, when we were hanging in JB's hotel room with the girls, JB came out of the bathroom naked with a pair of sunglasses on his dick. That was quite a funny way to come on! Ironically, I think it paid off for him later that night.

Skynyrd was a good, full-on band, not spectacular for most of their set, but solid, bluesy. They had the lead guitar thing in spades, three of them. They blazed away on the blues stuff— real swampy, rockin', Southern. No apologies, no bullshit. Their set was a bit long and repetitive for repeated nightly viewing, but it really came together at the end, with *Sweet Home Alabama* and *Freebird*. A good-old hippie mirror ball was hit with bright spotlights, sending thousands of rays of light spinning around the hall during *Freebird*. It was a classic rock-n-roll moment. Their current album was *Street Survivor*, and the cover showed the band engulfed in flames. I thought at the time, "Now that's a weird image." The tragic events of the near future would show it a sad premonition.

Artimus Pyle, our drummer buddy, was a notable wild man

in a band of wild men. In Newcastle, Skynyrd was invited out to some young lord's country estate. Apparently, the extensive acreage of the grounds beyond the house was a wild animal park, with lions and other big game. This was not the average Englishman's brick-walled twelve-by-twelve back yard with scrawny tomato plants and nosy neighbors looking down from the upstairs flat next door. The band was told to *absolutely not* venture out of the manor house. So naturally, Art dashed through an unlocked window, out into the wild animal park and was quickly gone. No one, including the presumably safari-outfitted big game wardens, could find him in the rapidly-falling dusk.

Hours had passed and the show was on. We finished our set. A half-hour, forty-five minutes went by. The Geordies, as the people of Newcastle are called, were stomping and shouting in the hall, going nuts, getting ready to be angry, which might be called a regional trait. Newcastle Brown Ale is one of the strongest beers in the U.K., famous for having so many victims of its abuse that there's said to be a special "brown ale" wing at the Newcastle hospital. The punters had been throwing down the brown that night. Both bands were in Skynyrd's dressing room, in full war-room crisis mode. Mickey Shine was going to sit in for Artimus, who had perhaps been eaten by a lion.

Suddenly, the door flew open and Art was wrestled into the room by three burly Skynyrd roadies. Like a bearded lizard being muscled by bikers. He was thrashing about like a drug-crazed madman, out of control. I was sitting in a chair against the wall. Art kicked and bit and punched his captors, who must have outweighed him by four hundred and fifty pounds. Then he looked down at me and gave me an exaggerated wink! He went out and played a great set. It was all a put-on. Artimus the Wildman.

We finally wound our way back to London, where the tour ended with fond farewells. We had a big time hanging out with those guys. Only Skynyrd could order a case of Moët & Chandon at three in the morning from a sleeping night manager at a small hotel and then say, "Oh shee-yit, if you don't got it then send up a couple of cases of fuckin' beer!"

Tragically, their plane would crash in just a few months, killing Ronnie Van Zant and several others. Their songs sure live on, though, don't they?

***

The review in the *New Musical Express* calling me just a journeyman singer made me very angry, and as you might expect, didn't do much for my already-strained sense of confidence. I don't know what it is that makes audiences connect to some performers and not to others, but in my case, I knew it was my own self-doubt that was the culprit. Yet how was I to overcome that? It had been in me ever since I was a chickenshit runt in middle school, ever since the wolf-spiders and H-bombs. It was hard for me to root out. You can't simply tell yourself you're going to dig yourself. Yet, that's the quality stars have. They have no doubt that people will like them. Look at Huey. He embodies self-confidence. He simply doesn't doubt himself much, though he keeps on his toes around accomplished people. His confidence draws people. The world has always thrown itself at him. He couldn't fail.

I had the looks, the voice, and the talent I needed to be a

successful rocker, but there was something missing, and that was unconditional self-love. And the balls to match it.

THE CHELSEA HOTEL
IN EARL'S COURT SQUARE

I'll always love Midnite
I love the way she leads me on...

ALEX CALL

Our album was out at last. Jacko had come up with a name for the record that we agreed to for some unknowable, influenced-by-aliens reason. "Right, chaps. Here's the thing: You've been unavailable for years, so let's call your album that. *Unavailable*. Yes? Yes?" His bug-eyed, gesticulating enthusiasm was infectious, and obviously it spun even McFee and Huey's heads around. This made sense? It was group psychosis. *Unavailable*.

What the fuck were we thinking? It seemed like a good idea at the time. Jake had a passion and an apparent genius for naming things and people. Like "Elvis Costello." Ridiculous, but it worked, if not all of the time. For example, Dave Robinson didn't have a *now, new wave* name, and frankly couldn't be bothered to create one for himself, so Jake took Dave's middle name, Watson, and dubbed him *Watson Television*. Dave just let that one slide off him. So Clover became *Unavailable*. Dave's name didn't stick; ours did.

For the moment we were actually quite available, waiting for the next thing on our schedule. We were now staying in Earl's Court Square, an area filled with foreigners of all stripes, at a tourist hotel called the Chelsea: *The Chelsea Hotel in Earl's Court Square*. Go figure. We could have as easily been in the Knightsbridge Hotel in Kensington, or the Upper Tooting Hotel in Brixton, or the New York Hotel in Philadelphia, but no matter. The Chelsea Hotel was a typical cheap tourist hovel, carved from the remnants of Victorian-era townhouses, which resemble the brownstones of New York, but are usually painted white. The interior was cramped and chaotic with narrow, ill-lit hallways painted war-surplus green, lukewarm baths down the hall (bathwater also war-surplus green), and a completely nonsensical floor plan. The rooms weren't numbered logically: Room one was across from room eight, but room five was on the floor above. It was quite a confusing place, it would have been like the Labyrinth if one were on acid, but for now it was home.

We designated it a temporary lawless zone for wild nights and steam off-letting. We'd met a lot of people in London now, and the hotel bar, which would otherwise have been empty, often had a good crowd. The Lizzys were there, Nick Lowe, Elvis, JB, various Stiffs, rockers, girls, and hangers-on of different stripes, from groupies to label people. There were enough wannabe models and music-biz girls to make the evenings interesting.

It was time to let off the pent-up, unspoken pressure. We'd been out there getting pounded by audiences and the press. Our internal springs had been wound pretty tightly. We were now aware of how much of a pressure cooker it was in which we were stewing. If you can't take the heat, stay out of the kitchen. Or, pour some vodka on the fire and see how hot you can make it burn?

Without the structure of a tour to keep us under control, we were running a bit hot and wild. JB introduced us to a place near Harrods in Chelsea called the Loose Box, which was a winebar literally jammed with swingin' singles, young bankers, secretaries, and the like, each pressing through the packed main floor or the equally-packed balcony clutching his or her own bottle of Liebfraumilch and a glass. It was a pick-up joint. Everyone knew what the action was. Suddenly, you'd find yourself squeezed face-to-face with a member of the opposite sex who might be interested, and away you went.

One morning after a Loose Box night, I woke up in an extremely hung-over state in an apartment I didn't remember going to the night before. The young lady was getting ready for work. I awkwardly excused myself and left. The flat was in one of those white three- or four-story walk-ups that are everywhere in London. The apartments, just like the hotels, had been created out of former Victorian townhouses which had once had bigger rooms. The floor plans, as in the Chelsea Hotel, didn't make much sense. I stumbled down the stairs and opened what I presumed to be the door leading to the outside, only to find myself in the flat of a couple having their breakfast. "Uh, good morning!" What's worse, I did that again before somehow finding the welcoming cold, gray, wind-blown street. Don't people lock their front doors, fer fucksake? *Ohhh, my head.*

Our old pal Marcus was hanging out with us at the Chelsea. He'd been trying to hook on with us as a drummer for a long time. He was a good guy, part of the family, but he'd never been—nor would he ever be—the drummer we were looking for. Marcus was known to keep a stash of nasal stimulants about his person, so we were always hitting him up for the same, and he was very generous. He and Ciambotti had a silly stoned thing going on. Johnny called Marcus "Harry the Hebe," because Marcus is Jewish, and rather hairy. Men will be boys. In the wee hours of the night, Ciambotti was often on the prowl, searching for Marcus in the warren of rooms we inhabited, while Marcus was on his endless, Sir Sleezalot quest: a panty raid.

One night I was lying in my little twin bed, trying to sleep. Our long, narrow rooms had four twin beds in a row, like a dormitory or barracks. I was one bed in from the window.

I awoke to find Marcus standing over me, breathless. He'd come in from the balcony, which adjoined the next room's balcony. You could easily climb from balcony to balcony.

He whispered breathlessly, "If Clambottle comes through here, tell him you haven't seen me!" With a furtive glance over his shoulder at the open window, he hustled out the door at the far end of the room.

Sure, yeah, whatever, man. Shit, can I sleep, please?

A few minutes later, my dreams were once again interrupted, by a wild-eyed Ciambotti, weaving as he loomed over me in the dark room, lit by the diffused glare of the Earl's Court streetlamps. He too had come in the window from the other room. He was waving his big folding knife around. His breath was like the bottom of a whiskey barrel. He hissed intently, "If I find Harry the Hebe, I promise not to stick this knife in his throat!" Then, like a psychotic combination of dapper vampire and mafia hit man, he was gone into the night.

The young, vaguely hip Lebanese guys who ran the hotel were glad to have us as paying guests in their otherwise mostly-empty establishment. They liked the women who visited us and they liked making money at their bar. They really did try to be cool, but they didn't have the stamina to keep up.

One evening they closed down the bar at midnight for some darned reason, perhaps the legal hours that a pub could keep, or something illogical like that. They didn't realize that though we'd run out of money and the bell had definitely rang, Ciambotti and I weren't near finished drinking and carrying on yet. The bar was, of course, locked behind those wooden shutters—which pull down like blinds from above and keep the bottles so inconveniently out of reach—that many British bars employ. After sneaking back into the bar and determining that the coast was clear, Ciambotti took a pool cue and tied a shoelace on the tip with a slip-knot hanging down like a little noose. He used the cue to pry up the bar shutter as far as it would go, maybe three or four inches, stuck the cue into the bar as far as it would reach, and angled the slip-knot over the neck of a liter of vodka. He raised the tip of the cue and the knot tightened. He had it! Down the big bottle slid on the cue into our waiting hands. We squeezed it under the shutter, and our problem was at least momentarily solved. The managers never did figure out how a liter of vodka disappeared from the locked-up bar, though I'm sure they knew who was responsible.

We were out clubbing around as well, hitting trendy Dingwalls, the Marquee Club, or one of the many clubs and pubs where bands were playing and boilers were in evidence. There was a chick from the label with a big set o'Bristols we called Rude Kathy, who always flirted around, daring one or the other of us to have a go. Well, one night we were at some club somewhere and I may have had a wee drop taken. I knew Rude Kathy fancied me, so I suggested to her that we slip out to JB's car. She said, "Sure, why not?" I got the keys, and shortly we were out there engaging in some awkward back-seat coed wresting. It was a small car. JB, Huey, Marcus, Hopper, and a couple of other guys came out of the club to smoke a spliff, and they saw this little sedan bouncing and rockin' around in the car park, its windows all fogged up, so naturally they came and stood around it in a circle. Rude Kathy shrieked and beat a red-faced retreat, but I thought it was as funny as hell. JB and the lads had a good laugh. JB called me "Mr. Love, Love," from my song of that title.

We were going back to the States to do a summer tour. Our single, the same *Love, Love*, was up for a slot on "Top of the Pops," the highly-influential weekly BBC TV pop music show. If we were allowed to perform the song there, we'd have a shot at charting the following week. It might change everything. There were both music biz "political" considerations and visa-work permit issues with getting us on the show. We had to find an English band with whom we could trade work-hours in the States to make up for the time we would spend shooting "Top of the Pops." It was also a question of whether our management guys had enough juice to get us on the show. Jacko and Robbo were at the BBC, working overtime, trying to talk the thing into happening.

It was all coming down to the last minute. While our mangers wangled and wheedled, we hung out at the fabulous BBC bar, having a few bevvies with actors and actresses, dancers, singers, and producers.

We flirted with the ladies and listened to amazing movie, theater, and other show biz tales from the highly-skilled raconteurs among the BBC bar regulars. JB was with us, asking both men and women if they were "firm!" As the evening moved along it became evident that we weren't going to get a shot on "Top of the Pops." So we had a drink. We were leaving for the good ol' U.S. of A. on the morrow, so why not have a toast? Or five? "Shall we, chaps?"

At two in the morning, "pissed as newts," as Nick Lowe would say, JB, Huey, and I wobbled our way back to JB's West End place. The entrance to his flat was through a big arched driveway that bisected his building. We were walking in when JB and Huey spotted two guys harassing a girl across the road. They yelled out, "Hey, leave her fuckin' alone!" The guys cursed back. Never one to encourage a fight, and thinking in any case that no one in their right mind would mess with Huey and JB, both athletic, good-sized guys in their prime, I stumbled down to JB's and took my shirt off, ready to crash. It had been a hard day's night.

Suddenly there was JB, the one and only six-foot-two chickenshit of Scottish descent, holding the butt end of a pool cue.

He pressed the cue on me, spouting excitedly, "They're beating up Huey!"

Without thinking, I took the cue and ran shirtless, and I think shoeless as well, out to the mouth of the driveway. The two guys were about fifty feet away at the other end of the archway, pounding on Huey. He was trying to defend himself, but he was outnumbered and they had him down. I raised the cue above my head like a samurai sword and starting shouting loud, phony Japanese Samurai-movie invective at them, charging at them waving this pool cue. It was something like "KoiYo! Kazumata! Shoi-Yudahhhh!"

They took a look at me and must have figured I was a fuckin' psycho, which description at that drunken moment I probably fit, and they took off. Huey was hurt. They'd broken a stout milk bottle over his head and he was pretty badly cut up. He'd have to go the hospital and get part of his long hair shaved and a get a few stitches. My Toshirô Mifune impersonation complete, and my head and gut full of scotch, I went back and crashed while JB and Huey went off to get doctored up.

We were out at Heathrow Airport in the morning. Huey had only slept for an hour. He had a bandage on the side of his head. My drunken samurai impression had at least partially saved the night. I'm not sure what might have happened if the punks hadn't taken off. Most likely, they'd have beaten me to a pulp with my own pool cue.

We had a couple of pints and got on the plane, going back to play for our fellow Yanks at long last.

We weren't the same guys who had flown off to England the year before. We'd been up and down and sideways. We'd been living on booze, smokes, coffee, boredom, anxiety, and wildness for months. We were as skinny and pale as any rockers. I was down to twenty-nine-inch waist Levi's. I had to wear girl's jeans. When we got picked up at the airport, our friend Hunter said, "We've got to get some cheeseburgers in you guys. Your veins are popping out of your foreheads!"

We may have looked out of place in tanned, fit California, but we were now battle-hardened veterans, ready for more rock-n-roll wars. Bring 'em on.

American Band

On the road again
Just can't wait to get on the road again...

WILLIE NELSON
(of course)

We were happy to be back in the land of hot showers and real cheeseburgers again. We hadn't been home for months. We hung out with our girlfriends and our pals. I got to see my goofy dog Abu, who had been with my dad. I'd missed him a lot. He was my solo-camping buddy. He and I had spent a lot of hours, just the two of us, driving down rutted dirt roads in search of fishing spots and seldom-visited wild places in the mountains, where he could chase deer and I could chase trout. Neither of us did as well as we'd have liked at those pursuits, but we were great companions. He'd flop his big lab-shepherd body down next to my sleeping bag under the stars. But there wasn't enough time for a camping trip right then. Clover squeezed in a softball game or two and then we were off in a station wagon to conquer America.

We had a hugely important Friday night headlining gig at the Roxy on the Sunset Strip. Wow. Clover was getting somewhere now. The Roxy epitomized what the L.A. scene was all about: long legged, enhanced-bosomed blondes, glad-handing handsome guys with sunglasses on at midnight, lights, camera, action. It was the most-happening L.A. gig of the time. There was buzz enough about us to pack the place with worthies: record company A&R types, publishers, publicists, wannabe singers, their managers and entourages, and dozens of women who were so pretty and flashy it was hard to know whose cleavage to stare at next!

We played well. It was L.A., baby. Bright lights, valet parking, drop-dead waitresses, perfect teeth, big boobs, phony smiles, handshakes with a dagger in the other hand. Man, it was all good. Jacko and Dave were pleased. People we didn't know plied us with coke and scotch and told us how great we were and how we should be doing business with them instead of so-and-so, who was a hopeless loser. It almost made you want to stay up all night and figure it out over a bunch of drink and drugs. Anyway, it was a fun night and we were off to a good start for our American tour.

What we were actually off into was the heat of summer in a rented station wagon and a Hertz truck full of gear. The Friday night Roxy crowd didn't need to know the details. Not exactly a Silver Eagle bus with a built-in stereo and champagne on ice, but that would come soon, we hoped. We headed east, to Phoenix, Albuquerque. Houston, New Orleans, Miami. It's a big country and we were going to drive it, seven wankers to a wagon with the back seat folded out backwards, legs hanging out in the blazing sun.

CB radios were all the rage that summer. *Roll that truckin' convoy, son.* We had one to communicate with the roadies in the Hertz truck and so we could hear the latest info on the

"Smokies." *Break one-nine, this be that one Johnny Reb. Mercy, how it be lookin' over your donkey? Kick it back. [crackle, buzz] How 'bout you, good buddy? You got the Okie Drifter. There be a smoky handing out green stamps at the three-six-two, don'chu see. Mercy, I be eyeballin' a seat cover in a red four wheeler at the three-five-niner....*

We were quite taken with this expression of Americana. We all had "handles." Frank, who drove the station wagon, was the "Cuban Cutie." I was the "California Kid." John McFee had the best: "That One Wacko Shithead." Huey especially got into it; he's very good at lingo and regional accents. He'd been talking a bit like a Brit, everything from cockney to member of Parliament, but letting the whole Brit approach color his language. In keeping with his perfectionist personality, he switched over and did CB lingo just right. He didn't want to be mistaken for, say, a rock musician in a station wagon. He did a funny bit where he hit his throat repeatedly with the side of his hand while going on in redneck-ese about needing a new set of load-levelers for his rig. He sounded like a guy thumping down a washboard road in a rig with bad shocks.

In Albuquerque, we had a gig at a roadhouse way out in the hills, which was called off because nobody—and I mean not one person—showed up. The club owner, a good-natured guy, gave us broke musos a couple of fifths of scotch. Huey uncharacteristically drank heavily and flipped over a foosball table at the club. Oops, sorry, we're just leaving, thanks for the booze man. Sorry about the table. We were staying at a big old motel just outside the Albuquerque city limits, a place that had an after-hours bar scene. We were told that politicos and organized crime figures hung out there, along with numerous hookers. It was kind of like Phil Lynott's mom's place in Manchester, but on a bigger, dark Cadillac, Wild West, New Mexico scale.

It was a hot June night. Doomed bugs circled in the parking lot lights. The scotch and beer had been flowing for hours. At three in the morning, Huey somehow managed to be out wandering around under those lights in the packed parking lot stark naked, bottle of scotch in his hand, shouting CB lingo. "Kick it back! Good Buddy! How it be looking over your donkey?" He decided it would be funny to break those little glass panels that say *Break Glass in Case of Fire*. So he broke them with his fists, shards of glass tinkling on the concrete. It was a wonder he didn't get his hands all cut up.

It was very funny, but eventually we stopped cracking up and McFee—the great calm voice in the night—talked him in, and Huey finally crashed out in McFee's room. But John liked having fun at Huey's expense, so he put the finishing touch on the evening by turning a mattress over on the sleeping lad, and packing his balls in ice. John found this to be wildly hilarious, as did we all. Today, we'd have captured it all on our cell phones and it would have been on YouTube by dawn. Thanks to that kinder, gentler, technology-deficient age, Huey was spared further humiliation for the moment.

The next day we had to drive all the way to Houston. That's like, fourteen hours. The merciless Texas summer sun beat down on the station wagon. Huey sat in the back, trying to sleep it off. The poor guy was not feeling well at all. After observing him puking on the side of the road, one friendly trucker called on the CB and said gravely, but with deep compassion, "Somebody needs to tell that boy to keep his liquor down." Huey didn't drink any more scotch for a long time. Like, maybe three days.

McFee was a great practical joker. Because he was outwardly so calm and humble, he could pull off major shit on the unsuspecting. One night he called our room and told Huey to come to his room "right now," he had to show him something.

Huey had just gotten out of the shower. He said, "Can't it wait?"

McFee said, "No, you've got to see this now!"

If McFee said it's important, then, so be it. Huey put a towel around his waist and stepped out into the motel hallway to John's door and knocked. John opened the door a crack and grabbed Huey's towel, whipped it off his waist, and slammed the door shut!

Everyone else, including me, Huey's roommate, had previously agreed not to let Huey into our rooms. Huey raged around naked in the hallway for a few minutes until John relented, laughing insanely. John always had this that-was-fucking-funny, don't-you-think conspiratorial look in his eyes. Huey had to laugh, too.

New Orleans, just like I pictured it. America's Alcoholic Disneyland, where the normally straight-laced Protestants of the Midwest and the South funneled on down the Missouri, Ohio, and Mississippi rivers to become momentary Catholic–Voodoo worshippers at the fire-fountain altar of the Big Easy. There were guys who were probably perfectly responsible accountants back home stumbling zombie-like down Bourbon Street at two in the morning, bare-chested with their t-shirts in one hand and a drink in the other. Normally staid, church-going, Jesus-loving, maybe not-so-sexually-repressed-as-you-might-have-imagined secretaries flashed their breasts and threw strings of beads from wrought iron balconies. The tide of hurricane-fueled humanity slogged past local passed-out drunks asleep in their own vomit. This was real, not Disney animatronics. Pirates of Bourbon Street. It was a wild opportunity, obviously, and quite a surreal scene. At our club gig on the strip in Fat City, a big-busted gal with an outrageously huge cone-shaped bouffant hairdo boogied down on the dance floor to a funky Naw'lins groove while a two-inch-long burgundy-colored palmetto bug walked around her hair like a living brooch.

We got a small cash bonus, which was unheard of, and three days off. It was Fourth of July weekend. I spotted a real hot but straight-looking Dallas business gal at an oyster bar. I told Sean Hopper I was positive she wouldn't even talk to me. But I struck up a conversation and we ended up eating a lot of oysters and having a big ol' Naw'lins time together. She had a penthouse room in the Sheraton with a view of the whole city. It was pretty up there. There were fireworks and forked lightning in the hot Louisiana sky.

After three wild days, including some more balcony-based shenanigans involving Ciambotti, fireworks (M-80 barrel bombs), and a police car, somehow Frank corralled us all and we headed off to Miami, another long-ass drive. There were seven of us in the station wagon. McFee and I generally sat in the rear seat that faced backwards, with the tailgate down so we could stretch our legs out. It was otherwise a really cramped ride. No one wanted to sit in the middle of the middle seat. You had to call "shotgun" first thing every day to sit in the coveted front passenger seat. Woe be to the guy who was too hung-over to think of calling at least a window. But John and I were the only ones who wanted to ride looking backwards.

Ciambotti, who was of course the last of the wayward partiers to be rounded up by Frank, was sitting in the middle of the middle seat the day we left New Orleans. We headed east, cruising along I-10 through the Florida Panhandle. It was an endlessly long, straight road, not too much traffic. It was a hot, muggy, cloudy day, with thunderstorms brewing. We came up on our equipment truck, with Cinque, Massive Roggie, and Lybo grinding along at fifty-five. Ciambotti lit a bottle rocket in a coke bottle and fired it out the window from his middle seat as we drove past the truck. It shot out and hit the truck right on the passenger door. Wow, what a good shot! But it was dangerous. We were going, "Fuck, Ciambotti, you're going to get us busted!" Frank was holding our stash of pot and a little of the white powder that makes those fourteen-hour drives bearable.

Suddenly, from out of nowhere, there was a Florida state trooper lighting us up. We pulled over on to the shoulder. McFee and I were sitting with the tailgate down, facing the square-jawed guy in his flat-brimmed Smokey the Bear hat as he walked up. He looked like an actor perfectly typecast for his role: thick-neck, military buzz cut, arms like legs. He looked like a big, mean version of Porky Pig. With a gun and a badge and cuffs on his utility belt and a shotgun in his car. Probably played tackle at Florida State.

He drawled, "Which one of you fellers been shootin' off fahr'wuhks?" He didn't sound all that friendly.

McFee, his hair hanging halfway to his waist, was wearing three-inch-long abalone earrings, a wild Hawaiian shirt, outsized women's sunglasses, and ripped-up shorts. He said, "I didn't do it, officer," from behind his Foster Grants.

The trooper glared at us. "Don't get smart with me, boy.

You watch your mouth. You're gonna wind up in a whole heap a trouble!"

Holy shit! He meant it, didn't he? We shut right up. Frank was out of the car, being cool, smiling and explaining that it was a bottle rocket, that it was our equipment truck we'd fired upon, and that we knew we shouldn't have done it. Our truck rolled up. So did four other state troopers. We were way fucking surrounded. Our hearts were thumping. Visions of smirking Southern jail wardens danced in our heads. We weren't in West Marin anymore, Toto. We were fifty miles from some nasty lockup in a small town in the cypress swamps somewhere west of Tallahassee. In 1976, long-hairs could still be still mistaken for commie- or faggot- or nigger-lovers in this part of the world.

The central-casting troopers were conferring, trying to figure out what do with us, when a blue dodge sedan rolled up and a short, beefy guy with long, curly hair, like an afro almost, and a '38 in the waistband of his plaid bermudas hopped out. He was the ATF agent who'd seen the incident and two-wayed the cops. He'd thought it was rednecks shotgunning a hippie truck. He was cool, thank God. He obviously outranked the troopers, who didn't want to deal with us anyway. We hastily autographed an album for him and we all apologized profusely to all the burly law enforcement guys. We were released from our doorway to hell and drove off at the speed limit, with the windows rolled up. When I drive around the South today and see people being routinely searched for drugs I have the feeling that we skated that muggy afternoon.

Johnny saved the rest of the bottle rockets so he could rain them down on Raleigh later from a hotel rooftop.

We wended our way through the South. The weather was

unbelievably hot. And so were the Southern girls. "Where y'all partyin' t'naht?"

"I don't know. Where are we all partyin' t'naht?"

Sounded like fun, and it was. We headlined clubs, which were more or less full, depending on the night, and also opened at a few arenas for the Atlanta Rhythm Section, a great, great band. The audiences weren't as doggedly hostile as the young British males had been. There were a lot more girls at these shows, which worked well for us handsome lads. It makes a big difference when you walk out onstage to an enthusiastic welcome instead of a sullen one. Occasionally we lit it up, had fun onstage, and got some encores. We were getting to be a real solid big-stage band. We wished our friends back home could hear and see us the way we were playing. We assumed that they would. Eventually.

After nights of fireworks and crazy young belles in Atlanta, Raleigh, and other sweaty southern locales, we finally headed north and eventually hit New York. There we got to play the Bottom Line, one of America's most prestigious gigs, a New York counterpart to the Roxy. We also opened for Alice Cooper, of all strange bedfellows, at the Nassau Coliseum on Long Island.

The Big Apple was a trip. We squeezed into a limo, which wasn't big enough for all of us, but no matter, it was out first limo, and were driven somewhere to meet our new manager. Our new manager? Was anyone going to tell us we had a new manager? The streets of New York produced quite an impression on all of us. There were so many people, all nationalities, giant buildings, brownstones, delis, Arabs selling stereos, yellow taxis doing sixty down the avenues, the Empire

State building, Fifth Avenue, Greenwich Village, and Central Park. It was coolly overwhelming. Just put an actor or two and a cameraman out there and you have a movie. Amazing women walked by, right next to bums and stockbrokers, all colors, shapes, and sizes. We did meet our new American manager, Alan, and witnessed a gun battle between police and a gang in the same day. We did a photo shoot with Annie Leibowitz. We were riding high.

Clive Davis, the legendary head of Columbia Records, was at the Bottom Line gig. The room was packed with music biz types and members of the press. We played pretty well, but towards the end Ciambotti and Mickey Shine got into an argument about something onstage. About what? Who knows?

"You're too fuckin' loud."

"No. You're too fuckin' loud."

We're talking about two guys who could be so stubborn that they'd have a public fight during one of our most important shows ever. Johnny started smashing Shine's cymbals with the neck of his bass and yelling, "Fuck you!"

Shine, a New Yawker himself, was yelling, "Fuck you!" back.

Hey, no worries lads, it was just fuckin' Clive Davis, one of the most important figures in American pop music sitting ten feet away, in the front row!

Clive thought this was great, authentic rock-n-roll theater. Or so we hoped.

Mickey had been a bit of a problem for a while. He was a fine drummer. His track record over the years speaks for itself. But he had some kind of persecution complex going. He always seemed to think that he was getting screwed in some way by somebody—the sound guys, one of us, or somebody in management. He'd been pretty hard to get along with. He had that New York attitude that doesn't back down. You couldn't reason with him. If he got a bad monitor mix, it had to be on purpose. And since we were generally *Support*, our needs were actually subordinate to those of the headliner. Did we get the short end of the stick sometimes? Absolutely. But it was something you had to roll with, it was part of being a pro.

I knew he was a good guy, but Mickey had allowed conspiracy theories about the band and management to ripen in his head, and he'd gotten defensive about it all. He was a late addition to a band that had been together for years: the outsider. As I said, he was also extremely stubborn. After a while, no one wanted to room with him, so I agreed to. I got along with anybody. But by the end of the first night of listening to one of his illogical rants, I was ready to punch him out!

It's just the way it is in bands. Someone's always a problem, or has a problem. Somebody's drinking, somebody's snorting (and won't share), somebody's girlfriend doesn't like somebody else's girlfriend, etc., etc., etc. There's always a crisis, there are secret meetings in one of the hotel rooms, factions form and dissolve.

Crashing bass necks into cymbals, onstage "fuck yous," and Clive Davis notwithstanding, the next night we opened for Alice Cooper. Boy, if there had ever been a mismatch on a bill, this was it. Bambi vs. Godzilla. The Nassau Coliseum was an NBA arena: There were thirteen thousand people there, not one of whom had come to see Clover. The bill was us first, our buddies the Atlanta Rhythm Section next, then Alice Cooper would go out and do his heavy-metal-theatre thing with dancers in black spider suits crawling along huge nets behind the stage.

The Long Island crowd decided, just for fun, to hate us from the start. Actually, those in the higher-priced floor seats, about three thousand people, were applauding politely, but the more vocal ten thousand in the cheaper side sections were going nuts, booing and shouting shit at us. I mean the *word* shit, as in "Yer shit! Yeah, I'm talking to you!"

As the set went on beneath the barrage of "Yer shit!"'s they actually began throwing M-80s—barrel bombs—at us. M-80s have maybe four times the power of normal firecrackers. They're silver, with a fuse sticking out the side. They look like little sticks of dynamite. You could see them trailing smoke as they arced down at the stage. *Boom!* Some hit the stage. It was dangerous, like a war zone, smoke drifting around the amps from the incoming explosives. We were somewhere between amused and pissed off, but were still trying to win over the crowd. Jacko and Dave pulled us after four or five songs. We didn't want to quit. We left to a hail of M-80s and choice epithets. Both Ciambotti and I wanted to go up after this set of jerks who were really giving us a hard time. Jacko had to grab Johnny to keep him from storming up into the bleachers after them.

No, I won't back down...

Backstage, the label folks and our managers were tense, thinking we'd be really bummed out about the fiasco, but after a minute or two we were all cracking up. It was just too funny. There was a big spread of food, another thing Clover didn't often get, and soon, cold cuts and spoonfuls of mayonnaise were flying. Everyone got into it, even the label reps. Before long, we were all collapsing in laughter. It was a memorable night. It's rare to actually be booed off a stage. It's a badge of honor, a rock-n-roll Purple Heart.

At the end of evening I met a Japanese fashion photographer gal. From that chance, brief encounter came the oft-repeated band phrase, "Oh Arax, that was so beautifurr!"

We went on to Boston, where Huey's Irish uncle had arranged for us to come out to Gloucester for a booze cruise on his big powerboat. We had a good gig the night before and we were ready for a fun day off with no responsibilities. On the way out of Boston, we stopped to see one of Huey's old school buddies. His place was right next to a freeway exit, which was t-shaped, not a big curving off-ramp. We decided to sneak back on the freeway by going out the exit. It was illegal, but there was light traffic and it looked safe enough. Our station wagon and the big Hertz equipment truck got safely back on the freeway. The road dipped down into a lengthy underpass. John McFee and I were sitting, as usual, in the folded-down rear-facing back seat, with our legs stretched out on the tailgate. We watched as our truck, behind us by a hundred yards, descended the down ramp toward the underpass.

I said, "Don't you think the truck looks too tall to make it?"

John stared at the truck and said, "I think you're right."

I was right. The truck ground inexorably down the ramp at fifty-five miles an hour. The top of the truck's box struck the concrete underpass with a grand smash and was shorn off, showering the roadway with pieces of two-by-fours and torn strips of sheet metal. There was no stopping or turning back, there was no place to stop. The guys had no choice but to power through the underpass for two hundred yards throwing off sparks, two-by-two splinters, and Hertz truck-top detritus. We pulled off on the other side of the underpass at the first exit. If we'd gotten on the freeway correctly, we'd have seen the height-restriction sign in time for the truck to exit. Oh well.

McFee and I were beside ourselves, laughing so hard. We felt bad for our crew, but that was unbelievable, like watching a car-crash scene from "The French Connection." The shocked, dazed roadies got out and surveyed the damage. The sheet-metal top of the truck was folded back in about thirty folds like the pleats of an accordion and the back gate was angled out at forty-five degrees. The cargo box was knocked way out of square, totally ruined. So much for the roadies coming out on the highly-anticipated booze cruise. We had a gig in Washington D.C. the next night. Now the guys would have to get another truck and explain this one to Hertz. To add insult to injury, the sky over Boston darkened and it began to rain on our now-exposed gear! The dejected roadies would have to get plastic tarps to cover it.

On their way to Washington, they rented a new truck, from Avis or somebody—anybody but Hertz—and paid some guy off the street twenty bucks to drive the wrecked truck into a Hertz parking lot in New Jersey and run for it.

Our American tour had been big fun, but now we were on our way back to England to do our second album with Mutt.

Kick it back, good buddy.

America is a great country, so big, so full of characters. I hadn't seen the South before. It was all very exotic, if a bit frustrating at times. Southerners move at a different pace than westerners do. You want that second cup of coffee to jolt you out of your hangover? Well, the waitress will get there when she does, but at least she'll call you baby or sweetheart. Who can complain? Still, I couldn't ever see myself living down there. I love the wide-open vistas of the American West; those fifty-mile views. In the South, all you see is endless repeating low hills, there's never a view that to give you pause. Maybe that's why it's less visionary as a place. Hills and hollers. Little did I know then that I'd move there one day.

THE NASHVILLE

I'm sittin' on top of the world...
    An old song, recorded by AL JOLSON, *among others*

I woke up suddenly. Somebody was shaking me by the shoulders. I peered through my foggy eyes and tried to engage my groggy mind. It was Elvis Costello leaning over me in my hotel bed. "Time to wake up, silly Yanks! Pub's opening." We'd flown in from the States and we were not only jet-lagged but hung-over from drinking late on our last night in the States and then carrying on, partying with the night-flight stewardesses, who seemed to have every pill known to the pharmacology of the era. We staggered out bravely under the London overcast. *The boys are back in town.*

We were going back out to Rockfield, to make our second record. *Unavailable*, with no hit single, had already tanked. But so what? We were all rocked up. We'd been out on the road with Lizzy and Skynyrd and the Atlanta Rhythm Section. We'd been melted down in the crucible of touring and forged into a hard-edged band. McFee had made me work on my guitar playing and I was getting better. I'd written some songs that reflected our touring band status: songs about southern belles and difficult, long distance relationships. Huey and I were singing more double harmonies, which was working for us. Huey and I wrote a rockin' song called, *I'm Still Alive*, which summed up where we were then.

Four A.M. phone call on an eight-hour drive,
Love on the wire, baby, I'm still alive,
I'm still alive.

Mickey Shine was still a problem. Mutt wanted to bring in a drummer he liked for the next record. Dave and Jacko put it on us and Dave especially put it on me. I agreed we should pull the trigger on poor Mick. The drummer had been a missing link for us ever since the Mitch Howie days. Mickey hadn't really done anything wrong, he just hadn't fully clicked with us from the beginning. But he'd been game. Lord knows, he hadn't been paid much. His playing had been good enough for Elvis Costello's acclaimed first album, *My Aim Is True*. But he caught a bullet. Robbo took him aside, "Mick, fancy a drink? We need to talk."

Mutt called in Tony Braunegal, the drummer for the Anglo-American band Night Crawler. Tony was an American guy from Houston, a great drummer who would go on to play with Bonnie Raitt, Eric Burdon, Ricky Lee Jones, and Robert Cray. He was a solid studio drummer, in addition to being a riot in the studio and a lifelong pal.

Working on this album was not as nerve-wracking. We were more confident in the material. The disco shit was gone, thank God. We had some better songs: *Hearts Under Fire, Ain't*

Nobody Own Nobody's Soul, I'm Still Alive. Even on the ones I wasn't sure of, McFee and Mutt did some magic stuff with multi-tracked guitars. Our singing was better. Tony Braunegal had Mutt's trust, which is a real issue in the studio. The whole process felt good.

We had an interesting studio mate in Ozzy Osborne. He was doing a post-Black Sabbath solo album. Ozzy's a wild man, very gracious and kind, but just full of energy. He laughed a bit louder, drank a bit more, and was more ready for whatever might materialize than the rest of the crew. He was a Brummie, that is, from Birmingham. Straight up and in your face, but friendly, with an accent like he had a mouthful of cotton-candy covered marbles.

The Yanks and Brits had afternoon soccer matches out in a field next to the studios. It was a cow pasture, with clumps of grass and muddy areas. I played in goal, since I didn't see much sense in all that running and I could utilize my ball-catching skills. Tony, Johnny, and Huey were good players. The play was fun, but it had its moments. You haven't lived until you've been confronted with Ozzy thundering down the pitch right at you with his big army boots on, yelling like a madman. I attempted to stand my ground, but, hey, it's only a game, right?

One day, toward the end of the recording, we were cutting an *a cappella* version of *Keep on Rollin'*, an old Coasters song. Huey would be taking the train to London to meet his girlfriend when the session was done. He and I walked into the studio together, the last to arrive. Everyone was naked. Mutt, the engineer, the tape-op, our road crew. Johnny, John, and Sean were naked in the vocal booth. Butt-ass naked. Huey was pissed off. He wanted to get the session done, he didn't want to waste time on childish shit like taking off his clothes to sing a vocal. I thought it was hilarious.

We were all buck naked, standing around a Neumann mic. Even funnier was Mutt sitting nude at the console, twiddling knobs and sliding faders around while massive Rogie and Superslab stood hugely in the background, like a pair of landlocked white whales sans speedos. We started doing takes, but I couldn't stop laughing. It proved to be infectious. Hopper intoned in his bass announcer's voice, "And now! From Rockfield: Totally Nude!" I tried to sing, but I was cracking up. Huey was getting even more pissed. He snapped, "Roll the motherfucker!"

I replied, "You'd think that taking your clothes off would make you looser, Huey!"

Ciambotti chimed in, "Not Huey!"

We all cracked up, our laughter echoing deep in the reverb. We finally got 'er done, the album was finished. Off to the big time.

We were going out on tour again, this time with Graham Parker and the Rumour. Graham, who was at the moment kind of the Bruce Springsteen of the London New Wave scene, was managed by Dave and Jake. Graham was an intense, wiry Yorkshireman. He was kind of quiet, not highly outgoing, but onstage he was a spark-spitting dynamo. His band was led by guitarists Brinsley Schwartz and Martin Belmont and keyboard player Andrew Bodner. They were all pub rock veterans. The band was powerful and exciting. Like Springsteen, their sound relied less on virtuoso soloing than it did ensemble playing. They were the band on Elvis Costello's fantastic cut, *Watching the Detectives*. We were doing the customary swing through the major cities of Britain and Scotland, plus dates in Paris, Brussels, and Amsterdam.

First we needed to solve the drummer problem. Tony Braunegal wasn't available to do the tour. Dave and Jacko came up with a brilliant fellow, former 5000 Volts drummer Kevin Wells. Kevin was a tall, blonde, young-looking Brit who was not only a great drummer, but also a solid writer and singer, and played other instruments well. Because he was a writer and singer, he instinctively understood songs in a way many drummers we'd worked with hadn't. We hardly even needed to discuss things like dynamics (the ebb and flow of a song, soft when that's called for and hard when it's time for that) and feel (the style of the song.) He just played the right stuff. Plus he was very bright and an extremely funny, wisecracking veteran who enjoyed putting the needle in when it would provoke a humorous response. His great playing and rock-star good looks added the final missing piece to the Clover puzzle, at long last. He was our guy, an instant perfect fit.

This was a better tour for us. Not that we were going to blow off Graham. As the British equivalent of the Boss, he drew packed houses and drooling reviews, and knocked the punters dead. But the audiences were much less hostile to us. Graham's punters were more sophisticated than Lizzy's or Skynyrd's. He was New Wave without being overtly punk. His crowd was much more middle-class. We even got a few encores. Plus, we were more seasoned and our songs were better. We were at the top of our game.

There was quite a bit less craziness on the U.K. part of the tour than in the past. The guys in the Rumour were less inclined to go for the full rock-star madness. It wasn't that they didn't like a pint or two, but it was a more working-man, slightly saner crew. It was up to us to create chaos and wild nights. And I was on the wagon for the tour, per band orders, so I was reduced to spectator.

It's when we got to Paris that things began to get livelier. There was a gig was at an indoor roller rink, with four or five thousand fans there. They were *les punks*, with purple hair and earrings galore. The stage was just a two-foot-high riser on the floor of the rink, so they were really in our face and vice versa. This audience did not like us. They wanted Graham's New Wave sound. In France, whistling equaled booing and they were whistling away mightily. They were also sullen and angry, plus they were only five feet away. We played our set, but it got worse as it went along. We were playing fine, so we got more and more pissed off ourselves. They hated us, we hated them back. We played louder and faster, they whistled more, and a breaking point was reached.

Right before the last song, Huey grabbed the mic and snarled, "We came all the way from fuckin' San Francisco to fuckin' Paris, France 'cause we thought the fuckin' people in fuckin' Paris had some fuckin' class. Well, you don't have any fuckin' class at all. And if you want to fuckin' do something about it, I'll be right fuckin' over here!" He pointed defiantly over at the side of the stage.

I might have left a few fuckings out in my retelling of his diatribe. He'd had enough. We all had. Huey glared out at the punters, who'd stopped whistling. They didn't know what to make of this crazy American, calling out the whole crowd. Then, slowly at first, then growing in a crescendo, they began to cheer and applaud. As we finished thrashing through our last song, we knocked over all the microphones, turned our guitars up to "eleven" and threw them on the stage, feeding back, and scattered the drums and amps all over the stage. We left to an ovation.

After the gig, Phonogram France hosted both bands at a big dinner at a *very* fancy restaurant in a grand townhouse near the Louvre. It was a great bit better than we were used to and definitely what we wanted to see more of. There was a waiter for every other person at the long table. One had only to lift a finger and a dozen more oysters appeared before you. The food was fantastic. There were also several intriguing women in attendance. Screw fish and chips, this is the life, brother!

The record company had a couple of cases of wine made for the bands and each bottle had a player's name on it. Pretty cool! The only problem was that the Scottish roadies and their partner in crime Johnny Ciambotti had somehow gotten the cases and absconded with them. This motley crew was holed up in a room on the third floor at the hotel.

We didn't know this at the time. The night was long and memorable, ending for me with a lovely café crème at a sidewalk café in the early morning with an attractive someone I'd just met, and a stroll down the Seine to visit Notre Dame de Paris in the pale winter sunlight.

A little later, back at the hotel, the bus was ready to roll. Both bands were already onboard. But the hotel staff couldn't get the Scottish roadies to open their room. They'd barricaded the door. Apparently, they'd painted the walls of the room a lovely shade of purplish red with our personalized bottles of wine, torn down the showers, and done the other creative stuff to TV sets and furniture that roadies liked to do when they were out of their fuckin' minds on sulfate and booze. At some point in the morning the staff became aware of what was going on and tried to gain entry to the room. This developed into a stand-off. To complicate matters, there was no electricity in the hotel due a rolling brown-out, so the telephones and elevators weren't working.

We watched from the windows of our tour bus idling at the curb as the roadies threw their bags out the windows to the street below. Then they made a break for it, pushing through the hotel security men in a flying wedge and racing down three flights of stairs and out into the street with a red-faced, angry hotel manager and a posse of irate employees hard on their heels.

We were all cheering them on, "C'mon Ciambotti! Run faster!" The bus started to pull away even as Johnny and the others scrambled on board. The cool driver jammed the door shut and we pulled away, with a dozen yelling, cursing Frenchmen trailing behind.

Johnny was willing to do things that mere mortals wouldn't dare. In Brussels he was rooming with one of our managers, who won't be named. Said manager had pulled a girl back to their shared room. We arrived on our floor from the bar and Ciambotti found the room locked. Our manager came to the door, breathless, opened it an inch and hissed, "Not right now, Ciambotti. Just give me a little time!"

Hopper and I had the adjacent room. Johnny went to the window and looked out. We were four stories above the city street. There was a two-tiered ledge no wider than a foot on each tier that ran along the building right below the windows. Johnny, who was in one of his wine-induced sideways moments, crawled out on it and edged his way along until he could look in the window. What he saw almost caused him to fall off! I was beside myself at Johnny's foolishness. If he fell, he'd be dead. He crept backward and crawled back in the window. Then he grabbed his camera (Johnny is a truly great photographer, he would have made a good war correspondent) and went out again. I couldn't fuckin' believe it. He was crazy! "Jeezus, Ciambotti!" He took a shot or two through the window and made his way, edging backwards inch by inch above the busy street with its oblivious strolling pedestrians and clattering trolleys far below. Then Hopper went out and had a look too, but Sean was so skinny the ledge could have accommodated two of him. I was sober: they were nuts. The photos, of what was certainly a most rude act, didn't turn out anyway.

Our last night of the long Graham Parker and the Rumour tour was in Amsterdam. After the gig, I tried to rip up the gold rayon shirt I'd washed and worn every night of the tour. The synthetic thing couldn't be ripped, so I cut it up with Ciambotti's ubiquitous folding knife. There were a few drinks and high-fives and hugs of brotherhood with the Rumour guys. It had been a good, solid tour. Clover had acquitted itself well throughout. Ciambotti, my roommate for the evening, ripped down the last shower stall of the tour at dawn. We left Holland for England's shores more than a little hung-over, but quite satisfied.

Back in London, Dave and Jake decided that we were ready to start some modest headlining: We'd host a string of Monday nights at a West End club called the Nashville, a high-ceilinged pub, with a huge, ornately carved mahogany bar with large mirrors. The Nashville held a pretty good crowd, but it was no longer big enough for us.

Clover had at long last generated a bit of London buzz. The

line of punters trying to get in went around the block. It was worth it for those who did. Nick Lowe, Dave Edmunds, and Billy Bremner had a new band called Rockpile. They were all, as players, the stuff of legend, real rock royalty. Dave Edmunds was a guitar hero from Wales and Billy Bremner did some of the classic Pretenders guitar parts. It was our gig, but they played as well some nights. Rockpile was flat-out rockabilly with Nick's great songs and droll humor thrown in as well. They were also loud as hell, I might add.

Southside Johnny and the Asbury Jukes had been playing some gigs with Graham Parker. They were part of the Bruce Springsteen orbit. Graham was similar to Springsteen in his ensemble-based band and driving social commentary. Southside Johnny had a six-piece horn section, led by a trombone player who went by the name, "La Bamba." You know him nowadays from Bruce's bands. They sat in with us regularly, playing old Clover standbys *Lovelight, Checkin' up on My Baby*, and other good ol' good ones. Clover with a horn section rocked out pretty well. The Lizzys were around. Brian Robertson sat in, and Phillip Lynott did a blues song or two.

Elvis Costello was there. After one set he told me, "I wish I could sing like you." Dead wrong, but flattering. The place was packed, hot and sweaty. I was drenched every show, my long hair hanging down my face. Just like at my social club dances when I was eleven. The girls didn't seem to mind. It was a scene. For a brief moment, Clover—the once-upon-a-hippie-moment band from Muir Beach—at the Nashville in Swingin' London was where it was at.

We were riding high, ready to conquer the world. We got set to go back to the States for a winter tour. We didn't know it then, but we wouldn't be back in London as a band again.

These were Clover's finest hours. We would all feel that our friends at home never got to see us at our peak. We were in a groove of recording and touring, meeting influential people, bringing in fans, attracting lots of boilers, and making good new friends as well. I don't think any of us thought it would end, but thought it would continue to rise up until we were among the famous, successful bands in the business, where we belonged. We needed to sell some records to make me personally feel more like a winner, but right then, my long-slammed confidence was building. Maybe I was a good lead singer, after all. Clover had a lot going for it. We were six good-looking guys who could sing and play. We had creative, even brilliant, management and a great producer. The label seemed pleased. Kevin Wells was absolutely the drummer we'd been looking for years. What could possibly go wrong?

The End of the Road

I want to chop off your head and watch it roll into the basket...
Elvis Costello

We arrived at San Francisco International Airport at the end of an eleven-hour flight. We were as skinny as Bolivian chickens. Rockers, like runway models, are obsessed with being ultra thin. When you live on coffee, cigarettes, and scotch you can achieve it. I weighed a hundred and forty-eight pounds, less than when I was a sophomore in high school. None of us could pinch half an inch on our waists. When I gained five pounds through actual good nutrition I felt like a whale.

We were going out to conquer America again, this time in the relative luxury of a fifteen-passenger van. The geniuses who booked us had us opening our tour out in Grand Forks, North Dakota, on New Year's Eve! Do you know how cold it is up there? The drive alone was harrowing. Crossing Nevada on I-80, we heard via CB chatter that the interstate was icy and that truckers were staying in Battle Mountain to wait for dawn before crossing a 7,000 foot-high pass ahead. We sat in a truck stop for a few hours, then said "fuck it," and forged ahead. It was icy, all right. Frank, a truly great driver, swerved us down the road in the pitch blackness. We tried chains, but they shattered—duh, they're for snow, not ice—so we tossed them into the roadside sagebrush. Onward.

By the time we finally got to Grand Forks, two days later, it was in the heart of an arctic cold blast: zero degrees with a wind chill of fifty below! We had to walk two blocks from our hotel to the city auditorium in our skimpy rock-n-roll clothes. We went on to make more frozen drives to gigs across the upper Midwest. We wore parkas, gloves, and wool hats. We sunny Californians learned about ice-scrapers and we learned to duck-walk on icy streets. I had a pair of insulated muk luks that smelled like bad farts after a few days. I chucked 'em for the sake of my compadres in the van.

It was bitterly cold and there were a series of severe winter storms that occasionally left us stranded. We spent a week in Chicago holed up in a Holiday Inn. The wind drove the snow sideways for days on end. You could look up and even see blue skies at times, but at ground level you couldn't see a hundred feet. In between the hotel and a nearby 7–11, there was a spot where you couldn't see anything but blowing snow: a white-out. It was kind of exciting for a California kid like me. I'd always been a weather nut. I love harsh weather and violent storms. There must be a dash of Nick Lowe's famous Viking chromosomes somewhere in my DNA.

We had some very good nights at colleges. We'd never been as tight a band as we were right then, and our material was closer to what we needed than it had ever been. We went on stage expecting to do well. We were even getting a little cocky. Huey and I started leaving the stage in the middle of a long

McFee solo to return to applause after having a smoke and quick snort. It might have been cold outside, but we were hot. This was what we had worked hard to get to. We wanted more out of our gigs; now we wanted to win.

We opened for a few different headlining acts, like Dave Mason, and played some clubs as headliners ourselves. We did a string of shows with Gary Wright, an Englishman who had a band that played all keyboards. He had a pretty big hit at that moment with *Dreamweaver*. It was a cool song, but his band wore their keyboards on straps around their necks. That's a tough proposition, wearing a keyboard like a guitar. You can't jump around or throw shapes. We, on the other hand, were mobile and energetic with our Teles, Strats and Les Pauls, not to mention Huey's dinky little harmonicas.

We shaped and leered and fist-pumped, and took the crowd for a couple of nights. We won. It wasn't a wipeout, but we out-pointed them. They had a hit radio song out and we didn't, so it was a moral victory. It increased our cockiness. After a couple of big nights, getting encores, we played a neato old theater in Wheeling, West Virginia. We figured we were going to blow them out of the room. But just when we thought we were going to cream 'em, wipe the stage with 'em, we came out and played lousy and they went on to get a big ovation and a couple of encores. Shit. But we stormed back and got right back on top of our world the next night. We headed for Chicago and our Mercury Records showcase. It was time to show our company just how ready we were to become the Next Big Thing.

We played the gig that would change everything in the Chicago suburb of Schaumburg, Illinois.

Why we didn't play well that night is one of those

unanswerable mysteries of life. The club was packed. We were absolutely battle-tested and ready. What could go wrong? For some unknown reason we were plain flat. Flatline. Less than zero. Couldn't get it up. The packed house was even primed by a little radio hype. The crowd welcomed us, they wanted to like us. But it was too tough for them: we were out of sync and boring. There seemed to be nothing any of us could do to get the energy going. The harder we pressed, the more it felt like we were being inexorably whirlpooled into a black hole. Then the audience went flat, too. It was like a football game where the home team can't possibly lose but plays poorly and loses to some bums. As we failed to connect, the audience became more and more silent.

But that wasn't the bad part. The Mercury Records Big Brass was there to see us. Mercury, the American branch of Phonogram, was based in Chicago. They were the company about which Graham Parker would pen the infamous *Mercury Poisoning*. The honchos were not as hip as they would be in New York or L.A. They were kind of Midwestern leisure-suit types. Chicago might have a blues scene, but as far as being at the center of hip rock music, their office might well have been in Ardmore, Alabama, or Nome, Alaska. In any case, they were finally catching our act in person and—as chance or karma had it—we sucked the big red ass. That's the way the dice roll sometimes. There was nothing we could do about it but play louder and faster, which didn't work, and pretend that it was cool, which also didn't work. The silence in between songs was deafening. If we'd listened close enough we might have heard the sound of Clover's death knell being intoned at the Mercury table.

Dispirited a bit, but still trusting in our overall level of performance, we trucked on through the snow and ice. Frank piloted the van through foot-deep snow to a college in northern Michigan. Students at Iowa State, Northwestern, and Slippery Rock State in central Pennsylvania dug us. Clover rocked on through the snow, sleet, and slush.

At a truck stop one night in eastern Ohio, we got hard looks from a couple of truckers. That wasn't that unusual, there were still a lot of rednecks out in Middle America in the winter of 1978 who thought long-haired hippies were pinko homosexuals. Actually, we were *heterosexual* pinkos. But rednecks just a half-step away from being Klan members probably wouldn't have been on our Christmas card lists, anyway.

When we got back out on the pitch-black, icy interstate, Frank asked for road conditions on the CB. A couple of truckers responded. At first it was a normal CB back-and-forth about the ice and snow, and the many abandoned vehicles off the side of the Interstate from the recent blizzards. Then the truckers asked if we were that band they saw back at the truck stop. Frank answered in the affirmative, being friendly and cool as usual. Then the two-way conversation got a little dicey. The truckers didn't like the way we looked, like god-damn girly hippies. It was hard guys all over again, 1978 version. And it seemed they'd penned us in, one right ahead of our van and one right behind. They were talking to each other hypothetically but pointedly about how easy it would be to crowd some long-hairs off the snow-covered Interstate and down the into frozen, snow-piled ditches. What's one more van off the road on a dark night in the middle of nowhere?

They were also calling Frank.

"Hey Frankie, we got your front door and your back door. Where you boys headed?"

Frank was cool as a cucumber, though the truth is, we were all on edge. We might be in deep shit. There was no way out, except one long shot. We had the maps out.

"We be rolling to that Liberty Town, don't you see," Frank replied. The Liberty Town was Philadelphia. The split in the Interstate that went southeast to Philly was a long five miles ahead. We were going to go northeast on I-80 towards New York. We hoped, anyway. It was night, it was cold, the snow was deep along the Interstate, and there wasn't that much traffic. We were at their mercy, those damned redneck fuckheads.

The truckers came back, "We be rolling with you, hippies."

We held our collective breath as we arrived at the split. We started bearing right, heading towards Philadelphia, still one truck in front of us, the other, behind. Then at the last second, Frank swerved on the icy pavement and bumped and swerved us over the snow- and ice-covered Philly-bound lanes to the New York-bound lanes. We watched the eighteen-wheelers roll away south, throwing off plumes of blowing snow.

We all got around the CB mic in triumph, "Fuck you, shitheads! Fuckin' redneck assholes!" We were shouting and laughing into the CB.

The truckers couldn't believe they'd been had. "Frankie! Frankie! Kick it back, Frankie! Aw, shit, go to hell, you motherfuckin' hippies!"

The U.S. was a tough country compared with the civilized environments of Europe and the U.K. In England, one might get the occasional head-butt from a drunk, like the one Lybo got one night at a gas station in Upper Tooting. I came out of the gas station's little store to find Lybo's face streaked with blood. A red-haired little guy was laughing as he walked down the street into the night. He'd head-butted Lybo for no reason. No words, nothing, the guy just walked up, reached out, grabbed Steve by his coat, and head-butted him. Go figure. But in general, one felt safe on the streets of a European city. Not so in our great country, land of guns, brainless truckers like those two, and random violence. We stayed in a high-rise Holiday Inn in downtown Philadelphia that had signs cautioning guests about being mugged in the hallways. There's a disconnect with the great things about America that happens sometimes.

We had great gigs in Philadelphia and New York with lots of plugged-in people in the crowd. Jacko joined us. We headed for Boston. We'd been getting routine encores. The record wasn't doing anything yet, but it was early in the radio portion of the great game. Clover was starting to make a name for itself now.

We played a sold-out club in Boston. It was a good night. In fact, most nights had been good. We came offstage, congratulating each other on a good set. But Frank had a strange look in his eyes. Jacko, who had flown in, looked tense as well. His eyes were kind of bugging out and he was wringing his hands, something I'd seen him do when there was a bit of unpleasantness to take care of.

He gathered us together. The room got suddenly quiet. "I guess there's no good way to say this. Those fucking cunts at Mercury have decided not to go ahead with promoting the album. You've been dropped."

What? Oh fuck! How could they drop us? It was that fucking bad gig in Chicago. We were in shock, stunned. No way. We were defiant.

"What the fuck do they know? Those assholes in their leisure suits?"

We were dropped. That was that. All those great shows, all that work. They saw us on the lame night. And there went the next album that wouldn't be, the magic third. In those days, it took three records to break a band. We weren't alone: history would show that Mercury fucked up the careers of many a band in those years.

But right then, we were three thousand miles from home and the show had to go on. We had a couple of gigs left on the tour, both taking us west. We got in the van and drove. Our spirits were low, but not extinguished. We still had fun spotting a guy masturbating in his car in rush-hour traffic in Worcester, Massachusetts. But it was a long, long drive all the way across the country on I-80 back to San Francisco. And what were we returning home to? Dave and Jake had shot their wad for us. They'd gone out on a limb and hadn't gotten a return for their efforts. We were a good band, a real professional band. But without hit singles and album sales that translated into ticket sales at venues a band couldn't survive forever. It had been eleven years for Clover. How would we go on now? We'd get another deal and make that damn third record, that's how. That's what we told ourselves.

After the last gig in Wisconsin, we hit I-80 for the last two-thousand mile drive. There was a sense of reckless freedom. I think it was a stage of the grieving process. We nearly ran out of gas in the wilds of Wyoming. We pulled into a tiny town where the only thing open was a cowboy-and-miner bar. We shot pool with the friendly locals, who called up the gas station owner. He came and turned on the pumps for us. We were all drinking our way across the country, except of course, McFee and Frank. But McFee had acquired a dick-nose, a fake pair of glasses with a huge penis where the nose should be. He chatted up some beavers on the CB on the stretch between Salt Lake City and the Nevada state line. They seemed to be excited about meeting a rock band on tour, so they'd see us at the state line casino in Wendover. Then McFee sauntered into the casino wearing the dick-nose and a midshipman's hat (with the top torn out) from our gig in Annapolis. "What do you think, ladies?"

After three depressing days we drove into the Bay Area at last. Under better circumstances, it would have been an exciting, happy event, a triumphant homecoming for our band. But we crawled in, heads down, our future unknown. I, for one, had no place to live. We'd been gone for almost two years.

Dropped again, just when we were peaking. It was a harsh shot. The reality was like falling into an icy pond and finding the only way forward was through an underwater cave, dark and endless, with no sure exit up ahead. The shock was almost too much to take in. Of course, for me, it all came down to my role in the band, just when I was finding my legs under me. I was the one who wrote most of the songs and sang them. The "Alex Call is a journeyman singer" review in the *New Musical Express* came slashing back up out of the darkness into the core of my being. Labels don't drop you because you're good. Quite the opposite. With everything we had going for us, there was only one explanation that worked for me: I wasn't good enough. I didn't have what it took, after all. The thin ice of my ever-shaky confidence broke apart beneath my feet.

It was doubly tough, because I'd allowed myself to feel

proud of what we'd become. We were a far better band than we'd been when this part of the adventure started. How could it suddenly be over?

The Bay Area didn't seem like a welcoming place. I had a sinking feeling in my gut at the sight of the familiar hills. Home were the vanquished, not to their promised fame and glory, but to barely-noted failure and ignominy.

BEYOND CLOVER

How does it feel, how does it feel,
To be on your own
With no direction home
Like a complete unknown
Like a rolling stone…

BOB DYLAN

Clover was at a fork in the old road of life.
Stick a fork in 'em, they're done.
It seemed a lifetime ago that we were mired in the dark muck of the Scoreboard days, though it'd only been four years. We'd gotten our proverbial shit together and gone off to London and had ourselves another major label deal. We'd learned a tremendous amount about life on the road, how to make good recordings, how to present ourselves to the world, how to rock the house, how to destroy a hotel, and how to say "Where y'all partyin' tonight?" in French, Dutch, and Southern.

But now we'd lost the keys to the fancy ride that would take us on down that highway to fame and fortune. The deal was dead. We could bravely go on trying, look for another label to take us on, or we could take our predicament as a sign that we were missing key elements in our makeup that would forever prevent us from achieving high-level success, and call it a night.

You acquire a taint when you're dropped. Other labels

would be wary. They'd look for the reasons we were dropped. Would they want to sign an artist who wasn't good enough for their competitors? There were hopeful, delusional rumors floating around.

"Hey, Humongous Records is interested."

"Irving Flatbar wants to sign you guys. Do some recording and let's see what you've got."

What we had? We'd just done a shiny new album. Well, any humongous record label would make sure there was a new, good direction on the new material. The old stuff, just months in the can, was crippled, stigmatized. It stank of the corpse of the old deal. We were radioactive for sure: deadly, deadly, deadly.

I was also in a stupid fix. I'd been living on the road for almost two years. I didn't have a place to stay. If Clover wasn't going back to England or out on the trail again, I'd have to figure out where to sleep. My dad had rented out the little house in Mill Valley that Huey and I shared as roomies. Andre Pessis and the Flying Circus guys invited me to stay with them at Muir Beach, so I made a bedroom out of a partially walled-in, non-insulated porch at their friendly but totally decrepit house. Beneath the warped and partially-missing floorboards lived a tribe of contentious raccoons. I dropped tidbits through the cracks in the floor and listened to them fighting each other over the crumbs. I learned a valuable lesson: Don't ever mess with raccoons. My oh-so-fierce-mighty-hunter dog, Abu, quickly hopped up on the bed when he heard the beasts scrabbling amongst themselves below. For the moment, I was back to being a hippie. The house, which was regularly flooded by a frequently rain-swollen creek, had been condemned and would be demolished soon. I'd have to find a better solution. But I didn't have one.

As the reality of losing our deal sunk in, of course I took it deeply personally. I was the lead singer. I was the main writer. It all came down to me. My dark side, banished by the bright lights of the stage and the road, emerged from the shadows again, told me to pour myself a few glasses of cheap red wine, and whispered conspiratorially, *Hey, I'm back, you fuckin' loser. Did you miss me? Ah, you knew I was there the whole time.* I'd tried to pretend my alter ego had been purged, killed off, blown away by the glare of the spotlights, by my aviator sunglasses, green satin baseball jacket, my two-inch blue suede lace-ups, and my blonde Strat.

Dave and Jake were gamely looking for another deal for us. But we were now rock-n-roll lepers. No one would touch us. We were just another band that hadn't clicked. Many are called, few are chosen. Dave and Jacko had put in their time as well. Elvis Costello was taking off, becoming a superstar as quickly as Clover was falling off the cliff. Graham Parker was breaking into the States as well. Stiff Records was the darling of the media. It seemed a new age had dawned and we were in the phylum of creatures who didn't survive the change, like Disney's cartoon dinosaurs dying off in "Fantasia."

As a cockney would sniff, "We still had our pride." We hadn't played for our home crowd since our great transformation in the rock wars. We all wanted them to see us at our peak. Our crazy friends in local Homegrown Productions put on a gig for us at the Odd Fellow's Hall in uptown Mill Valley. It was another little wood-paneled box with an American flag on a stand on the stage—under normal circumstances, a perfectly good place to eat a donut and sip a cup of weak, tepid Folger's in a styrofoam cup while listening to the minutes of the last

Odd Fellow's meeting being read by some Odd Fellow. It wasn't too different from the Outdoor Art Club where I'd seen my first band at age eleven. Hell, it was just down the street. Full circle in twenty years. Now I was the one dying, like those old rock-n-rollers who wouldn't grow their hair long and play hip music in the old days.

The tiny, ill-ventilated hall was packed with our old friends: Tam High grads, surfers from Bolinas, everyone from the extended Clover family. That was nice, but the hall was by its acoustic nature a boomy, bassy, echo box. You just plain couldn't sound good in there. We played our set, but it was a far, far cry from the triumphant return we'd hoped for. It was a bad, funky gig during which we drank, smoked, and sniffed too much booze, pot, and coke. We didn't know it at the time, but it was the last Clover gig. We ended not with a bang, but a crappy, lame, echoey whimper.

We got together for rehearsals after, but my heart wasn't in it. I couldn't see the band going on with me as the lead singer. It had been proven not to work. I'd had my chance, and that was that. I was sinking emotionally, and when I sink, I go down fast. I pulled the plug at rehearsal one day. The guys were talking about doing a new demo for some label or other and I said, "What's the point?"

John McFee had an offer to play with the Doobie Brothers. He had to take that. He was a new dad. I just couldn't see going on any longer.

If the horse is dead, get off.

Johnny and Huey were pissed. Giving up? Poor, amicable Kevin was confused. He'd signed onto a happening band just a few months before, bought into it heart and soul. Now, we were breaking up. I put my axe in its case and slunk off.

It was my fault: I wasn't good enough, never was. All that old crap came up and grabbed me by the ankles again and dragged me off my hard-fought-for but precarious ledge. Once I began to fall into depression, it was impossible to pull out of the slide. And it was an extremely deep, dark abyss. It was paralyzing. It was like my hands were frozen. I couldn't even pick up my guitar. All I could heft was a bottle. Why write another song? My songs were shit. I was shit.

***

Weeks dragged into months. I still needed a place to live. I pleaded with my dad to evict the very nice hippies who were living in the house Huey and I used to rent from him. He didn't want to evict good tenants, but finally gave in. I moved in, with a mattress from Goodwill and a bean-bag chair, the only pieces of furniture I could scrounge up. With my dad paying for the paint, I put some new off-white on the old walls of the little house. I had no idea of what I was going to do with my life. I was just turning thirty. My ticket to ride had been cancelled. My rock dream had been crushed. My delusion of confidence had been blown away like the dust it was. Twelve years, all for naught.

To top it off, I got popped for drunk driving the night before my thirtieth birthday. *Jeez, officers, what took you so long?* I'd been carrying a bindle of coke in my coat pocket, too. But the cops didn't find that when they searched me. They took me in and removed my cuffs for a few minutes while they processed me. What a great word. *Processed. Like lunch meat, or a German Jew.* I was put in a holding cell with no door, but out of the line of sight of the clerical desk at the jail. I got the bindle out and wet it thoroughly with saliva and stuck it to the underside of the stainless-steel table at which I was seated. It stuck, for a few minutes. The officer came back with the processing papers. I sat there horrified as the bindle dropped soundlessly from its moist perch to the floor at my feet. After a few minutes of my answering questions, the cop led me out of the cell and put me in the tank with the other night-afflicted idiots. Some low-flying angel watched over me, I guess. Maybe an angel who had his own secrets to hide, maybe one that owed me a favor? I don't know.

For some reason that had by then gotten lost in the depths of my consciousness, I'd always said I would die when I was thirty. All through my childhood I'd told people that. Why? Who knows? But here I was, turning thirty, and I was hungover and totally embarrassed. I think the Mexican term for hangover is La Cruda. The Crude. The crud. I was the Crude crud. I got out of jail at dawn and went dejected back to my little house. Of course, I had to swear off the booze, forever. In the afternoon, Dede said she had to go to Danny's house to pick up something. I rode along, feeling as low as I have ever felt. I was humiliated by having been arrested.

I should have guessed, but didn't, that she'd arranged a big surprise thirtieth birthday party for me. All the guys, all the pretty girls, everyone was there. There were gifts of bottles of this and that, and a whole gram of blow in a glass tube, just for little old me! Surprise! Oh shit. I felt like the proverbial turd in the punchbowl. And I couldn't drink, couldn't do the blow. Well, I put off that resolution for the morrow. I explained to a select few what had happened the night before. No one was very surprised by that, though most were sympathetic. I couldn't get in a party-hearty mood, despite the wine and toots. The topper came when they brought out an enormous, flat cake. On it were spread thirty-one candles, one for each year and an extra one for luck. I huffed and I puffed and I blew out thirty candles. One stayed burning. That was it: I wouldn't reach thirty-one.

Huey had quickly gotten a band going. He and Sean Hopper and some guys from a band called Soundhole had taken up Monday nights at a club called Macarthur's in San Rafael. They were called Huey Lewis and American Express. They were having a big time. Huey was out front, singing every song. I'd thought maybe Hopper and I might do a band, but there went that idea. Huey had the confidence, and a piece of his old yogurt business, too. I had nothing. My life had been Clover. I couldn't play music anymore, anyway. All I had was wine and pot. I went on the wagon again to atone for my drunk-driving arrest.

André came by the little house to see how the painting was coming along. We were standing in the kitchen talking about Gurdjieff and Sufism when the phone rang. For some reason I said to him, as a joke (as if something important could actually happen for me), "this phone call is going to change my life." How did I know? It was my girlfriend Dede. She was pregnant.

Dede and I had had an on-again off-again relationship for six years. It had been more on than off, but right then it was off. I'd been seeing a therapist, trying to deal with my depression. One of the outgrowths of therapy was that I'd decided to break up with Dede. Our relationship had been intense and frequently troubled, right from the beginning. My being on the road hadn't helped matters.

Well, in a phone call that all changed. I fumbled and stumbled as I felt the shockwaves of world-changing news, but I felt a responsibility toward the unborn child. Shoot, I had a house and a dog. Dede had a baby in her womb, and a cat. We'd get married and have our child. It's called doing the right thing. Dede's mom said, "What took you so long?" We got married at the Muir Beach community center in December of 1978.

Huey and American Express were the wedding band. I think they got paid five hundred bucks, maybe three hundred. Mutt Lange's ex-wife Stevie was there with her boyfriend, the lead singer for Manfred Mann. Huey and the guys honked through their pre-record-deal music: blues standards, a song called *Exodisco*, the "Exodus" theme set to a disco beat. *Hmmm*. Stevie sang *Natural Woman*, which she sang better than anyone but Aretha, no exaggeration. I croaked out a too-slow version of *Stand by Me*. I had the dubious distinction of being possibly the last person ever to tell Huey to turn it down, as my dad was complaining that that his older relatives couldn't hear to talk over the band.

Our son James was born in April of '79. I was there as he entered this world. When I watched Dede push him into this life, her eyes going bloodshot from the exertion, boy, was I glad I was born a man. Giving birth ain't for sissies. The doctor had me cut the cord, which was a tougher, more sinuous item than I'd thought it would be. Then he handed me the blood-and-blue-goo-covered tiny baby.

He was crying pitifully, tightly wound up in his yellow swaddling cloth. I looked at his red, bruised face, in his squinty little eyes, and I had a profound revelation. This was a complete human being: full personality, some history. Maybe you'd call it karma, but it definitely seemed to me in that moment that we're not born with nothing. We're born with everything. It was a moment of partial enlightenment. I can still see the whole scene today as if it just happened. This immediately deepened my sense of being responsible for him, for his future.

Beyond that, I fell instantly, deeply, in love with the little tyke. When he had high bilirubin counts and had to go under the french-fry lights at the hospital, I was almost beside myself with worry. The connection I felt with tiny James was far deeper than I could have ever imagined.

Being a dad awakened a part of me I didn't know existed. I'd participated in the universal mystery of creating a living being. Huey said, "Al's finally had a hit." I had a sense of validation that had been missing. It felt like my stock in the world had risen. There couldn't have been a prouder new dad. I was ahead of most of my friends, except for John McFee, who'd become a father the year before. I carried my little boy around with me everywhere I went, explaining the wide, wonderful world to this crying, pooping, uncomprehending infant. "This is yogurt, that's an airplane." I walked him around Mill Valley in his cheap little folding stroller. We couldn't afford one of the fancy new, big-wheeled prams that affluent people were parading their babies around in. We didn't have a dime to our names, but we had a beautiful son.

I hadn't touched music for almost a year. But now I got the itch to write and play again. Somehow I got my hands on a TEAC four-track recorder. It was the old kind, with big reels and synchronization switches. It had a high tape speed, so it sounded better than a regular tape deck. To overdub, you had to flip these synchronization switches that made the music sound like it was underwater. It made overdubbing a murky leap of faith, but when you flipped the switches back, it sounded like a million bucks. I picked up a pair of speakers, a beat up Shure 57 mic (I still have it), a tiny mixer, a spring reverb, and a cassette deck.

I also got a lounge-player's drum machine. It looked like a little suitcase and had just six beats: rock 1, rock 2, samba, cha-cha, bossa nova, and waltz. It was nothing like the programmable drum machines we'd have in a few years, but you could adjust the tempo up or down. I experimented: I hooked up all this stuff and recorded.

With the four-track, you could record the drum machine on one track, guitar on another, and bass on a third. Then you mixed those three tracks down to the one remaining track. Then you did two background vocals and mixed that down to the new one remaining track, then you still had two tracks left for lead vocal and lead guitar, or whatever, and so on. Then you could mix all that down to a cassette player, and put that back on the four-track stereo on two tracks and record more backing vocals! It was creative, though the sound got degraded and noisier with each generation of tracks—and you couldn't go back and change the tracks that had been merged—but you could get a lot of stuff on the tape. The state of the art then was only twenty-four tracks, which required the same kind of maneuvers when recording a full band. It was called ping-ponging. I couldn't copy parts and move them around the way we can today, with Pro Tools and other cool stuff we have now.

A crazy, wonderful friend of mine, Jim Hite, known as "Boom-Boom," had a funny rehearsal/jam party place in an industrial area of San Rafael. It was a one-room shack with a barely functional toilet and no other facilities. It was in the middle of a debris company's yard, surrounded by storage sheds, dumpsters, and the portable trailers that serve as on-site construction offices. There were backhoes and dump trucks and piles of rocks, bricks, and dirt. There were warehouses being built in the area, so all day long you heard the beep-beep-beep of trucks and heavy equipment being backed up and gears grinding on big machines. Jackhammers pounded, men shouted to each other, and girders clanged. It was one of those places where America went to work: an ideal place for making rock-n-roll music. I set up my funky, squirrel-powered four-track in the shed and got to work writing and recording.

Kevin Wells, Clover's last drummer, was hanging around. He'd hooked up with Ronelle McFee, John's ex-wife, one of the stalwarts of the Clover family. He and I and John Main, a bass player from Texas, started playing some gigs. We had a few different band members, including time-to-time guitarists Gary Vogenson, Jack O'Hara, and Mark Karan, keyboardists Kincaid Miller, Reid Whatley, and Austin "Audie" DeLone. One of our friends called me "New Daddy," since that's what I was, so that became the band name. Later, it morphed into the Love Dogs. Someone took a picture of me holding my baby boy James sideways like a guitar and that became my logo.

Huey was playing a lot at a club called Uncle Charlie's, in a strip mall in Corte Madera. He was building up a good following. Not surprisingly, his gigs were packed with young ladies. It was the new happening scene. Bob Brown, Pablo Cruise's manager, had taken Huey on as a client after hearing a five-song demo Huey did with his band.

As I watched Huey wow 'em one night, I said to Bob, "So you're going make our boy Huey into a star?"

Bob replied, "He already is one. I'm just going to help it happen."

My gigs at Uncle Charlie's started well, but I couldn't sustain the kind of following Huey had. Some nights it was packed, other nights it was sparse. It was just about the only gig in town and you couldn't expect the same people to come out over and over again. Uncle Charlie's was a dangerous place for me. Coke was the drug of the hour, and there were always petty dealers around who wanted to stuff our noses. I got off the wagon. Every gig, you'd end up putting in with the other guys for a half-gram. Then I'd have to drink to mellow out from the blow. Then we'd need more coke, then more booze. You know you're in trouble when Jack Daniel's tastes like apple juice. Somewhere in there, we'd play a set or two. It was a crazed party. Booze and blow do not make you play better, though you might think you do at the moment. It came down to an anxiety thing, a fear thing. *See the man with the stage fright.* Courage: in a vial and a bottle.

Our little family was struggling financially. I earned a hundred bucks here, fifty there. Dede was tutoring English at the community college. Often, I'd write a bad check at the market on Friday, hoping to make it good by Monday. That didn't always work. One day the Safeway wouldn't take my check, "Sorry, too many bounced checks." I walked away carrying my little boy and choking back tears, leaving a sorely-needed bag of groceries at the checkout stand as a line of waiting customers stared in silence.

Time was passing: I was almost thirty-two years old. I was driving an old Opel Cadet with a taped-up broken-out window. Half the time, I had to tell my dad that I'd get him next month on the rent. Without the help of Dede's folks, we wouldn't have had groceries on the table. I'd spent literally half my life doing music and I had nothing to show for it. Having struggled to within sight of the top rung on the ladder of success, I'd been kicked back down to the bottom. I found myself staring up at my old buddies, who were climbing back up toward the top rung.

I had a few allies. Kevin Wells and John Main were there. John was a business-minded guy who was intent on making it. He was a great big ol' Texas boy who loved the good things in life: great food, good pot, and good music. We spent a fair amount of time rehearsing and recording. He had dreams of being a producer. Then there was an A&R guy, Michael Barackman, from Clive Davis's Arista Records, who was a fan. He stayed in touch. That contact buoyed my spirits. Nick Lowe had married June Carter's daughter, Carlene. He produced two of my old Clover songs for her, *Love is Gone* and *Mr. Moon*. *Love is Gone* was released as a single, but fizzled. McFee played on her records and Ciambotti was playing bass and managing her as well. Johnny, who was living back home in Los Angeles, was also giving me business advice and helping me meet people and get in the studio. He was more of a mentor to me, now that Clover had broken up.

And there was Keith Knudsen, the drummer for the Doobie Brothers. Keith was a wonderful guy, a real talent. He married a girl from the Clover family, Tracy Collins. Keith was instrumental in bringing John McFee into the Doobs. He even nominated me for the band, but that didn't go anywhere. He also liked to produce. He took me into the studio several times. Keith liked the high life and could afford it—and might never have met a hit of stuff he didn't like—not too different from me, though our tastes in substances differed. Despite his occasional lapses, he had one of the biggest hearts I've ever encountered.

For one of our recording sessions, we were in a very nice full-on studio in the city. Keith had enlisted most of the Doobies to play on a demo of two songs. This included Michael MacDonald, Cornelius Bumpus, Tiran Porter, and McFee, with Keith playing drums. It was august company. The Doobies were on top of the world. Michael MacDonald was the biggest singing star in the country, the voice of the era, really.

We cut the tracks. I was in a vocal booth, playing guitar while recording a scratch vocal. Unbeknownst to me, I had a grunting problem. I'd never noticed it before. It was similar to Huey's breathing noises when he was playing harmonica, but mine was much worse. I kind of grunted along with the melody, but I was way out of tune. Every few notes, I'd hit a really high note in my squealing, usually following it with a really low one. The other guys were already in the control room, while I was still unplugging my guitar. Keith's deadpan voice came over the headphones, "You gotta hear this. C'mon in and have a listen."

I went in. Michael MacDonald—*ferfucksake*—was sitting there with the others. I was already nervous about the songs, wondering if these great players considered them really dumb or what. Keith said to the engineer, "Okay, roll it."

They had me soloed on the huge studio monitors, grunting away like a pig getting the business from an Alabama/Arkansas/Idaho/ you-pick-it farm-boy. It was unbelievably funny, though not necessarily to me. McFee and Keith were in tears laughing, MacDonald and the others were being more polite, but they were grinning as well. Okay, fair's fair. Huey got it that time, now it was my turn.

Despite my extreme poverty, I was having a blast making

my little recordings at the shed. I was discovering the joy of building tracks and I was finding out that I could come up with cool parts. I'll keep my pick, thank you, McFee and Mutt and the rest. I was playing a lot of bass on my old Fender Jazz bass, the one with the slim neck. Bass is my closet instrument. One cool bass riff led to a song called *New Romeo*. I worked out this insanely hooky riff. It wasn't difficult per se, but it was subtle and easy to get wrong. One mistake and it was start-over time. I must have played it for two weeks before I got it down.

Finally, I could do the entire song without screwing up the bass part. It was highly invigorating, the physical and mental aspects of playing something right. I recorded the bass part and the lounge drum machine. Rock 1 was the machine beat, as usual. Then I layered a couple of simple guitar parts over that. There was a great vibe there. I didn't have lyrics, so I kind of scatted along to the track. I really liked how the scat lay in the groove. So I translated the scat syllables into words. It took me some time, a couple of hours of concentrating on the sound of the scatted syllables. They turned out to be some of my best lyrics to date.

She came walkin' in clutchin' her silver collection
With her entourage in tow
With an immaculately fashionable cat that must be her new Romeo
I said, hello, I haven't seen you in so long seems like a dream,
Tell me, how long has it been, how long has it been,
And who's the new Romeo?
Who's the new Romeo?
Oh, man, I've had enough I don't know what she sees in him
With his pointed shoes and his poised expression
Well, I admit he throws a mean shape or two

But then again, my confidence is easily shaken
It never has taken much
Who's her New Romeo, who's her New Romeo?

The she looked at me with her bitter green eyes and said
Tin Angel, this is what I've become
And it's not for you to criticize me
Just look at me now, just look at me now

So I said excuse me and I got up and I
Crossed my fingers for luck
Then I started stumblin' and staggerin' through the shadows
Back behind me she was telling them, selling them
New and used faces around the dimly lit circle
Of the thunderstruck
And her New Romeo
Yeah, her new Romeo
Who's the new Romeo?

Creating these multi-track recordings by myself was a real breakthrough for me. It was songwriting without waiting for the band to give its approval and learn the song. I had the fire inside again, this time in spades. I couldn't always feed my family and I was driving the gold-and-rust Opel with the broken-out window, but I was getting the feeling that these songs might lead us out of the wilderness. Keith Knudsen paid for me to demo *New Romeo* and another song, *Annie Don't Lie*, at an eight-track studio. The tracks, with Keith on drums, John Main on bass, and John McFee on guitar, turned out great.

Through Keith and John, I met Marty Wolf, lighting director for the Doobies. He had managerial aspirations. He was working with an artist in L.A. named Tim Goodman who was being produced by John McFee. They were cutting some great stuff. Their eight-track living-room recordings were good enough to be records. Tim wanted to cut *New Romeo* and another song of mine called *Little Too Late*. It was a glimmer of hope.

Marty brought me down to L.A. He wined, dined, and tooted me up. I signed over half of the publishing to him, on the songs that Tim Goodman had recorded. Just being around the L.A guys swept me away into that world of nice houses, convertibles, real rock-n-roll duds, skinny girls with long hair and big, half-exposed knockers, drinks, and cruising to night spots, talking about deals and being on the inside. Well, kind of on the inside. I pretended to be on the inside while I was really a fish up against the glass of a fine aquarium, set in a coral reef. I could see all the pretty people floating around me, but I couldn't make my voice heard. They talked right through me, as if I weren't there. The Invisible Man. Sure, they wanted my songs. The rest was that typical insincere L.A. crap. But I bought into it, because I needed to buy into it. I sold one-half of the rights on the two songs for a couple thousand bucks, a pittance. But it was real money in my pocket. Marty said he might want to manage me, too. I could pay for groceries for a few weeks without writing bad checks. I flew back home feeling like I might just make it.

Michael Barackman from Arista Records was coming to the Bay Area and wanted to listen to my band. I'd sent him the recent demos, and I guess he'd been talking me up to Clive Davis. I wasn't taking this part of it as seriously as I should have, perhaps. Instead of setting up in a nice studio, I had him come out to the construction site. I hadn't seen him for a while, but as soon as I did, I realized that I'd made a huge error in my thinking. He was a major-leaguer, a heavy hitter. With the band packed in there, there was no room in the little shed for him, so he sat in the open doorway of the shed as we played, like the yard workers sometimes did on their lunch breaks.

We blasted away in our tight confines for a few songs. After five songs, he said he liked it but had to go, and he took off. Afterwards, I thought about what I'd done. What a moron. I should've scrounged up Marin Recorders or another studio location. I figured that was that. *Having the head of A&R for a major label listen to me out in a debris yard: What was I thinking?* Maybe it wasn't that bad a move. The English guys would've thought it perfect, "Let the wankers come to you." But Michael Barackman wasn't a wanker. He took me seriously when almost nobody else did.

The Love Dogs were getting to be pretty happening. We went through some guitarists and keyboard players, and the onstage results were a bit uneven, to say the least. But the nucleus of Kevin Wells and John Main and I had good energy. We played with our buddy Jack O'Hara on guitar at a big coke-and-booze-infused holiday bash at the Record Plant, the super-hot studio in Sausalito. We were rolling through *New Romeo*, rockin' along before a packed-out crowd of dancers. Jack, a great, great guy—and the guitarist for the American pub rock band Eggs over Easy, which had sojourned in London before Clover—took an extended solo. Jack didn't drink, but he was a pothead who liked the odd toot up the nasal cavity, as did many people in our scene, including me. When he got into a long solo, his jaw kind of dropped open and he beamed magnanimously at the crowd, as if to say, "Hey, dig me. How cool is this, folks?" During *New Romeo*, John, Kevin and I didn't miss a beat, but we gave each other raised eyebrows, because Jack was blasting away *one fret off from the right key!* He was so into his solo that he couldn't be reached by eye contact, so I finally went over and gave the bottom of his guitar a solid rap, sliding his hands up a half-step. Now he was in tune. He turned slowly, not missing a note, grinning like a pig in shit. *Right on, man!*

The Bay Area was heating up with breaking acts. Journey was hot, Santana was famous. It was turning into Round Two for the San Francisco Sound. Then Huey and his band had their first hit, *Do You Believe in Love?* Written with Mutt Lange, the song made it into the top reaches of Billboard's Hot 100. Huey and the boys, who were now called "the News," because American Express wouldn't let them use the name, had connected with their second album. I'd liked their first album, but they couldn't get a radio hit. They'd been out slogging around the country, mostly on the club circuit. It sounded a lot like an old Clover tour. They'd needed a hit single, because labels will only go so far developing an act, they must see results. *Do You believe in Love?* took off and *Bay Area Music Magazine* (BAM) ran a big picture of Huey Lewis and the News on the cover. I couldn't have been prouder if I'd done it myself.

The Love Dogs opened for Huey at Wolfgang's, Bill Graham's club in the city. It was a nice break for us, since we couldn't get into Wolfgang's on our own. We did well with Huey's audience. Strangely, we never opened for him again. Just a coincidence, I'm sure.

I now had a handful of songs that were my best ever: *New Romeo, Little Too Late, Annie Don't Lie, Blue Avenue, Going through the Motions*, and a hot new one, *Just Another Saturday Night*. It was a brutal, Springsteen-like flat-out rocker about ever-more-common teenage drive-by shootings. I wrote it while walking my two-year-old boy James in his stroller on a beautiful day in a lovely neighborhood in Mill Valley. Birds twittered in the green branches, hard-working honeybees buzzed in the roadside rose gardens and gentle breezes rustled the leaves of the bay trees along Evergreen Avenue. The setting for my creative moment couldn't have been further removed from the deadly subject matter of the song. Another new song I'd written in that setting bore a similar irony, but more on that in a moment.

The depression I went though following Clover's demise was a blurry dream. I don't know how that first year passed. I remember events and I can put together what happened, but how I walked through doors and drove down streets is beyond my comprehension. After all those years, it was as if I'd been shorn of my identity. I was no longer the lead singer for Clover. Huey was now the guy that people thought of as a good singer. It was like the world had been turned upside down, flipped over backwards, and plunged underwater. I tried not drinking, tried drinking. I tried to be positive. I let myself fall into blackness. Ever so slowly, I rose to the light.

Somehow I came out the other side with my creativity in full bloom. The break had been good. I had to lose myself to find myself. Starting to record on my own, with no McFee or the others to do the work for me, I had a better understanding of what it was that I did, of the music I wanted to make. For the moment, there weren't commercial considerations going into my music, it was just me being me. Now, where was the money?

Jenny, I Got Your Number: 867-5309

The song that saved my ass for a while

Jenny don't change that number...

TOMMY TUTONE

I wish there was a better story. What do you want to hear? Jenny was a girl that broke up with me and I wrote her number on the wall. Jenny was a good girl gone bad. Jenny was a black, transvestite hooker. But I have to tell it the way it was. I'm so sorry.

There was a pretty cherry-plum tree right out of a Japanese watercolor in my yard on Holly Street in Mill Valley. It was just passing out of bloom, leafing out, yet still drifting delicate white petals down on the light spring breeze. The sun was filtering through its green branches onto my shoulders as I sat on the wooden bench beneath it. Bees lazily worked the blossoms over. Does that sound Zen-like and pastoral enough for you? Yes, it was indeed just so.

I was out there strumming on my borrowed Ovation acoustic guitar looking for another song. The setting might have been bucolic, but I wasn't writing in reflection of that exquisite moment. I was looking to fuckin' rock out. I wanted to find

283

something direct, something like the Stones or the Kinks. There was an old Stones song called *Empty Heart* that had a cool four-chord progression. I always liked that sort of thing. *You Really Got Me* by the Kinks was another old fave, a timeless rocker akin to the archetypal rock-n-roll instrumentals that I dug when I was kid. I wasn't looking to copy those songs, but I wanted something that had that primordial rock vibe.

I tried various chords, just sliding around like I always did. How about F# minor, D, A, B? That's weird! That was kind of cool. It didn't go to the "normal" five-chord, E, so it didn't resolve, or lead back to the beginning again. It just hung there on the number two-chord, B. *Ta, tata, ta-ta, tata.* So I had this progression that was different; at least I'd never heard it before. It had a great rhythm and some unexpected tension. That number two chord just stuck out there like a rock-n-roll fist. *In your face, dudes and dudettes.* I played that a few dozen times, just digging it. When I hit on a groove, a chord progression, a riff, something I really like, I'll play it for a long time. Just like I used to throw the baseball against the school wall and catch grounders: over and over, because I really dig it. Each time around, a subtle variation emerges. When my son James was eleven or twelve, he came into my studio when I was working on a mix and said, "You play the same song over and over."

"No," I replied, "there's something different every time."

It needed a b-section, a part that takes it somewhere else musically, that leads to the chorus. I went to the "five" chord, E, then to D, and A. E, A, D. And again, E, D, A, and then back to the progression. That rocked! I dug it. It's not easy to find a good rock progression that hasn't been beaten to death already.

The music of the sixties broke apart many rules, and the

seventies were progressive, but by the eighties we were using all the known chord progressions in our hit singles. It took Nirvana in '92 to find new chords. Their dissonant but awesome music killed off a lot of eighties rockers. Post-millennial country and pop music has revived those worn-out progressions and pounded them into that Elton-Cars-Aerosmith-meets-white-trash-pickups-with-skanky-hair-products-and-jeans-pretorn-in-China music that now dominates the airwaves. Many of us have accordingly gravitated to old blues and music from other continents. But I digress. Let's return to those golden days of yesteryear.

I played my new progression and b-section for awhile and scatted along vocally and out popped this *telephone number* over the main progression. *8-6-7- 5-3-0-9. 867–5309!* Where it came from I'll never know. Maybe it was sent from the same deranged, earth-bound angel who made the cop look the other way when my coke bindle dropped on the floor of the holding cell. The number didn't make sense to me at that moment, but it sure fit the progression and the rhythm. My main method of writing is to let it all hang out, play and sing and see what happens. There's not a lot of thought involved. I don't even have a subject to write about most of the time. I simply strum and go blah-blah and decipher it later. It happens fast, at least when I'm getting the initial shape of the song. I'll chew the fingernails of the details down to nubs later.

What would go on the b-section? *Jenny.* You can't go wrong with a girl's name in a song. I saw her: She was five-six with green eyes and long, wavy, auburn hair. She wore a bun-hugging mini-skirt and a tight t-shirt that showed it all off. She chewed gum. I knew Jenny, or I'd sure always wanted to. In any case,

Jenny was and is a great rock-n-roll name and it fit perfectly on the b-section structure. I mean, Ashleigh or Whitney wouldn't do. *Ashleigh I got your number...* Sorry. Ashleigh is the girl you take to a nice restaurant and Whitney might discuss literature with you, but for a drive in a convertible to get late-night fries and some smoochin' on a moonlit Saturday night, it's got to be Jenny. *Jenny, dadada da-da.* Cool. I wanted to record this progression.

This thing needed a distinctive guitar intro. My intro model always was, and still is, *Satisfaction* by the Rolling Stones. The opening lick gets you right into it. You know what it is, instantly. What if I played the chords just up on the high strings? How could I make something that follows the progression? I goofed around with the existing chords in the new position and bingo, I had it. I knew it as soon as I figured it out. Man, that was a great riff. I played that for a long time. *867–5309, 867–5309.* Wow. I didn't have a clue how to finish it, but I thought I'd go record it and see what happened.

I went up to my shed in San Rafael, turned on the gear, and had a hit of pot. Pot: the music-maker. One hit and you're golden for a couple of hours. Two hits, same. Three hits, you're eating popcorn and watching "I Dream of Jeannie" reruns at two in the afternoon.

Pot is the most innocuous of all the mind-altering substances. The laws prohibiting its use are absurd. You can get a quart of vodka at any corner liquor store and get homicidally shit-faced in a few minutes. Alcohol is responsible for thousands of drunk-driving deaths each year. Spousal and child abuse and crimes of passion of all kinds are fueled by booze. We are a drinking and fighting society. Those pot-smoking hippies are a bunch of fag commie environmentalists who should be taken out and shot! They're un-American. Besides, the liquor lobby owns Congress. If people smoked pot, they might not spend as much on booze. Money might or might not be the root of all evil, but it's certainly down there in the dirt.

Silly old pot's about creativity, about getting into it. I took a little hit, just enough to make me frazzled and excited. I got the lounge drum machine crankin'. The beat, as always, rock 1. I added a bunch of reverb to it from my little cheap spring reverb until the snare sounded like a cannon being fired inside a high school gym. I played the progression some more. Shit, I needed a bridge. Quick: uhh...C# minor, E, F# minor A, B, repeat, back to the intro riff. Okay, that's done. I worked out some internal riffs for the verse on the acoustic guitar, added some bass. I was ping-ponging tracks down like crazy on the TEAC four-track. I was in hyper-drive. This was gonna be great!

I got the intro riff on there with my Strat. It fit fucking perfectly. I started singing, scatting along. The track rocked. *Jenny! dada-da-da. 867–5309, 867–5309.* I needed to find a story for the song, a central meaning. But by then, the dang pot was wearing off. That's the trouble with pot, which I later in life gave up completely—heck, thirty years is enough of anything—it wears off and the second buzz isn't the same. It was about two in the afternoon, almost time for those "I Dream of Jeannie" reruns. I needed verse lyrics. *Hmmm. What? What?*

Suddenly, there was someone in the open doorway. It was Jim Keller, the lead guitarist for Tommy Tutone. I'd met Jim through a friend recently. He was a very cool guy, well-educated and well-brought-up, from the high-toned side of northern New Jersey. He could swing a hammer as well as a six-iron and he was a good guitar player, too. He was a tall, dark, and handsome lady's man. His band had been playing around and I'd seen them at Uncle Charlie's. They had a deal on Columbia and also were supported by the Mendocino Brewing Company, one of the first successful micro-breweries. Now, that's how to have a good gig: have it put together by a brewery. *Cold beer and hot girls.* Tommy Tutone had a solid ensemble sound and a very distinctive singer in Tommy Heath. Jim and Tommy together had a unique vocal blend.

Jim had been listening at the door. He dug it. It was pretty damn infectious, even with just a name and number and no verse or bridge lyrics. The truth is, most hit pop songs are about melody, hook, and feel. The average person reacts to how a song strikes him, not to the complexities of the lyrics. There are of course exceptions, but in general, that's how it is. Just think about going to a rock concert. It's the big hook lines, either lyrical or musical, that stand out, like *8-6-7-5-3-0-ni-eeeyyyyeen!!!* That's what gets the fists pumping and the Bics flicking. Even with Bob Dylan, at first all you remember is *It's All Over Now, Baby Blue.*

"I just don't know what the fuckin' thing's about," I said to Jim.

In his sonorous, radio-jock voice, he said something that I'll never forget: "Al," he laughed, "It's a girl's number on a bathroom wall!"

Shit! Of course it was! How could I be so stupid not to see that? We both cracked up and blasted out some verse lyrics in about twenty minutes, finished the bridge with the *I got it, I got it!* bit, and sang it to the track. It was very fun and rockin'.

By five, we'd got it down on cassette and we headed off to my house. Dede was home with baby James. We put the cassette in the boombox in the kitchen and danced around, playing it over and over and over. It was funny and great. I laughed, "No one will ever cut that. It's about a girl's number on the bathroom wall!" But who cared? It was a really fun song.

At the end of the day part of me said, *Oh well, that was a blast. I'll write a real song tomorrow.*

So, there was no actual Jenny with that actual phone number. No esoteric mathematics around the fact that 8675309 is a prime number. No story of unrequited love or evil stalking or a flirty girlfriend of the lead guitar player or any of the other tales I've heard over the years. It would be more fun if there was.

Tommy Tutone had some story about a girl he knew who had a studio with that number or something like that. They needed a story because they were out in public, fielding questions about the name and number. It pissed me off when VH1 ran a show recently about the song and made that story out to be the truth, though. They came down and interviewed me in Nashville, and I told them the story the way it happened. But they liked the other version, Tommy Tutone's version. VH1 even claimed that Jim came to me to finish the song he'd started! It just goes to show you: don't trust what you hear just because it's on TV or the radio. The reality wasn't interesting enough to be told true. A plum tree under a spring sky. My version should have been that Jenny was a six-foot-six black transvestite prostitute who smuggled coke for Oliver North and the CIA. The number was tattooed on the inside of her/his/its thigh.

The truth: It's a rather amorphous and vague song about a weird guy in a stall fantasizing about a good time. And it's got a hook a first-time fisherman could catch a great white shark on.

Who'd have dreamed what would happen with this song? It wasn't even supposed to be on Tommy Tutone's record. It wasn't going to be a single, I've been told. It snuck out on the radio and stations got flooded with calls requesting it. It has had legs that have carried it—and me—many years down the road, and it looks to go a way further.

Maybe the secret is to just have a good time and not worry about the end result so much. We writers try to do that every day. We always start our sessions telling each other that we're done compromising, we want to write something great. But by the end of the day, we've acknowledged that radio wouldn't touch this phrase, publishers would ax this line, or singers wouldn't sing that word. So we usually don't let the 867–5309 Jennys even live and breathe. They become 555-5555 Jennifers. They become *Because I Love You*. They turn into *In the Heat of the Night*. It's hard to imagine this song being written in Nashville or L.A. today, that's for sure. Or maybe it'd get written, but it wouldn't get on a record. There are too many people going over the songs with a fine-tooth comb nowadays. Every word is scrutinized, challenged, and second-guessed, often by people who have never written a hit song in their lives.

Let's talk about songwriting for minute. Why do we write songs anyway? I think that for those of us who don't approach writing as industry—I hate the phrase the "music industry." What is it, factories belching out crappy songs? I guess there is that aspect, isn't there?—it's a genetic or karmic compulsion. I grew up with music, but I didn't write my first song until I was eleven. *The skies are cloudy and gray, it's a good time for goin' away...* Once I did that, the floodgates opened. I don't write for other people. I barely write for myself. It's not that conscious. I don't set about to craft a song or a novel; the ideas carry me away in a sudden, unstoppable flood. It's just something I do; it's always been inside of me. The process of creation fires off endorphins in the writer and (we hope) in the audience as well. There is fantastic joy in the intensity of the doing. We *play* music, we don't *work* music. People get that. That's why we listen to music. The places music takes us can be fun, sexy, heartbreaking, or profoundly spiritual. Music is about us and for us.

I think that in the earliest human societies there were Cro-Magnons around the cave who told stories and sang and danced, just as there were shamans, liars (sometimes one and the same), great hunters, drunks, and regular working people. The singers and storytellers told the tale of the people for the people and for themselves. Music and art seems to come from somewhere else, somewhere outside the person. That's why ancient people believed there were muses of music, dance, singing, storytelling, sculpting and so forth. Perhaps the muses exist. I'm a prove-it-to-me mystic, so I'll have my suspicions. Creativity certainly feels like a gift. It's tempting to believe in reincarnation. That would explain why we can sing and tell stories: we've heard it all before. One thing seems clear: people need music and stories. I have heard that the aboriginal people of Australia "sing" the world and the beings and places in it into existence with their songs. I can see that.

Say it for me, say it for me
Say it 'til we understand the meaning
Remembering the feeling of a simple life…

I am not a studied songwriter. There are songwriting students by the millions, some of whom are very great writers. They can tell you who wrote what song and which songs are on what records and all that in thrilling detail. I'm not one of them. I'm just a guy who has heard songs at various times that have turned me on. Lots of songwriters talk about their folkie roots, James Taylor and such. Those writers can fingerpick. They write clever lyrics. Many of them are much more accomplished than I would be if I had five lifetimes to devote to music. If there's anything I've *studied* all these years, it is world history. I just listened to the radio when I was kid and then was lucky enough to have buddies who found out about cool old music.

Everybody has a Top Ten list of this or that—books, movies, songs. My Top Ten songs are:

Satisfaction .... *The Rolling Stones*
What I say .... *Ray Charles*
Walk Away Renee .... *The Left Banke*
You Really Got Me .... *The Kinks*
Johnny B Goode .... *Chuck Berry*
Long Distance Love .... *Little Feat*
Subterranean Homesick Blues .... *Bob Dylan*
Turn On Your Lovelight .... *Bobby Blue Band*
Imagine .... *John Lennon*
Will You Still Love Me Tomorrow .... *The Shirelles*

Number eleven would be a whole bunch of country songs like *Nothin' But the Wheel, Pocket Full of Gold, The Race is On, Mama Tried, Ring of Fire*. Too many great ones. Number twelve would be a zillion other songs I've loved—let's not forget

Bob Marley and the Wailers, Latin music, Gypsy music, Mark Knopfler. Number thirteen would be the infinity of horrible, calculated songs that I've been stuck with thanks to the "music industry." But my Top Ten are all songs that influenced my songwriting, or were reflections of what I already had in my musical pocket. They just said it better than I could.

I like raw music that hits the gut. I love the early rock-n-roll guys like Buddy Holly and Chuck Berry, who would go out there and rip it up with just a guitar and an amp. *Roll Over, Beethoven*. *867–5309* is a bit like that, thank goodness. I also like music that says something about the state of humanity, which is so sadly underdeveloped at this late date in history. Lennon, Dylan, Marley. *Imagine*. *Blowin' in the Wind*. *No Woman, No Cry*.

In Nashville nowadays, kids take a few college classes, do an internship and take over the publishing and record companies. Believe me, there are very talented writers in Nashville writing amazing songs. But what ends up on records and the radio are hypocritically patriotic, pickup truck, beer-drinking, growing-up-out-in-the-boonies songs. Boonies, my ass. How about *Born in the Suburbs!*

Sometimes things got so tough
We had to go to Arby's instead of McDonald's
Out in the suburbs

That would be closer to the truth.

It's one thing to get a song right. It's another to bleed it to death from over-examination. The great thing about the classic rock era is that there was a tremendous amount of artistic freedom, and rock music was still pretty fresh. Everything sounds so recycled now. I suppose that's part of why the original 80s music is still popular today, even among young people.

Not made from overly-recycled materials.

In any case, at the time I didn't know it, but with *867–5309 Jenny*, I'd written the song that would save my ass.

For a while.

Are You Sure This Is Fertilizer?

I can't get no
Satisfaction...

Rolling Stones

It was fall of 1981. There was a deck party at Dede's parents' house. The McGuires, pureblood Irish—not, like me, a mix of Welsh, Irish, English, and twelve-year-old Scotch—had wonderful afternoon food and Irish music hangouts. Dede's brother Scoop played bass with frequent guest Shana Morrison, Van's daughter, and brother Tom played guitar. There were quite a few people over that day, including Jerry, the little Belfast refugee mick with green teeth, who played an old banjo while sitting with his back to the circle, his feet surrounded by a dozen empty Smithwick's cans.

Jim Keller stopped by. He and I had been writing more songs in the wake of *867–5309*. Tommy Tutone was making an album for Columbia Records. He said they might record *867–5309*. Jim is a great guy, but I wasn't so sure about Tommy and their manager, Paul. Tommy wanted me to put him on the song as a writer, but I refused. Jim and I had written the song: It was a sixty/forty split. I got sixty percent because I originated the song, had the music, the name, and the number. Without Jim it wouldn't have had its final form, but that was the way rock-n-roll splits were done. The Nashville guys have this one right. Everyone in the writing room gets an equal share. Or that's the theory; in truth, co-writers are always getting screwed. The music biz is virtual porn. But I felt our split on *867–5309 Jenny* was fair. Jim agreed to it as well.

Well, that fine afternoon he had news for me. It looked like Tommy Tutone would record the song but, as he put it, they felt it was a "marginal" cut and *it wouldn't make the record unless they got a hundred percent of the publishing.*

I had a quick answer: "How about zero percent?"

Jim was just the messenger, so I didn't kill him on the spot, but I was hot about it. I'd been around long enough to discern the unsubtly-perfumed aroma of bullshit. Mind you, I didn't blame Jim. When you're in a band, you have to go with the partnership, you have to try and get what you can. That also applies to the other parties. I had to stick up for myself. Hell, I was dead flat broke. If I kept my publishing share and the song made money, I'd make more for my family. The stiletto cuts both ways.

The way music publishing works is this: Every song is a juicy cherry pie which is cut in half: one half is the writer's share and the other half is the publisher's share. The writer's share is usually regarded as inviolate; it always stays with the writer, unless he decides to sell it. If there are two writers, they split it in whatever percentage they have agreed on, fifty-fifty or otherwise, depending on the contribution each makes. Titles that come from a third party are usually worth ten percent.

The publisher's half of the pie is owned by the writer, who often sells all or part of it to a music publisher, who promotes and administers the song and collects royalties out of which the writer's share is then paid to the songwriter. Publishers, having acquired for some small price a share of the publishing from the writer, collect all the money from sales and licenses (except for the radio and television performance income, which goes directly to the writer) and frequently give life-sustaining advances against future earnings to penniless writers (aka waiters, valets, Home Depot workers, dishwashers, lawn cutters, substitute teachers, cab drivers, housepainters, etc.), who then live on the advance until the "big money" kicks in (if ever).

So it is definitely in the interest of the writer to keep his share of the publishing, since that is his future bargaining chip. The publishing share on a hit song can be sold for a tidy sum many years later. Of course, the recording artists cutting the song and their managers want that publishing share as well, for the same reasons. If two writers split a song, and then one of them acquires the other's publishing share, one writer would have three-quarters of the song. Since a Number One song can be worth millions, it's a common cause of merciless greed, glad-handing subterfuge, and more or less open warfare. Many writers are coerced into surrendering their publishing to established hit artists for the sake of getting their songs recorded. Hey, half of *something* is worth more than *all of nothing*. So they will tell you.

If you understand all this, you have my sympathy, because you've been in the music business. Congratulations! I feel your pain.

As I said, in this case, I felt that Jim and I had a fair split. They had a share of the song and Jim's publishing rights already. I needed mine. Besides, it wasn't like Tommy Tutone was a household name. It might have been another thing if, say, Rod Stewart wanted some of my publishing before he'd record my song. Not that Rod would need the money. Guys like Rod shouldn't demand publishing from struggling writers who need the Rod Stewart cut to survive and raise families. Now, I'm not saying Rod Stewart engaged in this practice. He might not ever have done this, and I'm sure he's a lovely bloke, great bum and all that. I won't name here the stars I know of who do pull this shit. But there are plenty of them, rest assured. I am using Rod Stewart's name so you can get the picture of the level of star who might be doing this kind of thing. The band entity Tommy Tutone said *867–5309* was a marginal song? Well, Tommy Tutone, Inc., you're no Rod Stewart. "What have *you* done so far?" said I.

Tommy and his manager were not pleased. If they couldn't get my publishing, then they wanted more of the song. Tommy thought his voice was a big part of the record. Well, he was right: that's why their name was on the record and not mine. It was not the Alex Call album, it was the Tommy Tutone album. If they were successful, they'd reap benefits far beyond what I'd receive. They'd sell albums, get good-paying gigs, and sell merchandise, like t-shirts. They'd written a bunch of other songs on the album too. Just because he was the singer—and had even changed a couple of meaningless verse words here and there without my knowledge or approval—didn't entitle Tommy to a piece of my writer's share. I suppose I could have been more solicitous of them, but they had my dander up by saying the song wouldn't make the album unless they got the publishing.

After a long hassle that included a bunch of attorney's fees that I couldn't afford, I agreed to give them two and a half percent more of the song. So the final split was 57 ½ % and 42 ½ %. A ridiculous fight. I still retained all my publishing. It was a waste of time and money, and it engendered plenty of bad feelings on both sides.

On a trip to L.A., I heard the song over at Columbia Records. I'd gathered they'd put the album out to radio stations with minimal promotion to see what songs might surface as singles. It was kind of hanging around on radio, getting some airplay and surprisingly good phone action: People were calling in to ask if Jenny was there. A veteran A&R guy told me it might have some promise, but though he liked it, he didn't hold out a lot of hope. Columbia was unlikely to put a lot of money behind *867–5309 Jenny*. If it stuck, great.

Second- or third-tier artists have tough sledding with record labels. They promote—you might have heard the term "payola"—their established stars. It costs a lot of dough-re-mi to break a record on radio. The influential "parallel one" radio stations in major cities charge a lot to play a single, even by a big star. Of course, payola was outlawed years ago, sure it was. And those boobs in Playboy are real, right? The big stations know they hold the key to the kingdom. It's a golden key, and you have to pay to get to turn it in the lock.

Meanwhile, I'd written a lot of songs, including *867–5309 Jenny*. I had a good feeling about my music for once, though I was shit-dead broke. I was hopeful that soon I'd be on my way back to the big time.

I went out to my shed in the debris yard one morning to write and record as usual. I unlocked the door. My gear was gone. Stolen. A wooden panel on the side that was covered by a big heavy box had been pried off. The thieves had taken everything. Well, almost everything. Right in the middle of the desk was my TEAC four-track tape recorder. I had it covered with a black plastic garbage bag to keep it moisture- and dust-free. The idiots, jackals, bandits, bastards, druggies, or whoever they were didn't take it or the several reels of tape that had all my songs, including *867–5309*, on them. But everything else was gone. My speakers, my amps, my microphones, my little mixing console, my headphones, my stands, reverbs, even my silly lounge drum machine. What did they get for my gear? A hundred bucks? A gram of blow?

There was a heavy metal band that rehearsed in another shed next door. They soon had some new P.A. stuff. I imagined that they traded my gear for that. I'll never know. It wasn't much, but it was all I had. I'd added stuff piece by piece until it was fairly functional. I couldn't afford to replace it. The cops said, "Forget it, it's gone." Big John Main and I went over and visited the metal band. Big John had a way with people. He could have a quiet talk with someone and get results that might be prodded by the visitee's desire to stay alive and whole. But it was to no avail. They stonily denied knowing anything about it.

I was devastated. It was Christmas and I didn't have any money for toys for my son. I'd worked hard the last two years, writing and building up a catalog, and what had happened? I got ripped off and lost all my gear.

I couldn't believe it. I was as angry as I'd ever been. But there was nothing to strike out at. Faceless thieves had stolen my life, violated my space, man. I told myself I wasn't going to get depressed, but it was hard to shake off the gut-shot feeling that I was truly fucked. *You're a loser, Call. Don't forget.* Perhaps Music herself had abandoned me at last. The muse is fickle. She leads you on and then dances away while you hang on, withering away, waiting for her to call you back again.

I decided to take it as a sign. Forget the Tommy Tutone thing. That wouldn't go anywhere. It was time for something new, something that was more real. I'd had a little rock career, and I'd had a lot of fun. I'd gotten to live in England and toured the U.S. with my buddies. I'd made four albums for major labels. That's more than a lot of guys ever get. I'd have to rise above my depression. It was a god-damn pisser, but screw it! It was time to leave music and do something else.

My pal Curt was a carpenter, I'd apprentice with him. I could become a carpenter, learn an honorable trade. I like wood, I like tools. It might be nice to build something and walk way from it every day, a job completed, rather than wait endlessly for other people to justify my existence by doing one of my songs. In a few years, I'd become a contractor and have guys working for me. Forget that: I'd never had a job and didn't know how to do any of that construction shit.

I called Curt. Could he use me?

"Sure, we're working on Sean Hopper's house, fixing some foundation problems. C'mon down. You'll need an aspirator and some bandanas to keep the dust out of your throat. Bring some work gloves, too. And don't wear anything that you don't want to get filthy."

***

It was January, 1982. There were some good things

happening. My son James was a happy toddler, learning to talk. My beloved football team, the San Francisco 49ers, after years on the bottom, were going to the Super Bowl (which they would win.) And in many nice Mill Valley houses, I was sure, dogs and cats curled up by warm fireplaces and took comfy winter snoozes, while their owners opened nice bottles of cabernet after the kids were tucked in.

But I was thirty-two years old, working on a house that was eighty years older than me, in a cold and dark crawlspace, digging a foot-wide trench five feet deep in the hard earth along a concrete foundation wall with a trowel and a pickaxe with a sawed-off handle (so it could be wielded in tight quarters.) Sweat poured down my back, making the spiders that were crawling there a bit damp. I wore a bandana around my face, outlaw-style, to keep out the dust and drifting filaments of fiberglass insulation that filled the dank air. Outside, a cold winter rain endlessly dripped from the eaves and the trees. Everything was wet. We had to dig this trench under the house, paint the exposed concrete foundation with this horrible tar-like stuff, and then fill the trench back up with gravel. The gravel had to be hauled up fifty steep, muddy steps from the street in five-gallon buckets.

It was exhausting.

The company was good, though. It was Curt and Steve Bajor and a couple of other home-boy stalwarts from our hippie days, still doing laborer jobs, living for the six-pack at the end of the day. It was mindless but not too bad. At least I was getting paid something. I was through with music and it was through with me. As Steve put it, I was getting a muscle tan hauling the buckets and digging away.

The job dragged on and on. There was a lot of work to be done to this old house. Tommy Tutone's record was out. *867–5309* was getting some airplay, but I wasn't impressed. I wouldn't make any real money unless it got into the top forty on Billboard's Hot 100 chart.

Dede drove by in the beat-up Opel with two-year-old James in his car seat one afternoon to tell me that the song was at number eighty-eight. Eighty-eight. Not too bad. I figured I'd make a thousand bucks. Back to the buckets. Next week it was seventy-six. Hey, it was moving up, but I was moving on. Give me a beer, boys. Let me know if it hits forty.

The next week it moved into the top sixty. Now it was getting interesting. Marty Wolf, who had been "managing" me, called to say there was some interest in me on both the publishing and record deal fronts. Oh really? Hmmm. That was nice, but talk is talk. I'd heard a lot of talk over the years.

Talk doesn't dig a trench. Still, it was intriguing. Those buckets weighed a ton.

The song hit number fifty with a bullet. A bullet is a little circle next to the song on the Hot 100 chart that signifies a rapid rise in chart position. Jenny, my little rock-n-roll darlin', was starting to take off. Listeners were calling in to radio stations all over the country, requesting it like crazy. It looked like it might move up into the serious money zone. The house job was nearing completion, so Curt was looking around for the next one. There was always something, but often his jobs didn't require extra workers. Dede drove up on a Tuesday afternoon. The song had just gone to number forty-four. I could hear the buzz from the biz all the way out on that muddy hillside in Mill Valley. It was time to get back into the game. Six weeks was a long enough career in the construction industry for me. Hell, that was longest I'd ever been employed outside of music.

Marty had some serious interest from Chappell Music now. Chappell, nowadays Warner-Chappell, was one of the big publishers, an old, established house with offices in London, New York, and L.A. Clover had a group deal with the London office in '77. The L.A. office was talking about a writer's deal for me. I might get some real money to write songs. Michael Barackman was back on about a possible artist deal with Arista Records. Gravel today, sushi tomorrow. When you're hot, you're hot.

So, just as precipitously as I'd left music to become a grunt laborer, I now decided to rip up my roots and move the family to L.A. to take advantage of this song. I bought a gram of coke and a case of beer for my fellow compadres of the muddy trench and had a goodbye party at the job site. Goodbye mud, hello Hollywood!

I had to bum some money from my dad to buy a better used car, an AMC Pacer, one of those funny bubble cars. It was awesome, silver and red, like something out of the Jetsons.

The song was climbing the charts now, making good moves every week. It seemed destined for the top. We packed up our stuff. Chappell had made an offer. How the tides turn.

Had the Goddess of Music been plain fucking with me, or what? It was almost as if there was a cosmic law at work. This law isn't found in the physics books, but rather in folk aphorisms.

It's always darkest before the dawn.
You have to lose everything to get everything.

867-5309 JENNY

One door closes, another opens.

It certainly seemed as if I had to give up music before it would take me back. That's the way life goes. The seasons aren't always smooth transitions. Frequently they're marked by cataclysms, like the big, cold March storm that leaves gentle spring in its wake. In our lives, we often get piles of shit dumped on us, only later to find that it was fertilizer. Sure smells like shit at the time, though.

No matter, my little two-finger chord doodling had seemingly paid off at last. I finally had a hit record. It had taken me a mere fifteen years of trying. Now, would I be smart enough to keep repeating that formula, or would I be too stupid for my own good?

L.A. Lights

I crawl like a viper through these suburban streets...

STEELY DAN

We rented a house just below Mulholland Drive in Woodland Hills in the west San Fernando Valley. It was a big, rambling stucco job that looked liked it might well tumble down the steep hillside in a good earthquake. But it was like the Taj Mahal to us: big and whitewashed, a little bit Southwestern or Tuscan, with flowering vines growing up the corners outside and a row of those skinny cedars that I called the Jewish redwoods, for their ubiquity in the San Fernando Valley hills. The house was very almost-degenerate movie-star cool. Gulda, called Goldy, was our hip Israeli landlady. There was a magnificent view of the valley from up there: the red-rock Santa Susana Mountains in the west and the precipitous and lofty San Gabriels in the east. At night, the lit-up grid of the valley boulevards twinkled and shone like an enormous, flattened-out Christmas tree. The fabled lights of L.A.

The offer Marty had gotten me from Chappell was now competing with an offer from MCA publishing. Which publisher should I sign with? It was a tough call. Roger Gordon was head of the L.A. office of Chappell. He was a tan, energetic man, very positive. He seemed like a guy I'd hang out with. Leeds Levy at MCA was another go-getter. He was very complimentary of my writing, but personally a bit more distant. I chose Chappell. It was kind of a coin toss: the offers were similar. It came to down the personal hit I got from Roger.

My deal was a "co-pub." In other words, I kept half my publishing. It wasn't a bad deal: I'd get two thousand dollars a month advance against future royalties for two years, then a little more if they picked up my option. Two thousand dollars a month! Shit, we'd been living on four hundred a month, when we were lucky. In gross terms, the deal was somewhat more than that, but Marty would take his cut of the advance, plus I'd signed on to be represented by John Branca, one of the top music attorneys in town. He had Michael Jackson, among others, as his client. He was a bit pricey. But hey, I had some dough. Some actual money. So I had a little blow and too much wine to celebrate. My long efforts had been vindicated. I was on top of the valley; I was on top of the world. The neon and concrete palm-tree-studded oyster was at my feet.

I was introduced around the Chappell office on Sunset Boulevard. They made me feel like I was a star. Me and Richard Marx, we were the next big thing.

"We love your songs, can't wait to run with 'em, let's do lunch. Musso and Frank?"

There was a nice little studio I could use to cut demos. I put my feet up in offices and listened to songs and heard gossip about people that I didn't know, but should. I'd changed shoes: No more mud on my work boots. I wore my trademark purple converse low-cuts.

I'd never been a big follower of the biz. To me, it's always been about the music, not the commerce. In some ways "music business" is an oxymoron. These two words are antithetical. Music brings out the best—or at least the creative—in people, while business brings out the worst. I was embarrassed that I didn't know who the heavy industry hitters were. To the Chappell people, the successful publishers and label heads were bigger news than the musicians. I pretended I'd heard of these hotshots. I nodded and said, "Yeah, um hmm." Just fake it, Call, and get out of there before you show your ignorance. I truly didn't have any interest in that stuff. I just wanted to do my thing and get checks in my mailbox.

This is a weak link in my psyche, I'm sure. But what the fuck? That's me. The successful stars of music have a head— and a big boner—for business. They want to compete. They like it. I don't. If they don't want to sully their hands directly, they have the sense to hook up with ambitious managers who can swim in the shark-infested waters and come back alive. It's a cutthroat deal, baby. Do or die. Kill if you must, just don't get killed. It's called ambition, and I had the ambition of a floating duck. I grasped onto music way back as a kid as a way out of the tough-guy world. Now I was smack-dab back in the middle of it. I was like a little fish in Disney film with a fake shark fin taped to my back. All around me, the real sharks circled endlessly.

For the moment, however, I was having a blast. Roger took me out to lunch, Marty and Branca took me out to lunch, Jolene from Chappell took me out to lunch. There was Donovan over at that table, there's Irving Whats-his-name, Michael Whooz-it, and Gloria Katchen'fuque. The talk was of big stuff.

"Would you like to write with Bob Dylan?"

Jeezus! That'd be like playing baseball with Willie Mays! Not sure if I could handle that. "Sure, absolutely, fantastic!"

I'd brought in what I thought was a pretty good bunch of songs, and one of them was already a hit, so for now I was cool. Gorgeous, blonde Jolene, who looked like she should have had a record deal, went out and got me a cut by Pat Benatar with *Little Too Late* on Benatar's new album, which was called *Get Nervous*. That was hot. Pat had had a string of huge hits over the last two years. Benatar look-a-likes sat in restaurants on Sunset. I'd made the jump to a new speed and I thought this would happen all the time. My vast talent had at last been discovered and now everyone would flock to record my songs. I later heard that Benatar was pressured heavily by Jolene's big-time producer boyfriend to cut my song, that it wasn't a big fave in her camp. But at that time, that was knowledge I didn't have. Thank God for that.

This was heady stuff for me. Marty Wolf was angling in on Arista Records. Michael Barackman had gone to bat for me with Clive Davis. My demos had been well received; it looked promising. I had to go meet Clive at the Beverly Hills Hotel, in cabaña number five. I was nervous about the meeting.

Unbelievably, Marty had to go out of town and couldn't be there, so I had to make the cabaña pilgrimage by myself. *Gulp. Alex flies solo to face El Queso Grande.* I called up Johnny Ciambotti for moral support. He and Susan were living at his mom's house in Beverly Hills. I went by and we had a glass of wine and he gave me a big pep talk, "Take your balls in your hands and lead yourself through the world." Johnny might have made me feel small at times in my life, but this time he pumped me up and I was grateful. While I didn't take his suggestion literally, I tried to remember that I did possess balls.

I met with Clive and a couple of associates in his cabaña. The cabañas at the Beverly Hills Hotel are legendary. Many huge, historic deals have gone down there; many wild times have gone down there. Only God and the concierge know the details. At the hotel, everything is very discreet. It's all taken care of, quietly. The cabañas are little stucco houses set in palm trees behind the main hotel. I felt like I was in way over my head driving in there, like security was going to throw me off the premises for driving my used Pacer into the sacred precinct. The shades-wearing security guard would lean down, clipboard in hand, look at me and my car and say, "I'm sorry, sir, but even I can see that you're a fraud. You'll have to leave."

One of Clive's associates greeted me and I waited in the living room. I was trying to be cool, making small talk with my greeter, who could have been a personal assistant or an executive vice-president of Arista for all I knew, but inside I was sweating small rodents. Clive finally emerged from his bedroom. We chatted and listened to my demos. Some sounded good; others sounded lousy. I can't stand listening to my songs with business people. Let them listen on their own time and tell me what they think, but don't make me sit there and tap my foot awkwardly through the too-long verses and the unnecessary b-sections, the superfluous guitar solos, the lame choruses. I love my songs, even the crappy ones, but in the presence of A&R people or label heads, time seems to slow down to the semi-frozen molasses dimension. I just ain't that good a salesman to pretend I'm lovin' it.

Clive was gracious, because he is one of the most gracious

people you'll meet in the music business. For example, he always writes notes back to you when you send him a song, even when it's a rejection, where the standard protocol is simply not to reply at all. His manner put me at ease. He praised a few songs, made constructive comments about some others. He only creamed one. I couldn't have agreed more with his assessment of it. I didn't know he had a copy of that particular dud. We laughed about how bad it was—a gentle chuckle of mutual acknowledgement, not a guffaw. After about an hour, he reached out to shake my hand and said, "I think you're ready to make a record for us."

I said, "Wow, thank you so much."

I had a damn major label record deal as a solo artist. Alex Fucking Call of the Major Fucking Leagues, baby.

Holy fucking shit, I had a record deal! I drove my Pacer out through the palm grove, past the now-smiling security guard. *Fraud, my ass!* Actually, I don't even think there was a guard. I had gotten through on my own—no Huey, no Ciambotti, no McFee—by writing good songs. And also because Michael Barackman, who I'd made stand outside my shed in the construction yard to hear me play, had believed in me. It was quite a vindication after four long years of laboring in penniless solitude.

I thought I was ready for the big time, for financial reward as well. I couldn't see how it would all shake down, and I didn't want to look too closely. I'd gone to gigs around L.A., where the men and women all looked like movie stars and the bands were as polished as the chrome on a Corvette. I was an AMC Pacer—a little sideways, not quite a standard-issue rock star. But somehow that would all come together for me.

When I signed my contract, I was paid a fifteen thousand dollar advance. After Marty had me cut him a check for his well-earned commission and John Branca deducted his legal fees, I took the remaining seven hundred and fifty bucks and bought two badly-needed new tires for the Pacer and a pair of unfinished bookshelves for our living room. I splurged on a can of mahogany stain. And a brush. Life in the fast lane. I should have looked at the date when I signed. I did later: April 1. Alex's record deal: signed on April Fool's Day.

Well, Roger Gordon was quite pleased. Chappell's investment in me looked good, with *867–5309*, the Benatar cut, and my record deal. If things went well, they'd have signed me for a pittance. He'd found a couple of writers that he thought I should hook up with to get the hit machine pumping.

One guy had a hit. Should I name it? I think I will. It was called *She Talks in Stereo*. So off I went, guitar case in hand, to his little house in Hollywood. He came to the door wearing rainbow-striped suspenders and a spandex t-shirt and oversized sunglasses with just a tinge of pink in the lenses. He had a hundred-dollar rock-star spiky hairdo going on above the glasses. There were two leggy girls with him who looked like models. They were checking out a photo album from a recent shoot and I sat across the living room from them while the three of them looked at pictures. I sat there, a nervous smile pasted to my face, next to my guitar case. They weren't even talking to me. No: "Hey, can I get you a coffee?" No: "Sorry man, we'll get started in a minute." They just totally ignored me. I waited there patiently for a few minutes, then half-an-hour, then a bit longer, my mind being blown.

It was fucking unbelievable. Here I was in this guy's house.

The writing appointment had been set up by higher powers. Shit, my hits were bigger than his little forgettable ditty! What the fuck was going on? *This is the L.A. shit we'd always railed about up in Marin, the Hollywood plastic star thing.* After a long while during which my incredulousness smoldered and then iced into a calm-so-what-who-gives-a-shit dismissive anger, I picked up my guitar and walked out. They hardly acknowledged my going. No apology, nothing. Welcome to Hollywood, motherfucker! Hope the guy enjoyed the models talking in stereo.

That writing appointment notwithstanding, the pace of the action picked up. Arista wanted to find the right producer for me. Marty dealt with them. I didn't know who would be good. I didn't know that world, didn't know who the honchos were. Hell, I still don't. To be perfectly honest, I don't pay that much attention to music. I read books, mostly history, and listen to NPR. When I do get into music, it's very intensive. I'll play an album over and over again. But it has to be something that really grabs me. Bob Marley, Peter Gabriel, Sting, Stevie Wonder, Merle Haggard, Vince Gill, Los Lobos, Paul Simon.

I don't listen to keep up with the biz, because I have the disgusting habit of subconsciously copying songs I can't stand. That's not the worst part. The worst part is that I do a lousy job of it. I've written some horrible stuff that apes hits that I hated. Go figure. Ask my therapist, if you can find him. I think he's out driving his Porsche around his ranch in Montana.

So, since the business abhors the vacuum of ignorance, Arista picked Ron Nevison, a producer-engineer who had worked with *The Who, Led Zeppelin*, and *Bad Company*. Ron was a solid pop-rock guy who'd go on to have many huge producer credits with Heart and many others. Right then, he was recording some tracks with TV heartthrob Rex Smith. As it turned out, they were cutting my song *New Romeo*. So I went with Marty down to a big studio somewhere out in the massive terra incognita grid of endless, faceless L.A. boulevards and met Rex and Ron.

Rex actually had a DeLorean parked in the alley behind the studio. He was soap-opera-star handsome, which made sense, because I think he'd been on soaps. He had a starlet-class babe with him on the studio couch. Ron was a good-looking guy himself: black hair slicked back, nice clothes. There were a couple of session players and a couple more hot girls in the control room. It was a real slick Hollywood scene. I felt like a spud-field worker from Pocatello who'd accidentally walked through a space-warp and found himself in the Barbie and Ken Go Hollywood Galaxy. But I was cool, dude. We went to an upscale bar nearby and Ron ordered something called a *kir*. I knew all about *beer*, but I'd never heard of *kir*. I thought I'd better get used to it. Ron had some high-falutin' tastes.

We chatted in the bar. I had a ginger ale. Ron and Marty talked about more big music biz names I should've known and didn't; deals going down; guys getting fucked over; the usual Hollywood stuff. I finally got around to asking Ron about using my band on the record. That's what Huey did. Ron nixed it out of hand. He had great A-list players, he said. We had to make a great record. End of subject. I insisted that I had a drummer I wanted to use, Tony Braunegal. Mutt Lange used him. Ron didn't like it, because he wanted to use Steve Price from Pablo Cruise, but he finally gave in. I could tell this rubbed him the wrong way. But part of me wanted to have at least *some* say in what went on my own record. I now had a tough phone call to make to John Main and Kevin Wells. Big John had been counting on making the record with me. He'd put in some years and he deserved it, but it was truly out of my hands if I wanted to make a record for Arista. Deal or no deal.

Ron was a realist who played in a bigger league than I did. He knew how to make great records, and he knew who was paying him, and it wasn't Alex Call. He had to answer to Clive, and Ron wasn't going to monkey around with a bunch of Marin County musicians. He was going to use A-teamers he could trust. I understood. In a similar situation, Huey had said "no" to his deal if he couldn't use his band. But Huey and his manager Bob Brown were way tougher than I was. It wasn't the worst choice I ever made, since Ron's session players were fabulous, but it was like caving to my hard-guy nemesis Alan Acree back in seventh grade. It was the beginning of a process that would chip away at me until eventually I wasn't sure who I saw in the mirror. Looking back, I don't think I knew who that was in the reflection anyway.

Ron did the budget and booked the Record Plant in Sausalito. That was great, as I'd be back home. Dede and I had now bought our first house, a little fifties ranch-style in Canoga Park, down on the flats far below the lofty heights of Woodland Hills and Tarzana. It was a small house, but nice inside. All of the San Fernando Valley used to be orange and lemon orchards before they planted a million or two houses there. We had two big lemon trees in our backyard. Now we'd be going back to Marin for the fall and early winter while I recorded. We'd rent my dad's house again, and actually make the rent payments, since that was in the album budget!

John Main didn't take the phone call well at all. The only good news was that a song we had co-written, *Love Dogs*, would be on the album. It was little consolation for Big John, who'd faithfully put in a lot of time, effort, and his own money into making our band work. There was no choice for me, unless I didn't want to make the record. But I desperately wanted to. My publishing gig and my new house, my family's future, was tied up in making the entire project work.

Michael Barackman, Ron, Marty, and I chose the final songs to be cut. Of course, Clive Davis oversaw and approved everything. The feeling was that it was a good list, with a few possible singles. We had to start cutting to see what jumped up or fell down. It's not always obvious where the magic will strike or fail when you record. Some songs start out as the lead contenders only to fall by the wayside when other songs work better. Ron had chosen the players: Peter Wolf on keyboards (he'd be the de facto musical director), Peter Maunu on guitar, John Pierce, the bass player for Pablo Cruise, and my choice, Tony Braunegal, on drums.

We packed up the old Pacer and drove north. I had a little money in my checking account and two new front tires. I was gonna be huge.

What a wild time this had been. In a few months, I'd gone from digging ditches in the freezing mud under an old house in Mill Valley to meeting Clive Davis in his cabaña at the Beverly Hills Hotel. It was like I'd been cast in a movie that accidentally starred me. But it felt right. When Huey got signed, he definitely deserved it. But I didn't think that Huey had anything on me as a singer and writer. He was a strong personality and the girls loved him, but I wasn't too bad looking myself. I'd had two hits, with the Benatar single getting up to number twenty in the charts, and her video played on MTV every hour. *Jenny* made it to number four for an entire month. It was kept out of number one by the vapid *Ebony and Ivory* and a handful of other songs. Number four for a month isn't too bad! It was on the charts for forty-two weeks, almost a whole year. Southside Johnny was cutting *New Romeo* and would have an MTV video as well. Then I would have one, too. I had a good bunch of songs. It was my turn. I'd had to cut John Main and Kevin Wells—my buddies in the Love Dogs—loose, which bothered me, but maybe I was in that higher, Ron Nevison–Clive Davis league now. Maybe I was destined to get back on the big stages, the ones with flashlight-wielding roadies and a roaring, squealing crowd of pretty girls right up front, waiting to throw their underwear at me.

I had to take care of Alex Call. *Sorry guys.* When I went on tour, they'd be my band, unless there were higher-up guys that I could afford. Time would tell, but right then, I thought I was going to hit it big. *Huge, I tell you.* Well, I was a huge asshole, anyway, one who was being led around by the fuckin' nose, like a stupid cow.

THE RECORD PLANT

So tell me who I see
When I look in your eyes
Is that you baby?
Or just a brilliant disguise...

BRUCE SPRINGSTEEN

We set up shop at the Record Plant in Sausalito. It was a major studio. Dan Fogelberg, Joni Mitchell, Pablo Cruise, Bonnie Raitt, Huey Lewis, and Sly and the Family Stone had recorded giant hits there. The interior had that faded-redwood-planking-drug-dealer-pad vibe: unpainted, dark, no day, no night, just stoned. Sly's circular, sunken listening room/drug den was a well-known feature. There were three main studios. I'd made demos, played parties, and been to sessions there many times before. But it was big-time to be making my record there. I knew many of the locals, guys in bands around Marin County, were jealous of me.

"Fuckin' Alex Call? Give me a break."

Very sorry, but eat crap, peons.

We were going to rehearse for two weeks before running tape. Peter Wolf, the blonde Austrian *wunderkind* was playing keyboards. Peter was from Vienna, where he'd been a child prodigy, going to conservatory—say it with an Austrian accent, please—at age six; another Mozart in the making. But he'd dropped out of the classical music machine and switched to jazz and pop music in his teens.

He was a graduate of the Frank Zappa player-testing labs. Zappa's bands were legendary. Apparently, Frank wrote insanely difficult charts just to see if his players could cut it. All the guys who played for him were big-time session cats now. To have Zappa alumni status was like having your PhD from the Harvard of Insanely Cool. Peter was personally a charming, smooth customer. He loved the ladies and the good things in life. He also really loved making music. It almost seemed like playing was a sexual act for him. He got orgasmic over his sounds and the stuff he created with his fingers on the keys. He had a thing about being Austrian. He said the Swiss and Germans were as lively as corpses, but Austrians were like blacks: they dug music and women and good times. Well, I don't know about *being* corpses, but the Germans were good at *making* corpses. They proved that a few times.

Pete Maunu, the guitarist, was a skinny guy with glasses. He also absolutely loved what he played, as well he should. He and Peter W. were old compatriots, they'd done many sessions together; they were like a team. Pete M. is a very funny dude. He got into diatribes that were like stand-up monologues. The two Peters were both guys on a big roll: they were in demand and they were lovin' every minute of it.

John Pierce, bassist, was on loan from Pablo Cruise, the Marin County band that had scored a handful of hits like *Whatcha' Gonna Do When She Says Goodbye*. I knew David Jenkins and Cory Lerios from around, but John was new to me. In addition to being a great bass player, he was a droll crackup. He just had a funny way of putting things and great sense of timing. He was a master of both headphone banter and the practical joke, so he was invaluable in the studio. He and I hit it off from the start. Tony Braunegal fit right into the witty crew. He was also a seasoned veteran, and even if Ron Nevison would've rather used Steve Price from Pablo Cruise on drums, Tony was right there with the team, both musically and humorously.

The pace was pretty damn leisurely. You *play* music, you don't *work* music. We'd drift into the studio around ten in the morning, talk and laugh about the previous evening's capers and start making some noises, and then it was time for lunch. After lunch, we'd regroup and make some more noise, usually working over one song for a couple of hours, then do another. Around four in the afternoon , someone would invariably say, "Where's Chuck?" It was a reference to a guy well known at the Plant for directing folks to a source of reasonably-priced nasal stimulants. So there'd be another break while Chuck was rounded up. Then after a toot or two, we'd crank up again for a while before calling it a day and going out into the night.

I'd head home to Dede and James most evenings, but the rest of the fellows were on the road, so they were eating sushi, hitting Uncle Charlie's, or hanging out in groups in the studio with Chuck's products until the wee hours.

There was a table-top Galaxians and a Xenon pinball machine in the hangout room at the Plant. Evenings there ranged from quiet to festive, depending on who was working there. If there was someone recording, there was usually some action, a few girls coming by. But many nights, it was just a few guys waiting for some blow to show up, for something funny to happen. As

I said, making a record is both boring and intense. Everyone is acting like they're having a great time, and they are in one sense, but there's a whole lot on the line with these recordings. Many futures are at stake. The pressure is underlying and subtle but real, like a huge shark camouflaged in the waving kelp, hence the never-ending desire for drugs and alcohol to provide a squid-ink cover, a way to deny the danger.

Ron Nevison had his own schedule. He kept somewhat apart from the players. It made sense, as he had to oversee the asylum and make sure the inmates did their proper parts. He, Tony, and the two Peters were staying at the house owned by the Plant in Mill Valley. That was another well-known party spot made infamous by Rick *Superfreak* James and others as a den of wildness. If the carpets could talk! There were probably a couple of pounds of blow down in the roots of the plush '70s shag.

The Pablo Cruise guys were winding down their session. They'd been cutting what they hoped would be a comeback album. Despite their big hits of the previous couple years, they'd fallen out of the good graces of their label and were on the way out of the picture. The label chiefs came by and didn't dig what they'd recorded. *What have you done for me lately?* I found it hard to believe that they could be so dissed by their label. What a business. Bob Brown managed both Huey and Pablo Cruise. Huey was hot, riding a career-breaking first hit, *Do You Believe In Love?* and also *Workin' for a Livin'*. The News was coming in to cut their third album for Chrysalis. That would be fun, to be right across the hallway from my old chums. The Pablo guys could see the writing on the wall and were a bit down.

It'd been two weeks since we'd started rehearsing. We were about to go red on my project.

We moved from the rehearsal room into the studio proper and started cutting tracks. It was an even slower pace than the rehearsals were. We started by getting the drum sounds, which is excruciatingly boring for those not involved. Drumheads were tightened and loosened and changed. Microphones were changed and repositioned, endlessly. Our engineer, Mike Clink, was one of the best. Ron, who'd started as an engineer, was a hands-on producer like Mutt was, so he and Clink knew what they were doing. Ron had an issue with Tony's kick drum. It was on the small side for Ron's taste. Ron was still obviously miffed about my having chosen the drummer. Mr. Nevison has a reputation as a bit of a curmudgeon. He certainly doesn't mince words when stating his opinions. I had to grin and bear it. Tony was my choice and I was sticking to it. Too late to change by then, anyway. Besides, though we all joked around and acted on the surface like equals, I still felt like a bumpkin guest at a fancy-pants party where everyone knew everyone but me. I wanted my little say in the project. *I still had me pride.*

Ron and the two Peters had done a lot of recording together, so they were thick as a junior rat pack. That's why I felt a bit left out of the joke, like they were cutting a record on this guy who they didn't think had what it took to make it. As I wrote in *New Romeo: My confidence is easily shaken, it never has taken much.* Regardless, at this point, we'd cast off lines and we were sailing across that ocean of fame and fortune. We'd have to wait and see where the boat floated us.

I had my hopes up for two songs, *New Romeo* and *Just Another Saturday Night.* They were both rockers, especially

Saturday Night, which was originally called *High School Killing*. It was about senseless slaughter wrought on the streets by boy-men with guns. *New Romeo* had been cut three times by then, but none of the recordings had matched the great groove put down by Keith Knudsen and John McFee on the original studio demo. That recording had a slap in the rhythm which seemingly couldn't be duplicated. The more groovy stuff was added to it, the more off it got. It seemed to start with singers not quite getting my timing on the lyrics. That bled into the feel of the track, and each recording got further from the original, like a game of "Telephone," the kids' game where a whispered sentence goes around a circle and by the time it reaches the last person, it's a very different sentence.

There were a few other good ones: *Blue Avenue, Annie Don't Lie, Goin' Through the Motions, There Goes Another Fool In Love*, and my take on Pachabel's Canon in D, *Dark Side of the Night*. There was one dog that I couldn't stand, kind of a rock anthem called *Hungover You*. It stunk, I hated it, but it had been chosen. I guess the powers-that-be felt it filled a hard-rock void on the album. I wrote the stupid piece of crap; now I was stuck with it. I'd written a lot of bad songs in my life, and this was definitely one of them.

Once again the problem arose, the great white shark lurking out in the waves that no one would acknowledge in my presence. Who was I going to be? The rocker of *Saturday Night* and *New Romeo*? The Michael MacDonald-style crooner of *Goin' Through the Motions*? Or the vapid, insincere rock guy singing *Hungover You*? Different people had different opinions. My writing covered a lot of ground. If I'd been strong, I'd have stood up and said, it's *Saturday Night*. But I let myself be influenced by the voice speaking at the moment. If Marty Wolf thought I should be the hard-rock guy, then I'd rock. If Michael Barackman though I should be the crooner, then I'd MacDonald it to death, baby. Of course Arista had to go with what they felt could draw a larger acne-and-hair-products-buying audience to the radio stations.

The failure of this thinking, both theirs and mine, was essential. In order to succeed in music, an artist has to know who *he* is and what works and what doesn't. He can't let himself be blown around like a leaf on a pond, because, there's a lot of wind a-blowin' every time someone opens his mouth. I was acting like I was in control. But I didn't know who I wanted to be. Deep down, I wanted to be more like Springsteen than MacDonald, and I sure wanted be more like McDonald than some big-hair guy with a black-leather metal-studded jock strap and eye shadow. But even deeper down, so far in there that I couldn't even see it—was afraid even to peek at it—maybe I didn't want to be there at all. Maybe I liked being in my home-studio-cave making little recordings and getting checks in the mail. It'd take me quite a few more rounds in the ring to see the truth in that, and a lot longer to come to the point where I wanted to be on stage, delivering messages I deeply believed in.

But right then, I was thirty-three and this was my last, biggest, and best chance to make it as a performer. And the project was off to a good start. The tracks were hot. We were cutting one song a day. We'd straggle in as usual around ten in the morning and Ron would be bringing up the board mix from yesterday to have a listen. I took home rough tapes at night and listened to them. I tried to have some constructive comments in the morning. The funny thing was that Ron didn't give a flying crap about my opinion. He'd make a face that was imitated by the other guys: one eyebrow would go up and he'd peer down the console at me and say nothing, which simply meant "no." The look said to me: What the fuck did I know? Ron knew best. After a while I gave up and went with the flow. The truth is, he *did* know best, and we were highly unlikely to re-record anything that was done anyway. A lot of work went into each step, and we weren't going to go back go back and start over for the sake of one of my observations.

"Can I borrow your ear, Alex?"

Every day we'd get some sounds again. Keyboard and guitar approaches change with each track, and the drums need to be dialed in on a daily basis. We'd have lunch and then start doing takes; two, three, four. Then around tea-time someone would make the call in the headphones, "Where's Chuck?" Some blow would arrive, lines were snorted again off the grand piano, and the track got cut, usually in one or two takes. Somebody laughed, "Is this a cocaine record?" It wasn't anything like a runaway coke bender, but there was blow being snorted. Truly it wasn't wild high-end rock band freebasing or even more than a few toots, just enough to fire up the little deuce coupe for that quarter-mile run.

Whatever the pharmacology, for the moment, over those big speakers above the mixing console, the stuff sounded shit-hot. Peter Wolf and Pete Maunu made daily magic in there. Wolf had a new synth called a Chroma that made some amazingly gorgeous noises. Pete M's leads were searing. John Pierce was world-class, and Tony was a funky bad-ass, no matter what Ron thought.

There was a vibe. Guys from other bands, other projects, were stopping by and digging the tracks. Huey and the News were across the hall. They were cutting a collection of little ditties that would eventually be called *Sports*, and sell eight million copies. But right then, they were down a little bit. Not about their music. They'd been hassling with their label. Their record would end up not coming out for a year. Sometimes it felt like the positive energy was in my room. Of course, Huey's tracks were unbelievable. We all wandered back and forth a lot, stopping by to listen. One day they were singing backgrounds on a song called *If This Is It*. Holy crap! I'd never in my life heard anything that sounded more like a hit coming over those big studio monitors.

There was a funny competitive spirit in the studio: our team vs. their team. We wanted to get them with practical jokes and vice versa. Ron came up with a great one. He made a phony coke bindle, the folded-up paper that blow came in. He put about a gram of baking powder in it. It looked like blow; close enough, anyway. We hung out in the game room. There was no one there yet, but the News was working down the hall. Someone would be in within a few minutes, no doubt. Ron placed the fake bindle on the floor by the pinball machine. He sat at the table-mounted Galaxians, blasting away aliens. I sat at a booth, pretending to read a magazine. Bill, the News' drummer, came in and started playing pinball. He was pounding away, racking up points. Then he saw it. He glanced around surreptitiously to see if anyone was looking. I had a good angle on him: it looked like I was reading, but I was almost ready to pee on myself. He bent down and picked the bindle up and slid it into his pocket. He played a little more pinball, as if nothing had happened, and then quietly left. Ron grinned. Now we just had to wait for the payoff.

Later, we were back in the game room and Bill and Johnny came barging down the hall. Bill said with mock anger, "What shithead put the phony blow out?"

Ron shrugged from his station at Galaxians. We all had a good laugh. One point for our side. There would be revenge.

That night we all went down to Uncle Charlie's. It was the happening spot in cocaine-and- booze-drenched Marin. Huey had put Uncle Charlie's on the map, and now all the better bands played there. It was packed with hot, permed-up, cleavage-drenched chicks and penny-ante dealers with tumblers of Jack Daniels and half-grams of blow for sale.

Ron had new twist on the fake coke bindle. He'd scotch-taped a ten-foot-long black thread to one. We got a table near the bar. Ron dropped the bindle on the floor in the heavy-traffic area between us and the bar. It didn't take long for the first coke-whore to bend over and reach for the bindle. But just as the guy's fingers neared it, Ron gave the thread a subtle jerk and the bindle slid a foot. The guy started up, nearly knocking over a waitress's tray of drinks. Then the deluded nose-monkey tried again. Ron moved it another foot. Freaked, the guy stood up and walked away, nervously checking to make sure no one saw him. We were about dying laughing. It worked a couple more times before everyone got wise to it. Good joke.

The morning after the fake coke incident, we arrived at the studio to find Ron's chair missing. It was a special chair, a black leather swivel office chair with arm rests that Ron brought specially, wherever he was booked for studio sessions. It was Ron's chair and nobody else sat in it, period. On the console, there was a Polaroid photo of the chair with duct tape wrapped around it, like it was tied up. An ominous message was scrawled in sharpie on the photo: *We've taken your chair hostage. Pay a pound of coke ransom or you'll never see it again!* Underneath that it said, as if the chair were talking, "Please do what they say! They mean it. Help!" We poured out a pound of flour into a plastic bag and dropped it outside their studio door, and the chair was returned, no questions asked. Ah, there's nothing like maturity.

The cutting of the basic tracks took about two weeks, and then we got into the overdubs. We had to get all of the two Peters' parts down before they moved on to their next projects. Hour after hour we sat in the control room and honed the lead guitars and extra keyboard parts. It was like eating a box of exquisite chocolates: pure ear candy. We decided to bring in John McFee to do some leads on *There Goes Another Fool In Love*, a song I wrote with Tommy Tutone's Jim Keller. John was spectacular, as always. Ron was blown away. He said something like, "Now here's a guy from Clover who I'd want to make a record with." Bill Gibson, Johnny Colla, and Chris Hayes from the News contributed background vocals. We had some women singers as well: Sharra Penny, Rahni Raines, and Lynne Ray. We watched them ooh and ahh through the smoky glass of the control room window.

Then everyone was done and gone and it was down to me and Ron and the all-important lead vocals. I think Ron had been hoping that some of my scratch vocals might hold up, the vocals I sang along with the basic tracks. But that didn't turn out to be the case, so we started in on the whole lot.

Doing lead vocals is exacting. Each word has to be in tune,

in time, and have meaning and spark. A few guys I talked to thought it was nuts to do all of the leads in a row. It's such a workload that it should be spread out. But there was no other option. We did nine vocals in a week. Each one took three or four hours of hard singing; line by line, word by word. I had to go back in and tweak the takes afterwards, too. My voice held up pretty well, thank goodness, because when it goes out, I have a peculiar trick: I blow out-of-tune octave notes. Think of a clarinet being played by a fourth-grader: *Squeak, honk*. It's no fun when that happens, especially because it means that I will need some recuperative time.

With two or three songs to go, I got a cold and we had to call it quits. I sensed Ron's frustration with me as a singer. He didn't say anything, but there was a vibe. I can only do what I know how to do. I'm not Steve Perry or Sting. I was happy with some of the vocals. On some of the songs, I wasn't so sure. Some of it had to do with the songwriting. A great song can be sung by anyone. The melody, which is the biggest part of a song, will carry the day even if the singer is not the best. Or lyrics can save it. But though I liked many of the songs on the record, I didn't know if I had even one song which might be considered a timeless classic. It seemed more about me and my voice: If you liked it, great. If you didn't, you could melt down the edges and call it a Frisbee.

We went back to L.A. and waited for my throat to recover. It was winter now. We arrived back at our little boxy house just off Winnetka in the valley. Our formerly-green lawn had gone into tawny dead Bermuda hibernation. After being in northern California, L.A itself seemed biologically dead. It was windy and dry, hot at Christmastime, dust blowing around the billboards and little cookie-cutter fifties ranch houses.

There was some sudden, major bad news. Roger Gordon was fired by Chappell the week before Christmas. I was shocked. I mean, Christmas, Hanukah, whatever. Is that when you fire people? The guy had a family. He was upset, but characteristically optimistic. He'd catch on somewhere. Roger was a survivor. *Aren't we all?* The good old music business: it's good at *giving* people the business, for sure. But it was a serious blow to me. Roger was the guy I related to at Chappell. He was the one who'd signed me, and that was important, as you shall see. Ah well, the other friendly, sharp, and effusively supportive people were still there. They were my buddies, they believed in me. Or so I thought.

After the holidays, Ron and I went back to the Plant to do the remaining vocals and mix. We were going to drive up in his baby blue Rolls Royce—I told you Ron had highfalutin' tastes— but we were turned back by heavy winter tule fog at the downslope of famous Grapevine hill, where I-5 drops into the Central Valley. It was so thick I had to open the passenger door and watch the edge of the road as we crept along at walking speed.

Back in Sausalito, we finished up the remaining vocals. It was eerie being there with just a couple of people. What happened to the party? Where was Chuck? After we were all done, Ron, Mike Clink, and I had a drink in the bar at the hotel in which we were staying. We'd finished a big task and were sitting there, it was time to say, "Well done, good luck to the album." Instead, Ron looked directly at me and told me matter-of-factly that in his opinion, I didn't have what it took to be a great lead singer. He didn't want to say anything while we were getting vocals, but there was no point in holding back now.

I was floored, staggered. My knees buckled. I reeled back and hung onto my glass like it was the ropes around a boxing ring. Mike Clink looked away, embarrassed. But he wasn't going to be my corner man. I was on my own. Ron could be pretty damn cold. I fumbled out something about how I was sorry he felt that way. End of conversation, end of evening, end of album.

So much for a little afterglow, a quick pat on the back, a high-five, a "Job well-done, mate." The night was unfortunately, desperately young. I went on to over-serve myself.

The next morning I woke to a thin winter light coming through the parted curtains of my motel room. I had no memory of the end of the evening. I got up and showered, though there was no washing away what I did remember. I crammed my rumpled clothes into my bag. Who gave a shit at that point? Not me. I found my wallet: empty. But I couldn't find my rental car keys. I had that panicky feeling that always comes with no keys. When I went to the bar to look for them, the pretty waitress, already back on the job again after the night shift, laughingly told me I'd offered to take her to Bali the night before. Bali. Well, at least I was imaginative. Most guys would've said Hawaii or Mexico, or just a motel room number. The keys were gone.

Well, fuck a dumb duck! Ron's pronouncement of my unworthiness cast a pall on everything. Shit, here I was thinking we had done a good job; that I had done a good job. Oh well, Ron would be Ron. It wasn't like I hadn't gotten to know him after three months in the studio. He wasn't one to pull his punches when he decided to throw one, that was for sure.

I went back home to L.A., trying to put it out of my

mind, while also trying to back-burner the importance of my publisher's firing. Surely, it would all work out. The future was so bright, wasn't it? I was the hot new kid in town. It was supposed to be me and Richard Marx, right?

Ron mixed the record on his own. I had a good idea of how it would sound, because he kind of mixed as he recorded. He didn't like to have any surprises to deal with, didn't leave anything in "fix it in the mix" mode. Maybe I should have been there, but the way I was feeling then, like I'd been ball-kicked by several cold-hearted mules, I just left him to do it. He didn't want to listen to what I'd have to say, anyway. He knew far more about mixing than I ever would.

But if I'd been insecure before, now I was lost. I told others about it and got some encouragement. "Ron is just Ron," they said, "don't let it get to you." But it got to me. Another example of my letting others chip away at me. Now I was really unsure of who I was, or if I was good enough. His tell-it-like-he-saw-it comment was the last thing I needed.

When Ron returned to L.A. with the mixes, he had me come over to his condo in Brentwood for a listen. The record sounded spectacular on his fine system. I thought maybe there wasn't enough of John Pierce's bass in the mix, but I bit my tongue. Ron knew best. Maybe there was enough bass. If I wasn't a good singer, then I probably wasn't a good judge of the proper mix for radio.

Nothing was going to change at this point, anyway. Ron was warm and friendly. Maybe he'd forgotten what he'd said to me. His girlfriend was there. She had a bunch of blow and there was vodka. She liked to drink as much as I did. Ron wasn't a big drinker. She was hot to party and it turned into a long, stupid night of pointless blow-induced yammering and bottles of vodka. I'm a beer and wine man, really. The high octane stuff blinds me early. The night was a horrible unconsciously-conscious fall on my part.

This is a very hard part for me to tell you about.

The next day we were supposed to play the final mix of the record for Clive Davis, who was in L.A.

I came to on Ron's couch. I was fucked: so hung-over that I knew it would be a terrible mistake to have Clive see me that state. I wouldn't be able to play the record for Clive. He'd see right through me, he'd know how fucked up I was. My wife and son had gone back to Marin County. That would be my excuse: my son had a high fever and I needed to fly there that morning. *Yeah, and the dog ate my homework.*

Ron handed me the phone: it was Clive. I went through my lie. "It's my three-year-old. He's running a 104-degree fever and is going into the hospital. I've got to fly back up there right now." Clive said he understood, but I could tell that he was miffed. I'm sure he did understand me, or was beginning to. *You don't stand up your label head, asshole!* Of course, the worst and most telling part of this was that I got that fucked up knowing I had to see Clive the next morning.

Despite my wretched performance and non-attendance, Clive liked the record enough to give it his blessing. So maybe I snuck though that hole in the fence. Maybe, barely. There's a right way to handle yourself and there's a wrong way to handle yourself. This time I was the Wrong Call. But for the moment, I was off the hook. Or maybe I was dangling on its point.

Chappell Music had chosen a new guy to head the L.A. office. He was the son of a famous film producer. From the very get-go we were at odds. When a new person takes over a company or department after a purge, there's a blood-letting. The new head wants his or her own signings, not the baggage of someone who was just canned. That only makes sense. I was Roger's signing, so this guy would just as soon that I disappeared. After all, Chappell didn't fire Roger for doing the job they wanted done, right? Therefore, Roger's signings were suspect, tainted. The music biz is built on taint: layer after layer of different colors, like an apartment that a new tenant takes over every few months and repaints. That's why everybody in the biz plays their cards so close to the vest. No one wants to acquire too much of someone else's office furniture, too much of the other's stink. I had eighteen months left on my deal, and the album was about to come out, so there was nothing the new guy could do but let me ride. He was quite clear about what he liked: Motley Crue and Olivia Newton John, who'd just had a big hit with *Let's Get Physical*.

Did I have stuff like that? Well, I'd try. But we both knew I didn't have that kind of material.

One day I was over at the office and there was a meeting going on with a couple of the other staff writers and Ira, the new head cheese. I was not included. I stood out in the main office wondering what to do with myself. There was one glam L.A. writer gal in particular who I'd met like nine times but who still couldn't remember my name. A blind man could see how chummy she and Ira and the others were. They had a nice little clique going on there, and I wasn't in it. And I wasn't ever gonna be in it. My status at Chappell had changed overnight. Even the chummy admin gal who'd been so friendly and kept me up-to-date on office gossip had been canned. "Merlene is no longer with the company."

Michael Barackman called me to talk about a video for the first single, which was *Just Another Saturday Night*. At last, some hot news. Arista would come through with a video budget. They thought enough of the record to put another chunk of money into it. Marty found a director who had done a couple of videos already.

This was 1983, the early age of music videos on MTV. MTV was on fire right then. The genre of music video had just been invented as a marketing tool. It was a home-grown thing still, but everyone was aware how important it was. The videos hadn't taken on that vapid rapid-fire vague images thing that soon they'd all sport. The early videos didn't take themselves too seriously. There was a lot of humor, something that disappeared in time. *Fish-heads, Fish-heads, Roly-poly Fish-heads*. Huey's videos were funny and so was the Tommy Tutone video of *867–5309*. MTV could make hits out of songs like *I'm on a Mexican, Whoa-oh, Radio*. We, that is, Marty and the director, with powerless me nodding in assent, decided to do a spoofy take-off on the evening news, shot with video cameras instead of film, in a real TV newsroom so that it would replicate the look of the local six o'clock news, only whacked-out. It was a funny idea that appealed to me.

The director got KTLA to rent us their newsroom. I became Tom Mudd, slightly graying anchorman, with a beautiful Asian actress as co-anchor, a black sportscaster, and a bow-tie-wearing geeky weatherman. *Good Evening. I'm Tom Mudd, TV Wankerman.* I had my own make-up gal, my own wardrobe gal, even a nice-looking lady who did nothing but handle my toupee, as it were.

We did a six o'clock news bit to the song, which chronicled the then-new phenomena of high-school-age drive-by shootings. There was nothing funny about the subject matter of the song; it was straight off the evening news. But just as *Mad Magazine* used to do, when you put truth in a funny setting, it becomes more palatable. That was the theory, anyway. We might have done better with a serious, stark video, but that would have framed my career from then on. Anyway, MTV was mostly funny back then. I wasn't unhappy with the ironic depiction of the brutal killings that were just beginning to rage out of control. They came from American culture, and sensationalist news coverage was part of that. It was the same subject matter as Don Henley's *Dirty Laundry*.

In addition to the full-blown TV evening news set scene, we shot two outside scenes. The first one was in a West Hollywood neighborhood, with the cops arresting a crazed teenager who'd shot his parents and buried them in shallow graves in the family backyard so he could collect the insurance money and buy himself a TransAm (based on a true story.) I played an on-the-scene reporter.

The other scene was shot at the corner of Sunset and Vine on a warm L.A. Friday night. We had a fake shot-up car halfway up on the sidewalk, an outline of a victim in chalk on the pavement, an ambulance with lights blazing, and lit-up cop cars and motorcycles with off-duty cops in full gear. A big crowd of street people and tourists and other passers-by gathered as we shot video under the klieg lights. I, your faithful roving reporter in a beige camel-hair sport coat and blue tie, walked down the sidewalk with Mrs. Miller, an oddball local who was then a semi-regular on "The Merv Griffin Show." She happened to live in the neighborhood and was out walking her little dog, so she invited herself into the video. While we were shooting, on-duty cops arrived with sirens blazing and lights flashing, responding to what someone thought was a real incident. It was a good addition and a good laugh.

I was the center of the action and attention, yet I had no responsibility other than to walk around acting like a reporter, which suited me just fine. KTLA's station manager even suggested that I do an audition reel for an anchor position. I should have taken him up on it, but hell, I was a rock star. We also did a shoot on a stage with the band for some "live" music shots to be interspersed with the funny stuff. The whole thing took four or five days to shoot. They were probably the most fun days I've ever had in my whole career.

It took a while for the director to put the video together. I thought it was pretty funny, though I didn't like the shots of me and the band playing music. They looked phony. The black actor playing the sportscaster did the splits on the news desk, the Asian beauty did her nails while we were singing about murders, the young actor playing the kid who shot his folks looked quite deranged, and the weatherman fell down, taking the cumulous clouds from the weather map with him. It was good fun. The video went out to MTV as the single was released to radio. Here we go.

Rolling Stone gave me a great review on the album, three and a half stars. It said, "Move over, Michael MacDonald." There wasn't much mention of the single. They played up the more Michael MacDonald-aspect of the album, not the Springsteen. At least they didn't mention *Hungover You*. Ah well.

Initially, radio picked up pretty well on *Just Another Saturday Night*. Mike Bone, a very talented Arista promotions V.P., was running it the way he knew how to. MTV had the video in light-to-medium rotation. My single was getting added to the playlists of many smaller market stations in medium-sized cities like Akron and Spartanburg and Spokane, but would have to crack through to the more important stations in the bigger markets, like Atlanta and Los Angeles, the stations that were called "parallel ones," in order to push the video into heavy rotation on MTV. The big major market radio stations always require convincing before they'll play a single by a new artist. That's what they say payola, er, radio promotion, is all about. I didn't know about payola directly, but I'd heard stories about how much this or that station required to grease the wheels. I hoped that Arista felt my record was worth it. Labels put out a certain number of records per year. They have established artists that they *have* to push, as they try to take advantage of the wave the artist is riding. Stars, no matter how big, only have a half-life of a few years. Think how big Prince was, or Stevie Wonder. Their talent hasn't gone away: their audience has aged and stopped buying records. They're not heavily marketed anymore. Most big artists don't even have major label deals after seven or ten years. New artists are the life-blood of the industry. But new artists have to succeed. Most won't have even one hit; others will be one-hit-wonders like Tommy Tutone. Only a few turn into Elton John or Sting. Most will just get thrown against the wall and won't stick.

There was radio resistance to *Just Another Saturday Night* in various important markets. The content was too heavy for some programmers. Teenagers shot each other every day, but songs about it probably didn't sell acne products very well in Dallas and Indianapolis. Some programmers thought the song glorified drive-by shootings. The problem might have been that it was all too darn ironic for its own good. The music wasn't dire-sounding. It was powerful and fast. Maybe it sounded too much like a positive song: a happy song about killing. I think it's amazing that anyone would think that. If Bruce Springsteen were singing it, there wouldn't have been any such consideration. But Alex Call didn't have a reputation as a social commentator yet. And Springsteen would've shot a gritty, mean-streets video with images of inner cities, not a farcical take on the local six o'clock news.

The song had been out for almost a month. Airplay growth had been steady, but we needed to break through to the big stations. Mike Bone had me come down to the office and get on the phone, to call program directors at stations across the country to schmooze and make my case about why the song should be played. It was a grueling day. Some program managers were receptive, but some were not. The song didn't "fit their station profile, their demographic." One guy heaped praise on me, thinking I was from *the* Call, an unfortunately-named band that had released a record the same week as mine.

"No, I'm Alex Call."

"Oh. Well, we love the Call."

Good timing, no?

We were *bubbling under* at number 101 on the Billboard Hot 100. The record was still alive, but we had to fight to make it happen. The label would have to step up with more promotion.

I was right there: On the verge of success, so they said. It was gonna be tough, gonna be close. As I drove away from Arista after spending the day talking to program managers, I was glad the day was over. I wouldn't want to spend my life doing that. But that's what it's all about. It's calling radio, it's schmoozing the labels, it's brown-nosing publishing guys. It's about gig promoters and managers and booking agents. Were these my people? I'd rather be up some creek in the Sierras with my flyrod and my dog. I like people who work at grocery stores and restaurants more than I like music biz people.

I thought I'd made a good record, though more than one person told me they thought there wasn't enough bass. Some who'd been privy to the project and the personalities went so far as to say they thought Ron did it on purpose. Had Ron intentionally undermixed the bass to make this album fail? So he wouldn't have to make another one with me? That was crazy. No professional like Ron would do that. Still, I wished I could hear more of John Pierce's low frequencies on the record. Ron had sure nailed me hard with his comments. I needed not to take it personally. I didn't think he meant it personally. He was just speaking his mind, the truth the way he saw it. It's a cold, hard world out there. I'm too sensitive for my own good.

"So sensitive it makes your feet hurt," as Huey was fond of saying.

My confidence is easily shaken, never has taken much.

Well, look out confidence, because a mountainside of boulders was about to roll down my way.

THE COLD HARD TRUTH

I can't make you love me if you don't...

Have you ever rolled a big rock down off a mesa just to see what it will do? I have. A boulder not much bigger than a beach ball can take out a hundred-year-old juniper without the impact even slowing the damn rock down much.

The phone rang. It was Mike Bone, head of promotion for Arista. He and Michael Barackman were the gents at the label I spoke to most of the time, though Michael was the A&R man, so he was about creative stuff. Bone was sales, the promo V.P.

"Hey, man, I need to give you a heads-up about something."

"Okay," I said. *Is this good or bad? Good, right? Right?*

"I'm leaving Arista to take over as head of RCA records. I'm sorry."

I was stunned. Not again. Not so soon. Roger Gordon fired at Chappell, now this. Even an idiot like me knows that when the head of promotion leaves a label, the projects he's been pushing will be regarded as having leprosy by the new guy.

But I didn't miss a beat. Hey, I'm a pro. "I understand,

Mike. That's a great gig. You have to do what is best for you. Good luck."

"Yeah, well, thanks. Like I said, sorry."

I hung up the phone. Shit, I was fuckin' sunk. Torpedoed. Dead in the water. That was it: Life support had been pulled, tell the family. The single was sitting there at number 101, the video was being played on MTV. But the cold, hard truth was: It was over for my record. Timing was critical. When you're going for adds at radio, trying to get your single played by more influential stations in bigger markets, momentum is everything. Once you lose that forward motion, you've had it. Stations watch each other's playlists. My little single was gonna die.

RIP: *Just Another Saturday Night*. Vaya con Dios, Alex Call's Arista album.

Stick a fork in it, folks. It's done.

Marty had brave talk. We were going to keep it afloat. Arista would plug in a new guy and we'd roll. But we both knew that was bullshit. First Roger Gordon at Chappell, now Mike Bone.

With all this going down, I had three gigs booked in the Bay Area with the band from the record. More brave talk from Marty, "We'll pull it off." We rehearsed, played the shows, but three gigs? It takes months to get a show working. There was a lot to think about while doing those shows, too much. The process made me nervous. I went out there and tried. I thought I did pretty well. But Marty told me after the last show, "I see a guy on stage who doesn't want to be there."

Touché!

It was unanimous: I wasn't cutting it. My single wasn't cutting it. *Jeezus, how the fuck did I ever get those other hit singles? Was there someone else in my body?* Everybody around me seemed to think so. I guessed they must be right. There was a guy on stage losing his idea of who he was or was supposed to be.

The record fell off radio within three weeks. It was as if it never happened. Birds went on chirping, the world spun around, babies were born, and old people died. But the *Rolling Stone* review, the MTV play? Never happened. Marty suddenly had a new band he was all hot for, a hard-rock affair lead by a German guy named Lenny Wolf. The band was called Stone Fury. Marty was suddenly very busy with that project. Too busy for me, apparently.

A previously-friendly rat slinking away from your ship saying, "call me" over his shoulder as he disappears into the maze of the docks is not a good sign.

There was nothing I could do but try to pretend it was okay. Maybe they'd do another single. *Blue Avenue* or *Annie Don't Lie*. My record, my shiny new record! But Arista didn't even name a new head of promotion for several weeks. When they did, there were no calls to me, there was no talk of Alex Call. I heard through the grapevine that Michael Barackman had bet Clive that I'd sell a half-million on this first album. I hope Michael didn't have too much riding on it.

The truth was that my record was falling away because of conditions beyond my control. This happens to most records. Almost all records. But I took it personally, as I always do.

Marty had me write with Lenny Wolf. We wrote a song called *Break Down the Walls*, which would be Stone Fury's first and only single. I was trying to be a team player, but I was losing my mind. And that wasn't all I was losing.

Suddenly, I was the odd man out. At the time I finished my album around Christmas, I was riding high. Now, just weeks later, I was persona non grata around my publishing and record companies. *Hello Hollywood: Good-bye*. Ira, the new head of Chappell L.A., had only thinly-veiled contempt for my writing.

"Why can't you write some Motley Crue? What happened to something like *Let's Get Physical?*"

It only takes one prick to burst a bubble. Holy shit. No more lunches at Musso and Frank's. My former buddies were always busy when I called. Marty had his new heavy metal German.

It was a big lesson: Nobody loves you when you're not going to be the next big thing. People will tell you you're the best new artist they've heard in a long time when they think they can make a buck on you. If you're naïve like me, you'll imagine that they're your actual friends, your compadres. You'll imagine that they like you for who you are, that you are one of the in-crowd, that you are one of them. But when you fall out of favor and luck, your new friends will avoid you like the plague, fearing taint by association. All at once you're up shit creek with no canoe, much less a paddle.

Jenny, Jenny, who can I turn to?

Well, I could always turn to the bottle. There was a friendly liquor store right down the street. The Lebanese guys who ran it started to see me on a daily basis. I had a coke connection down off Vanowen in Van Nuys, fifteen minutes away. His place was inhabited by well-known musicians who seemed to be on semi-permanent benders. They were always lounging like lizards on low, beat-up couches around a table completely covered by full ashtrays and two-thirds empty Corona bottles, staring at the guy's big fish tank between two huge speakers.

They squinted at me and grinned burned-out grins: "Hi, man!"
It was slimy, sleazy, and gross (now, there's a good name for an
L.A. law firm.) But, guess what? I was part of it! Friday nights,
I'd get a gram. Stay up all night, drink two liter bottles of cheap
red wine and everything else in the house, smoke three packs
of cigarettes and pretend I was writing cool lyrics. My little
boy was just a toddler and he couldn't tell dad was whacked. I
wasn't out of it. I was just trying to relax.

Just keep lying to yourself, pal.

I needed to keep up the phony bravado. I was still collecting
my two grand a month as a staff writer at Chappell for the next
year and a half. I told myself I'd write a lot of great songs and
have more hits. Shit, I'd just had two. Pat Benatar's album
went triple platinum. *Little Too Late* reached number twenty in
the Hot 100, respectable. It was all over MTV for months. Why
couldn't I get more of that? I didn't think that was anything
like one of my best songs, but it was good enough to get to
number twenty.

I had a song that I thought would be perfect for Tommy
Tutone called *You Never Really Loved.* It was very hooky. In
my mind's ear, I can still hear Tommy singing it now. There
was a section that went *na-nana-nana-na* that I guarantee
would've had audiences chanting along. But when I gave Jim
Keller the demo, Tommy passed along that he "didn't do 'na-
nas.'" Tommy Tutone didn't do any more Alex Call songs. And
they didn't have any more hit singles. They did have internal
problems that I heard rumors about. They slipped and slid off
into that whatever-happened-to-old-what's-their-name nether
region from which they'd emerge only as candidates for One
Hit Wonders on VH1 twenty years down the road.

Chappell still had to pay for demos on my songs. Jim

Keller had a pal who had a funky looking, but good sounding demo studio over in Glendale. Glendale was an older L.A. neighborhood locally called Frogtown, for the homeboy gang and for the frogs that live alongside the homeless in the weed-choked concrete-walled L.A. River channel. Jim and I wrote a bunch of nondescript songs and recorded them there. Many nights we knocked off at two in the morning. I'd drive back through the hot night to Canoga Park on the astoundingly-crowded Ventura Freeway. It was amazing: Always jammed, even at two A.M., everyone doing seventy-five. Who were all these people and where the fuck were they going at that time of night? Beats me. I just don't get L.A.

One day I needed to get out of the blight, so I took my dog Abu and drove out into the Mojave Desert. I pulled off on a dusty road and bumped my Chevette up towards a little canyon. I let Abu loose and started walking in the dry heat. About a half-mile up the canyon I heard gunfire. Around a bend, there were a bunch of Chicano yahoos shooting machine guns at TV sets and old cars. Disgusted at having my solitude disturbed by a bunch of potentially-homicidal maniacs, I trudged back to my car. Abu, who'd been chasing rabbits, finally came back, trailing his tongue in the dust. He was happy. As for me, someday I'd be out of that place.

My songwriting was all over the map. Not that that was so unusual. I had the habit in those days of writing two songs of a given style and then moving on to something completely different. I should have written two *867-5309*s. Actually, the na-na song was the second like that. But I'd been hit so hard from so many directions that I was wobbling away from whatever center I might have had. My top was spinning out, like a gyroscope that's been knocked on its side. It somehow stays up until it runs out of torque, then it falls, spinning around in crazy circles while it sputters out. I kept coming up with stuff: everything from Michael MacDonald-type grooves to Tom Petty rips. Nothing too great. I was imitating, trying to find some way to get a hit. No one at Chappell liked the songs, in fact. I often got no comment at all when I turned them in. My deal was just playing out. When I went to the office, I was generally ignored. Sometimes I went and hung around just long enough to see that no one was going to talk with me, I wasn't going to get an invite into their offices. I hadn't heard from Michael Barackman in awhile. Marty was basically gone, out of the picture of playing with his heavy metal Germans. No more commissions: No more manager.

My older brother Lewis had moved from far northern California to God-awful Whittier to work in a buddy's machine shop. He and I got together and snorted coke and drank once in a while. At least he was there. He didn't dig it there either, but he needed the work. For us both to be in Southern California at the same time was a strange parallel *El Alien* experience.

Dede and I were fighting a lot. The money from *876-5309* and *Little Too Late* didn't seem to go very far. I suspected I'd gotten short-changed on both songs, but I couldn't prove it. It wasn't as much dough as one would expect, and after paying manager's commissions, legal fees, and taxes, it was gone. Our bills weren't that high, but we were still having a hard time making ends meet. Dede took a job working at a bed-and-bath place. I refused to get a job. I was a god-damn songwriter and artist, for fucksake. I still had a publishing deal and a record deal. On paper, anyway. This caused a great deal of tension in our house. There were lots of arguments that quickly morphed into profanity-laced shouting matches. Our son was caught in the booze-fueled crossfire. Alcohol is closely related to gasoline. Dede would find me half-drunk sometimes when she came home from working across the valley. It was pitiful. I was pitiful.

My much-vaunted album had tanked, but Huey's long-awaited third album *Sports* finally came out, and it was a smash hit. All the hassling they did with their label ended up producing enormous results. *Sports* had seven hit singles on it, which was amazing. It was the kind of success everyone works for. Huey put me on the guest list for a sold-out show at the Universal Amphitheater. I mingled with the incoming throngs outside the venue. It was like a carnival: so many people so excited to see Huey and the lads. It was a grand triumph for my old roomie and comrade-in-arms. The adoring fans showered him with ovations. The backstage was incredible. There were hundreds of dazzling, big-boobed, tight-assed, shades-wearing, glad-handing Hollywood types hanging out. I was dressed up like the rock star I still imagined myself to be, tight jeans, rock boots, and cool jacket. In the press of flesh Huey introduced me to this guy wearing a checkered flannel shirt and sporting a beard. He looked a bit like a lumberjack. "Al, this is Bruce. You guys should write together."

I shook his hand. *Write with a lumberjack?* I took his number, but I didn't call.

A few months later, Huey phoned me to say he was in town, down the street at Captain and Tennille's studio, doing some overdubs with that lumberjack guy Bruce, Bruce Hornsby. They were working a song called *That's Just the Way It Is*. As it had been with Elvis Costello years before, I grokked in one instant just how great Hornsby was, and what a fool I'd been. His album would sell millions and his sound would define an era. The lesson for me was: When Huey Lewis says write with a lumberjack, you grab your fucking axe and write.

Time crawled by. Week after week, month after month. Months dragged into a year. L.A.'s non-seasons passed by in a well-fingered-wine-glass blur. My album had become a distant memory, a shooting-star Camelot. Once there was this young, good-lookin' prince, old fuckin' what's his name, but he fuckin' died.

I was writing and demoing, but my forgettable songs were going into the great dumper in the void where they belonged. The phone wasn't ringing. My writing deal with Chappell would be up before too long now. I sold my Pacer to a Guatemalan family of seven before it died, too. I hoped it served them well. I was driving a beat-up kelly green Chevy Chevette with no air conditioning. I was putting on weight. Sometimes I wore sweatpants when I went to the store.

You know who cared?

Fucking nobody, that's who cared!

I wasn't drunk when I got the call. I was in hyper mode, being positive, writing away, recording on my four-track, trying to come up with a deal-saving hit. I'd had 'em before.

Ira was clear and chipper and seemingly quite pleased to tell me that I was not being re-upped with Chappell.

I told him I was writing some good stuff.

"Everyone has a hit or two. You'll never have another," he said.

Click.

Well, fuck you very much, you little prick-head.

Later that night, I didn't need the clock to tell me it was 2:30 A.M., Standard Blackout Wakeup Time. Adrenaline pumping, heart racing. Shit, at least I was in bed. In the spare room. My wife wasn't having this. Not after all day folding fucking towels at the bed-and-bath store across the Valley.

"You're fucking drunk. I come home and you're fucking drunk."

"It's just one bottle." *So far.*

"You're lying on the floor and you smell like a distillery."

My boy was jumping on my big fat stomach. I was tickling him, he was laughing. But I was drunk. I needed to be drunk.

It's all right. Fuck the little dickhead. I'll get another deal.

No you won't, you loser. You're no fucking good. People just don't fuckin' like you. They never have. You're not a cool guy. You're a fuckin' wimp, a zero, an invisible shithead.

No, no, I'd be all right. No, I wouldn't. Two fuckin' thirty. Shit. I was gonna be throwing up right around the time I'd have to take my little boy to school. They already looked at me like I was a suspect in a child abuse case, no matter how much I talked like a yuppie and tried to act sophisticated and urbane. My boy looked like he was being abused. Because he was. My fucking drinking and the endless fighting going on the house was too much for a five-year-old. He had sallow skin and little bags under his eyes, like a homeless kid. His face strained with a tight, forced, phony smile. We were screaming and throwing things and slamming doors. He was never touched: we treasured him. But what I did is child abuse, pilgrims.

My brain clicked relentlessly back and forth from self-recrimination to the previous day's phone call from Ira.

That fucking little asshole publisher. What songs did he ever write? None. He's got his job because of his famous daddy or grandfather or whoever it was. Fuck all those pretentious, cliquey fuckers. I should've understood when they fired Roger Gordon right before Christmas and brought in this little, swaggering jerk.

"Why can't you write like Motley Crue? What about *Let's Get Physical*? Something like that?"

Over and over.

"Imitate whatever is a hit right now. What's the matter with you? Don't you get it?"

God-damn it, it took me years to get to a place where I liked what I wrote. I had hits with my music, my lyrics. Now I was trying to copy shit I hated on the radio. I would always be really bad at that.

Shit, there was no more wine. Two big bottles by myself. I lay there and fucking hated myself until six and then got up and pretended that a shower would wash away my sins, my failure, my endless wimpiness.

I went and puked in the bucket in the garage so my boy wouldn't hear me.

"Daddy?" He stood there silhouetted in the doorway, the light from the alley shining behind him like an aura in a medieval fresco, "You okay?"

"Daddy's fine," I stood up, wiping my mouth with the back of my hand. "It's not time to get up yet. Go back and get in bed with your mom. I must have eaten something bad."

His innocence was being ground down, the shining edges of it slowly worn off by the endless flow of drunkenness, vomit, and anger.

"Okay, daddy."

***

Sunset Boulevard. Not a street for beat-up kelly green, dinged-up Chevettes unless you're a Mexican going somewhere to wash something or cut something or bus somebody's overpriced, under-eaten endive and arugula salad with seared ahi slivers and a drizzle of Thai peanut sauce for 26. Not $26. Just 26. We don't stoop to cents here, or even dollar signs.

The illegals' cars were better than mine. Hell, I had the worst car on the road. No air conditioner, the driver's window taped up. I'd had one of the top songs in the country three years before. A shiny new-artist deal with Clive Davis, the hit-maker. Now I was sneaking along in this piece of shit, going to Chappell to pick up my last check.

I parked next to a Beamer and Jolene's new VW Bug. Hot blonde with the top down, so LaLaland. I once had had fun going with her to lunch, glitzing in to all the hip see-and-hope-you're-seen places around town, to talk about my Arista deal, all the good shit that was coming down.

"There's Donovan over there."

"Oh hi, Frank. Have you met Alex Call? He's a new hot writer we signed, you know *867-5309?*"

"You wrote that? Fuck you! You did not!"

"Well, someone had to." My big phony laugh. Hell, not phony. I was inside the joke. It was my joke. My joke!

"Congrats, I love that song! Hey, you should write with our new kid Michael, he's going to be hot. Jo, call me about Saturday. Nice to meet you. I'm serious, Jo will set it up."

The joke was on me now. The new, hot receptionist at Chappell never gave me more than a perfunctory, "Hey, how ya' doin'?" on the best of days. She'd seen I was dead meat, but now she was really cold. She handed over the sealed envelope.

"We'll miss you!" Her teeth were so perfect. That *miss* was like a little death in itself.

"Don't you hate to have to use that word?" she might tell her friend over margaritas.

"Yeah, but he's kind of old, isn't he?" Her friend would say, "like thirty-four or something? Hey, there's Kim. Kim!"

Miss, hiss, fake kiss. Snake tongue. Se habla L.A. aqui.

Miss me? *Sure you will.*

No one came out of their windowed-sanctum offices, many doors of which were open. I could hear traces of conversations

"He is fucking not gay!"

"Haha. You are a real fucking shithead. That's why I love you!"

"So, call me and we'll get that together...."

"I love his energy."

"Yes. Fine, fine, okay. Sure."

I was cut out, the ghost of the new kid in town, standing out in the open area between the formerly-friendly offices, holding a folder with some papers and a small box of cassettes. The ice-foxy receptionist was busy making cassette labels for Mademoiselle X, the one who couldn't even remember my name after two years in the same office.

"Oh. Oh, you write here?"

"Yes," I said. *For the ninth time, you cunt.*

Two other nobodies scuttled by without looking at me. I was invisible now. My contract had run out yesterday. I waited, lingering for a moment to give them a chance, but no one came out to wish me well. No one had returned my calls for months over there. I shuffled off, feeling the sloppy bagginess of my fat jeans and the crappy cheapness of my old purple Keds.

But, you know what? Underneath it all, I have a real gift. It took me a while to recover my senses, but on one otherwise formless, purposeless day, as I drove somewhere to do something, I had a new song in my head. Shit, this could be big. I'd never heard that title before.

***

For some time I called around a little, trying to find any interest in me out there in LaLaland. There wasn't any. Once again, who wants you if you've been dropped by a competitor? Not good enough for them, not good enough for us. It's also hard to sell yourself when you don't believe in the product. It's even harder when you have trouble picking up a telephone. Someone pointed me towards these two guys who had some sort of publishing company. I guess they had some catalog stuff, but it wasn't a legit house with other staff writers. I took a few meetings with them, enough for them to determine that I was still under contract to Arista. If I made another album, these guys would get mechanical royalties when the record was pressed and shipped, an easy buck for them. They signed me for a year at a thousand a month, not a co-pub. They got all my publishing rights. It was a classic horrible, crap-ass deal with people I couldn't relate to, didn't like, and didn't trust, but I had to take it. My performance royalties from BMI weren't adding up to much. With the Chappell money gone, we were really going to be scraping by.

I took the contract to John Branca's office for review. He

was way too busy to see the likes of me. He had an associate meet with me. This associate attorney drove a purple Porsche convertible and looked like fuckin' Sting on steroids. I felt like a fat fool with a bad haircut and ill-fitting clothes sitting in his fancy office as he told me what a lousy deal it was. He said, "We could find you something better." But Branca's office had already called around and hadn't found anyone who was at all interested in me. I had a bad case of music-biz cooties. I was also financially desperate. I signed the god-damned deal.

Jim Keller knew this manager, Bob B, who met with me occasionally. He wasn't managing me per se—we didn't have a deal on paper—but he did give me regular advice. He thought he might be able get me another record deal if Arista didn't want to make another album. Since I hadn't heard from Arista in so long, I'd assumed they'd written me off. He wrote to them, asking for my release and they agreed to drop me, though this brought a call from Michael Barackman, "What gives? I thought we were making another album?"

I was taken aback. I told him I was following the advice I've been given. It was a lame moment for me. Barackman had been the biggest ally I'd had in my career and now I was asking to be let out of the deal he'd engineered. Truly, I didn't think Clive had much interest in another Alex Call album anyway. I hadn't heard from Michael for some time and nothing from anyone else at Arista.

I struggled to write more songs. I didn't have a demo budget anymore, so I was back to making recordings on my squirrel-powered TEAC in my garage, exactly like before any of the L.A. nonsense happened. *867–5309*. Pat Benatar. Chappell. Arista. My MTV video. My lunches at Musso and Frank's.

My new-kid-in-town status. All that glorious shit was gone, and I was just another fat fuck out in Canoga Park, fending off crazy-eyed gang members when I played basketball at the local playgrounds, and driving around in my non-air conditioned kelly green Chevette with the taped-up window, wearing sweatpants.

You remember that "Seinfeld" where George starts wearing sweatpants? "Sweatpants mean you've given up. Or you're really, really rich." I didn't fall into the latter category, that was for sure. I had a few guys to work with: Dean Cortez was a great bass player who hung out. Keller came by a little. I was still trying to imitate what was on the radio. Prince was big. The Jackson Five were happening. Madonna was huge. Ronald Reagan was president. It was all very depressing. I was way out of my element now, grasping at straws. And I was now living in Canoga fuckin' Park. No offense, Canoga Park, but you sucked.

In an extended reprise of Clover's miserable *Scoreboard* period, I was becoming a bloated mess. Our home life was terrible. I was, in fact, the total loser I'd always thought I was. Ironically, the same loser my wife told me I was. I had my big chance and it went nowhere. All my so-called friends in L.A. had turned their backs on me.

"Whatever happened to Alex Call?"

"I don't know, maybe he moved back to Marin."

In my dreams.

The next year was a gigantic, slowly spinning, nothing, nowhere nightmare. Bob B. got a gig as label head. But I never heard from him again. My new so-called publishing deal ended. I had nothing going on but intermittent drunkenness and the occasional toot. It was as low as I'd ever been, but I hadn't even hit rock-bottom yet.

L.A. is a lonely, lonely place when you're not happening. The fancy restaurants, the high-class women, the nice houses might as well be behind bullet-proof glass. I crawled through each day, taking my son to preschool, trying to write songs, waiting for the phone to ring. It just didn't. Where we lived out in the flats of the San Fernando Valley, might as well have been in New Mexico, not two miles from Ventura Boulevard in plush Woodland Hills, except that I like New Mexico a lot. When I ended up in the wealthier neighborhoods on errands, I felt like an illegal alien in my junker Chevette, wearing my sweatpants. My little house should have been an oasis, but our home life was far from a refuge. Lack of money is one of the hardest things a family can go through. Dede was working and I was still hanging on to my fading musician façade. My so-called career was like one of those movie wild-west sets: Open the door and there's nothing behind the false front.

THE POWER OF
LOVE AND SOBRIETY

Love will make you do right...

It was a Friday night. Dede was in tears. We'd hocked her wedding ring at a pawn shop in Reseda to keep the electricity on. I had a small check coming Monday, so it was temporary, but I was ashamed and embarrassed. I didn't have a publishing or record deal. She'd been slaving away at her job while I'd been drunk a lot. I'd gotten amazingly overweight. My face looked like it was painted on. I looked like a weighted punching bag that keeps rolling upright when you hit it, like a piñata full of shit. It had been almost four years since we'd moved to L.A. We sure weren't living the life we dreamed of.

All we had to do was look down the block.

Our boy James had a little girlfriend who came over unaccompanied sometimes. She lived one street over. She was an awfully precocious six-year-old. One day I found scrawled drawings she had done, of a penis and a vagina. The images were the crude scribbling of a six-year-old, but they were unmistakable. Her mother was some sort of biker chick. They lived in a house that had several beat-up cars parked around it.

There was another house down on the corner that had become a Chicano gang house: Canoga Boys. The cops were frequent visitors. One morning there was a burned mattress on the roof. It stayed there for weeks. Motorcycles and primered muscle cars raced up and down our street. The neighborhood had changed since we moved in. It had been working-class, but now it was plainly trending downward. The guy across the street, a real law-and-order type, had a fit of anger and hurled an axe handle at one of the hot-rod bikes. He missed, thank God. He just flipped, it wasn't like him.

We worried about James in this environment. He was nearly plucked from his schoolyard by a stranger. He told us he ran away when the man wanted to play a game of grabbing hands. The teachers didn't take it seriously, but the police did. That kind of stuff was becoming more and more frequent across L.A., across the country. One hot, smoggy Saturday morning, James was suddenly missing from our house. I raced across to the neighbors. Someone had seen him walking down the street with the little girl. I ran around the long block to their house. The door was open. I knocked and called out, but no one answered. There was a shrieking electric guitar coming from a bedroom. I ventured in. The place was a mess: beer cans, ashtrays, a TV was blaring away in a corner. In one bedroom, a long-haired high-school-age kid with no shirt on stared at me wordlessly from behind his electric guitar. James was sitting in another filthy bedroom with the little girl. I told him it was time to go home.

It was time to go home. We needed to get out of there.

Before Christmas in 1985, we finally had some good fortune. It came in the form of a surprise sale of some stock that had belonged to my mom. My siblings and I would get some much-needed cash. The check was going to be fifty-five thousand dollars! My dad decided to let us have the dough, though technically it should have gone to him. After being broke for two years, we were suddenly in the clear. I bought a new car for the first time in my life, a Jeep Cherokee. The Cherokee was the first generation of SUVs. I was thrilled to be driving something that was actually new, with air-conditioning. Bye-bye green Chevette!

This was a cause for celebration, so I celebrated, of course, to wretched excess. Beer and wine were my staples now. I was so bloated that I wouldn't go near any music biz office. I didn't look out of place in lower-class Canoga Park, but just on the south side of the Ventura Freeway, in Woodland Hills, anyone that noticed would see me for what I'd become: a broken man, a fat slob.

Ah, but there was still my little gift. I was still writing songs. I had this idea for a song called *The Power of Love*. It was meant to be an Aretha Franklin-style gospel power-ballad.

With the power of love to guide us
The power of love inside us
The power of love

I set to work making a track on my rusty and trusty old four-track. My big gospel choir vision for the song was a bit grandiose, as in: What you thinkin', white boy!? But I was pretty excited by the song. A few years later, Celine Dion would do Luther Vandross's *The Power of Love*, which was in the same ballpark as my song. After years of trying to sound

like Prince and Madonna, *The Power of Love* felt more in tune
with my inner being. There'd always been a spiritual side to my
writing. That's why I liked Dylan and Lennon and Springsteen
and Sting and Peter Gabriel. Music should be fun, but more
than that, it should shape our psyches, wake up our souls, and
make us treat each other better.

I got a call from Huey. He was just checking in. He called
every couple of months. He and the News were having a *huge*
time. They'd had hit after hit and had reached the true upper
echelon of the pop music world. I went to a sold-out gig at the
Inglewood Forum, the arena in which the L.A. Lakers play. It
was a humongous, Roman Empire-sized event. Hundreds of
Hollywood poseurs were crowded into the backstage. There
were fifteen thousand ticket buyers at, what, $35 each? Do the
math. Of course, those ticket prices are nothing compared to
today's over-expensive tickets. I said to Huey's manager, "You
guys are really doing it now."

He said, "Well, there are a lot of stupid people out there, and
we need to take advantage of that."

That gave me a shiver, it was so cold, so calculating. But
there was truth behind it. I never cared for the truth in that
way. Often when I talked to Huey, I came away depressed.
Not because he was successful and I wasn't, for the moment.
It was because he knew where all the bodies were buried. I
wanted to retain an image of a good world, where people had
fine motivations and there was progress being made towards a
better future. The cold hard truth is that greedy, power-hungry
egomaniacs run the world and always have. I was a history buff.
I knew it was true, but I didn't want to hear it. It's interesting
when it's ancient Greece, but disheartening when it's right now.

As I looked at the size of that crowd there to commune with my old band mate, I was amazed. What was this? What makes a star? Why do people idolize stars? Part of it is that performers are speaking for their audience, singing their tribal life stories. They're up on the stage, leading the way the members of the audience never could. Another aspect of the star thing is that ancient primal desire to push through the throng and touch the hem of the Anointed One's robe. I suppose it makes people feel like they're in touch with something higher, something beyond their reach, beyond their humdrum lives. Think about the way people respond to the Pope. Now, there's a star! I admire the work of many musicians and actors and writers, and I know there are incredibly talented people in this world in all fields, from art to science to spirituality, but I have no desire to crowd together with a herd to see someone a hundred yards away, who looks like he's four inches tall, prance around on a stage. I get a full-access backstage pass or I stay home. What a snob I am!

Huey, on the phone, asked me what I'd been writing. I told him I had this new song, *The Power of Love*.

He said, "Ooooh. *The Power of Love*."

I sang a little of it to him.

He said, "Uh huh," a bit dismissive of the melody, but I could tell he dug the title. I could almost hear the ka-ching going off in his head. We chatted and he was off, he had to get back to attending to the throngs of gorgeous women who flocked to his gigs. He was very busy.

When he answered the phone, he'd say, "You got him: Go!"

I was still dreaming of getting another publishing gig to help pay the bills, and this song reignited that idea. But I wasn't even talking to any publishers or managers at this point. For the moment, we had a bit of lucky, fall-from-the-heavens coin and besides, I was too busy overindulging to contact the music business. Soon, I said to myself, I'd quit drinking, go on a diet, and get out there again.

The New Year came. 1986. My twentieth high school reunion at Verde Valley School in Sedona was coming up. I wanted to take my son to see the Grand Canyon and the red rocks. We'd drive out there in our new Cherokee. James would be turning seven and would probably be able to appreciate the sights. But I needed to lose *fifty pounds* before then. I didn't want my old classmates to see me like that. I was a fat slob. I was gross. But I couldn't seem to get started with any program. I kept making pledges of good behavior, only to see my resolve washed away by liters of merlot.

Dede decided to take James up to Marin to see her folks for a long President's Day weekend in February. I was staying in Canoga Park for an unspoken reason: to go on one last bender. The moment she left, I stocked up with bottles of wine. I'd have some freedom. *No ball and chain this weekend. I'll have a blast. I can do what I want. I'll play golf and have drink or two. Yeah, that's right, just a couple of glasses of wine.*

I got really, really drunk for the next four days. I don't recall much of that time. Did I play golf? Did I drive? I was extremely hung-over when they arrived back home. There was barbeque sauce on the kitchen ceiling. I couldn't explain how it got there, because I couldn't remember. I was feeling sick, very sick. I needed to keep drinking, but Dede crossed her arms and put her flaming Irish foot down: no more booze. I just wanted one more big glass of wine to mellow me out, but she said, "No way."

I went into the spare bedroom and sat on the edge of the bed. I felt quite ill. It was just my vivid imagination, but I saw an ice-cold, claw-like hand come right out of my chest and reach up and grab me by my throat. *This is a warning! You will die if you don't stop drinking!*

Thank God, I had no choice. Dede would force me to stay straight. The first day was rough, but after that I got on the program. I even went to a couple of AA meetings, though that wasn't my style. It's a great program of enormous benefit to millions, but AA was not for me. I just don't like meetings. You either drink or you don't. You live or you die. You have a family or you lose it. I'd wanted to stop for a long time. The lost weekend had sealed the deal.

Three weeks later, I was starting to feel good about myself, because when you eliminate booze, you get immediate good feedback from your pain-wracked body, so I took a chance and glanced in a mirror when we were at a shoe store. For many months, I'd avoided mirrors and plate-glass windows in which I might see my reflection. I didn't want to see the bloated asshole looking back at me. Now I snuck a peek, expecting to see handsome Alex, the rock star. He had a deal on Arista, a video on MTV. But I was dismayed by the enormous porker I saw in the shoe-store mirror. After three weeks of not drinking, I was still a fattened hog, jowls and all. This was a shocking wake-up call, but there was a stronger one to come.

A couple of days later, I woke up in a strange room. It was pale morning. I lay there, absolutely terrified. It was strange, but real enough. I had no idea where I was. I stared at the walls, at the windows. Suddenly it came to me. I reached over and shook Dede hard.

"Dede, Wake up! Wake up! We live in L.A.! We live in L.A.!! We have to get out of here! We have to get back home!"

At last, I was coming out of my self-induced alcoholic coma. We were in L.A.!

We had to get back home right away.

With this realization, things started happening fast. Dede readily agreed that we should move back to Marin. She missed her family. We'd managed somehow through all our hard times to make our payments on our little house. It had gone up in value. We'd paid $108,000 for it and now it was worth $132,000. We started showing it. We'd painted the interior with nice, subtle colors and bought a hot tub. The house was in good shape. We found a buyer right away. Dede went up to Marin to find a house there. It took a couple of trips, but we came up with a little fifties ranch house in Tam Valley, part of Mill Valley. Not the ritziest of neighborhoods, but it'd do.

It was ironic, but once we decided to leave L.A., good things started happening. Huey called. The News had cut a song called *The Power of Love*. It was going to be the big song in a new movie called "Back to the Future". It was their own groove, melody, and lyrics and all that, but they'd used my title and they were cutting me in for ten percent of the song, which is the standard share for a title.

I said, "That's great!" I didn't really understand how great it was. I didn't know what kind of money Huey had been pulling down. Huey technically didn't have to include me: You can't copyright a title. But it was definitely the correct thing to do. Besides the fact that he got the title directly from me, I'd taught Huey a lot. He learned the basics of songwriting from me in the Clover years, but even more importantly, in terms of the music business, I'd shown him exactly what not to do.

Ha.

All I knew is that we were getting out of L.A. and somehow things would get better. If Huey had a hit song with *The Power of Love*, so much the better.

My lost weekend had been the bottom of the bottom. Even when we had a little money, I'd still sought to self-annihilate. I truly had had my head down so long it had become lodged up my own ass. Thanks to Dede, I was seeing the haze clear a bit. I still had no idea what the future would bring, but at least I wasn't hung-over, at least I was leaving L.A., a place where I truly didn't fit in. I was thirty-seven, an old man in the world of record deals. I'd been seeing my life as over, but maybe I was wrong. Maybe it was just beginning.

Livin' In a Perfect World

Somewhere over the rainbow
Bluebirds fly
Birds fly over the rainbow
Why then, oh why, can't I...

JUDY GARLAND

Iconic majestic spires of red rock towered over the mass of signs and buildings that cluttered Sedona. I couldn't believe how much the sleepy little village had changed over the last twenty years. The population had gone from fifteen hundred to fifteen thousand. There was a factory outlet mall where the once-unpaved Verde Valley School road met the main drag. There used to be a ruined stucco shell called the pink house there, nothing else for miles. Now there were several pink stucco subdivisions and two golf courses. Sedona's McDonald's had teal arches, in a bow to the rich, artsy-fartsy so-called New Agers who'd overrun the town. There were billboards advertising vortex tours by pink jeep. Never mind that the vortex thing was invented by the gal who now ran the Chamber of Commerce. Ah well, life goes on and things change.

An attractive thirtyish brunette gave me a flirty look as I walked to my Jeep from my motel room. Now, *that* hadn't happened in a long time. I was in Sedona for my class's twentieth reunion at Verde Valley School. I'd lost thirty of the fifty pounds I was on my way to losing. The brunette's smile told me I was returning to the world at long last. The sweatpants era was history. I was getting in shape. I now could look at my reflection in a mirror and not blanch. It felt good, very good. We were moving to Mill Valley as soon as we got back from Arizona.

Free at last, Lord, I'm free at last!

While Sedona was overdeveloping itself into a premier tourist destination, Mill Valley was in a bit of a golden age in 1986. The old town, including the Two AM Club and Moon's Chinese Garden eatery, was still there, but there was a new overlay of fancier restaurants, espresso places, and sidewalk cafes that made life there very comfortable. You could sit out beneath the redwood trees at the red-brick-paved Book Depot plaza (formerly the train station, then the bus depot, now a book store and café), have a Peet's latte (not yet passé, not yet replaced by the two-splenda-double-shot-caramel-Americano-macchiato-with-low-fat-whipped-cream), and read the paper as healthy and hip-looking women and men walked and biked by. Okay, so the Old Mill Tavern had been converted into some nouveau cuisine joint and there was a Whole Foods grocery, called "Whole Paycheck" by locals, where the old Top Hat Market used to be. So, now there were no parking places downtown, and the Sequoia Theater, where I used to go for kid-silly Saturday matinees—where once, during "The Tingler," someone had thrown a Sugar Daddy up on the screen where it stuck, to our glee—now hosted a film festival.

Like everything that once was cool, Mill Valley would soon be ruined and gone. The price of being cool is death by coolness.

My hometown was in the process of being discovered and turned into a completely unaffordable playground of the ultra-rich, where the "hardware" stores sold paintings that cost ten thousand dollars and where old-timers sold their places for ten times what they paid for them and moved sixty miles or even across the country, looking for a place that was like what Mill Valley used to be. This bright, shiny darkness was coming. I could feel it and it made me unaccountably queasy at times, but it wasn't there quite yet. That was four or five years off. By 1990, I was telling friends that this mad rush for wealth was unsustainable and it has proven to be just that. But in 1986, Mill Valley was just about perfect.

The little tract house we bought in the Tam Valley section of Mill Valley backed onto a tidal slough, an arm of San Francisco Bay. The slough was full of fish, rays, and ducks. It smelled of the sea. Muir Beach was fifteen minutes away over the hill to the west, the hiking and biking trails of the Marin County headlands even closer. James was enrolled in a wonderful, safe, public school just down the street. I was back among my chums. I could play a round of really inept golf with Danny Morrison anytime our wives let us.

I looked back in amazement and regret at the way I'd lived for the last three years. I had truly wasted precious life time. I'd put my family through hell with my drinking, with my depression. I'd gotten so far from the music of my heart that I was going to have to find it again, somehow. All I could do was emerge as strongly as I could from that nightmare and just live. There was no going back and changing anything.

I loved the clean air and open spaces of northern California and beyond. I never was nor could I ever have been an L.A.

kind'a guy. I'm a Giants and 49ers fan. I couldn't have become a Dodgers fan if I'd lived there for fifty years. I know; I tried. The Dodgers sucked. I went to Dodger's Stadium and was happy when the blue guys lost. I wanted to put the whole L.A. experience far behind me and never look back at it again, if that was possible. It would be ten years before I went near that smog-infested blight again. Even then, as I drove down to Arizona in '96, I looked southward toward the San Gabriel Mountains and shuddered at the thought of what lay beyond. Someday I'd return to visit and have fun there, but that would be another lifetime from '86, or even '96.

I hooked up with Big John Main and Kevin Wells again. We enlisted Gary Vogenson on guitar and Kincaid Miller on keyboards and started a new band called Alex Call and Real Life. It was a bit of a group grope, with various players coming and going as their schedules allowed, but it was good. I was out playing again, something that had disappeared from my life while I was in that supposed-mecca of the music biz called Hollywood. Huey had been using the Tower of Power horns, which is like having an outfield of Ruth, Mays, and Mantle for your softball team, so I put a horn section together as well. Tim Larkin on trumpet and Alex Murzyn on sax anchored what would be called The Real Life Horns. It was usually three guys, but sometimes as many as five. Annie Stocking, queen of the local background singers, led a threesome of Call girls including Jeanette Sartain, Lynne Ray, Lorallee Christiansen, and other cuties with great pipes. It was great to play with a band again. I'd only done a handful of lousy gigs in L.A. in four years. Now, here, I played every month at least, sometimes more. The songs came tumbling out again. I was working long hours, learning to record with midi and a multi-track.

Huey's publisher, Ronda Espy, called to tell me the figure for the first big radio performance check from *Power of Love*. It was more money than we'd ever had, enough for a couple or three years, enough for me to start a pension fund! I paid more in taxes than I'd made most years. Dede bought me an eight-track tape machine for Christmas and I started putting together a viable home studio. The squirrel-powered four-track went into the corner and gathered dust. We had a big bonus room off the garage, where a former owner had run a carpet company out of the house. There was both rehearsal space and a big room for the studio. Kevin's drums were set up there, along with my P.A. and various amps. I liked to sit in there at night with the lights out and just look at the little jewel lights on the amps shining in the dark. A musician's Christmas tree.

I had enough money to even pay guys to rehearse, which they appreciated. Most musicians, stars not included, are seriously underpaid: fifty bucks and a meal. We spend our lives practicing and making music for people, yet people seem to think music should be free, or at least cheap. You know the old joke: musician gets to the Pearly Gates, Saint Peter checks his list and says, "Ah, that's right. You're a musician. Yes, you're on the list. You just go around the back, there's a little side door..."

I put out a spread of baguettes and brie and made everyone lattes. For rehearsal!

This was the life. The band sounded good. There was a new club called New George's in San Rafael. Old George's was a sleazy pool hall, so there was little transition needed to make it a perfectly normal place to rock-n-roll. There was a little buzz around that I'd returned. We played to packed houses. I was now sober, so I could enjoy it a bit more, though I have a penchant for making things more difficult than they need be. I was writing so much that I made Real Life learn up to ten new songs for every gig. We had a lot of train wrecks, and guys grumbled that we should just play the same songs twice to get them down. But that was okay. When it clicked, it was very cool.

We also played the Sweetwater in Mill Valley. It had an ornate old carved wood bar and walls covered with autographed photos and signed guitars and other star memorabilia from the sixties and seventies. It was owned and run by a glamorous Southern belle named Jeanie who had deep ties to the New Orleans area. The Sweetwater had a lot of truly wonderful artists playing there, alongside local bands. It had become an insider's venue where Elvis Costello and Bonnie Raitt would play with John Lee Hooker and Aaron Neville.

San Francisco in the mid-eighties was a rock-n-roll paradise. Journey, Santana, the Grateful Dead, Huey Lewis and the News, Night Ranger, The Doobie Brothers, Neil Young, Starship, Marty Balin, Boz Skaggs, Greg Kihn, Grace Slick, Sammy Hagar, Eddie Money, Clarence Clemons, Bobby McFerrin, and Bonnie Raitt were all part of a big family-style scene. *Bay Area Music* magazine's Bay Area Music Awards, or BAMMIES, an annual gathering of all the local wankers, was frequently hosted by Robin Williams, a Redwood High graduate from Tiburon.

The '60s might have been more colorful and earth-shaking, but the '80s scene had better bands who made a lot more money. There were plenty old-timers left as well, so there was a sense of a continuation of the flower-power era. Another cool group of celebs were Joe Montana, Dwight Clark, Ronnie Lott, Roger Craig, and the rest of the 49ers, Super Bowl heroes, who were the darlings of the Bay Area. Huey had them come up and clap and stomp around on stage when he played *Hip to Be Square* for one of his encores. Huey and Dwight were close buds. They were dubbed the Lewis and Clark Expedition for their famous late-night ramblings.

I might not have been in quite the same league as the heavy hitters, but I sold out the Sweetwater and New George's on a regular basis. The other guys in the club scene were the Edge with Lorin Rowan, and Austin DeLone and his band. Players from the bigger bands were always around the clubs when they were off the road, so you never knew who was going to sit in. It was a happening time. I didn't personally know all the guys in all the bigger bands, but everyone kind of knew who everyone else was. It was a far cry from the closed-door cards-close-to-your-vest scene that I'd encountered in LaLaLand.

With money in the bank and no crying need for a style-cramping publishing deal, I felt that I could cut loose in terms of my writing. With my new studio setup, midi synths and all, I could make decent recordings with a full band and horn parts all on my own and then have Real Life play them out live. I found one cool horn line that led me to write a song called *Perfect World*. It had an unusual beat that people told me was ska. To me, it was a combination of half-time and double-time, one of my favorite beats. I could do that with drum machines. The horn line was highly strange, but it made sense in the song. The bass part was pure Bob Marley, *mon!* When I first tried doing the song with the band, the drummer (someone subbing for Kevin, who was off with Carlene Carter) threw his sticks down and said, "This is fuckin' Chinese. I can't play it!" I had to walk him through it, beat by beat. If I could think of a part and play it on a drum machine, there had to be a way for a decent drummer to replicate it. At one rehearsal, when I was talking about the melody of *Perfect World*, Big John drawled, "If you call that a melody!" Okay, I made up stuff that was different. Everybody's the same. I don't ever want to be just like everyone else.

There was a live radio broadcast from New George's one night. Several of the songs came out quite well, especially *Perfect World*. I thought it would be a cool song for Huey, but I was also thinking of a record deal for myself again. I knew I was getting a little long in the tooth for such show-biz shenanigans, that thirty-three was sort of the unofficial cut-off date for aging rockers, since it takes three or four years to break an artist, but I just couldn't help myself.

I also happily couldn't believe the money coming in from my little ten percent of *Power of Love*. Huey and the lads sure baked a way bigger pie than Tommy Tutone did! Naturally, some of my songwriting was pointed toward the News. In the wake of the quadruple platinum *Fore!*, Huey would be putting out another album soon. Andre Pessis — who scored along with his co-writer Kevin Wells on Huey's big album *Sports* with *Walkin' on a Thin Line* — and I wrote a bunch of songs that were aimed for Huey. As with almost everything I've ever written on purpose *for* somebody, the songs kept coming up short.

Ah well, I still had very good royalties coming from *Power of Love*. Once again, I'd been rescued from oblivion by luck and timing. You have to be good and lucky to succeed. That is, you have to be good and you have to be lucky. It also doesn't hurt to know the right people, the guys cutting the record, that's for sure.

My new-found elation aside, my son James was having a bit

of a tough adjustment to his new school. He was in second grade, which in some ways was like the first year of junior high. Kids were forming cliques. James was an outsider. He was a gifted child for sure, but his personality was quirky. Three weeks into the school year, at an open house in his classroom, he surprised us and everyone else by suddenly performing the entire poem "Jabberwocky" to the tune of *La Cucaracha*! We could only blush and smile and say, "That's James!" Most kids his age couldn't even read the poem, much less recite it to music. He related well to adults, who recognized his intellectual and artistic brilliance, but he had trouble connecting to the kids in his class. He was on his own wavelength and his modes of communication were highly idiosyncratic. Sometimes he'd hop around like the video game character Q-Bert and go beep-beep as he hopped. He was also the new kid in his classroom. The other kids had all gone through preschool, kindergarten, and first grade together. I felt his pain, but all I could do was tell him that things would get better with time. The frame of reference of a seven-year-old is not broad enough to handle that kind of platitude.

He'd been stressed out from his earliest days. I'm afraid we might not have taken the burdens on him as seriously as we should have. He took comfort from our pets. One day, a stray dog we'd acquired right before we left L.A. got out of the yard. Spot, as James ironically called the all-tan ridgeback, was a wanderer by nature and didn't like being behind the fence. He came home, a little dinged-up. I thought he might have been in a dogfight, so I tied him up to keep him from getting out again. We had to go out for the afternoon. When we came home later, Spot was dead. His dings must have been caused by a moving car. There were no major obvious wounds on his body. I felt terrible, though I doubt that there was anything that we could have done to save him. James took it hard.

One afternoon a few days after Spot's death, James was invited by a classmate's mom to go over to their house. While playing basketball, he got bonked on the head by the ball. It seemed to make him ill. The mom brought him back home. He was woozy. I thought he might be getting the flu. He had a fever. He projectile vomited, which was strange. Within half-an-hour, he'd lapsed into unconsciousness. Dede was in the city taking a class. This was before the era of cell phones, so I had no way of reaching her. When I realized James was incapable of talking, I called 911 and the ambulance arrived. James was breathing, but was otherwise completely non-responsive. The EMTs said it might be a fever seizure—whatever that was—as he had a high temp. I raced up the freeway following the lit-up ambulance to Marin General Hospital. Dede finally got word from her parents of what was going on and arrived, frantic and concerned about our son.

James had been unconscious for almost three hours. They ran tests for drugs and did a CT scan. All negative. A doctor came out and quietly told us they didn't know what had happened to him, and they couldn't give us a prognosis. They couldn't say whether he would live or die, or if he'd be brain damaged if he survived. It was like a scene from a movie, but it was real. It was our precious boy lying inert but strangely rigid on a gurney under the fluorescent lights of the ER. The doctors simply didn't know how to proceed.

We sat in a side room by his gurney for hours as he lay there, breathing shallowly. He couldn't be brought back from unconsciousness. At least he was breathing, but it was uncanny. I'd never seen a person in a state like that. It was very much like he wasn't there in his body. Dede talked to him softly, telling him gently over and over to come back. After several long hours, a tech came to take yet another blood sample and suddenly James reacted to the needle, sitting up and crying, "No!"

He was conscious! He was present again. He was still woozy, but he recognized us. He'd come back from wherever he'd been.

The doctors didn't know what to make of the episode. Their best guess was it had been some kind of seizure, but they couldn't say for sure. He stayed in the hospital for two days and then went home. They did an electro-encephalogram which showed that some abnormal brain waves had occurred, but they couldn't draw any firm conclusions from it. We were in the dark.

Weeks went by without any further signs of anything wrong. The incident receded somewhat from our minds. I was getting ready to play at New George's on a Friday night. James started acting funny again, woozy. I instantly knew that he was heading into a repeat. He was still talking, but he wasn't right. We rushed to his pediatrician's office. She examined him. During the exam, he suddenly sat up and said in his little voice, "I don't want to die."

I felt like a steel rod had been run through my heart. My little boy.

The elderly doctor said, "Now, now, you're going to be fine." She thought he had had a seizure and that he was past it, but maybe we should take him to the E.R.

We got in our car and headed for Marin General Hospital.

It was rush hour and the only road north was jammed, so we were stuck in stop-and-go traffic. There were no other routes. It was extremely frustrating. James was sitting on my lap as Dede drove. I could see he was slipping away. I tried to keep him talking, but it was no use. He began to have a seizure in my arms. When we finally got to the hospital, I ran through the ER reception area and took him right into a room and put him on a bed. I don't remember who directed me. I only knew that I wouldn't be stopped by anyone. I was at his side while he had a major seizure, his body spasming wildly. An emergency doc was there with a team of techs and nurses. They struggled to hold him down long enough to get an IV started. She injected him with Valium and Dilantin, an anti-seizure medication. After a few excruciating minutes, he went limp and unconscious. He'd stopped seizing.

He had had a grand mal seizure. Now we knew: Epilepsy. The doctor asked me who I was, because she'd assumed I was a doctor. She said she'd never have allowed me to be there if she'd known I was the father. I thought this was very strange. Who else should've been there at that crucial moment?

James came to some hours later. He didn't know what had happened, why he was in the hospital. His memory of the event was zero. He was lying in the hospital bed with an I.V. and oxygen tubes. It was very difficult to see our little boy like that. He recovered, but we had to face a condition we knew nothing about. A pediatric neurologist told us James would have to take Dilantin. It's a major downer. It made him uncomfortably dizzy. He'd be on it for the next six years.

I couldn't help but think that the seizures were at least partially a response to the stress of moving, being at a new school, Spot's death, and living with the chronic tension between me and Dede. We'd had some big problems at home. Despite our newfound prosperity and my sobriety, we'd still been fighting. About what? It's hard to say. It just seemed to be a way of life for us, somehow. I think it was very hard on James, but that didn't stop it from happening.

It doesn't matter if you have all the money in the world; if you can't get free of your neuroses, you're stuck in a shithole. There's a *New Yorker* cartoon that shows a guy striding purposefully along a country lane. The sun is shining, there are birds singing in the trees. He's well-dressed and there are no obstacles in his way. His hands are on an iron birdcage sitting over his head, on his shoulders. The door of the cage is open. His face shows worry, anger, and panic.

We're all caught in our own cages. They exist only in our minds, but they might as well be made of iron and have locks on them.

When I write lyrics, I try to just let them out and decipher them afterwards.

Ain't no livin' in a perfect world
There ain't no perfect world anyway
Ain't no livin' in a perfect world
But we keep on dreaming of livin' in a perfect world

Our expectations put us in cages. But we keep on thinking that if we can just have more money or lose weight or have different friends, we'll be groovy. It doesn't work that way. It's all internal, not external. I wasn't free of expectations and desires, and neither was Dede.

But we keep on dreaming of livin' in a perfect world

Months passed. I was playing the usual haunts, still pulling good crowds. The money was still rolling in, but I knew that the royalty checks would eventually dwindle. Huey was cutting another album. I'd given him every song I could think of that might work, including *Perfect World*, but nothing clicked. I'd kind of given up on the process. Something else would have to happen. I'd been recording with the band in a very cool studio out in the hills of West Marin with a producer named Carl Derfler. There was still that glimmer of hope that I'd score another deal. My energy was high. Money may not buy you love or health, but it sure takes away the endless dread that comes with poverty. I was jazzed about my writing and recording and playing out.

My band, Real Life horns and all was playing the Sweetwater one Saturday. Bob Brown, Huey's manager, stopped in to have a drink on his way home from the studio, where he'd been with Huey. He came up to me between sets and asked if there was a demo of *Perfect World*. I told him there was a live recording that was pretty close to what we were playing that night. He said that Huey was basically done cutting, but they were looking for maybe one more song. Bob couldn't promise anything, but he'd play it for the band.

I dropped the tape at Huey's office. I'd given Huey the song months before, never heard a word about it, and assumed he didn't care for it. In our biz, no news is no news, but you never know. Sometimes it takes a couple of listens. Word came back through one of my roadies, Ed Gibson, who was the brother of

Bill Gibson, the News' drummer, that Huey and the boys had cut my song.

Be still my beating heart.

That was truly exciting, but I didn't want to get caught up in putting the TransAm in front of the engine. I didn't hear much else for a couple of weeks. I was dying to know how it stacked up with the other songs on the record. Ed came up to me as we loaded in for another Sweetwater gig and congratulated me for having the *first single* on the new album. I said, "Yeah sure, nice try Ed. Pull the other leg."

He said, "No, it's true." He'd just come from Huey's rehearsal space. It was going to be the first single.

Holy fucking guacamole. First single! And I wrote it by myself! I had all the publishing. It was all mine. *Mine, I tell you!*

The news was confirmed. It was incredible. Huey was at the top of his game. His previous album had sold four million. If my song went to number one, it would earn at least a half-million, maybe more, maybe much, much more!

I hadn't heard the cut yet. I didn't want to force myself on Huey. I wanted to be cool, though it was tough. They were shooting a video out at the garbage dump, of all places. I guess the juxtaposition of Huey and piles of refuse highlighted the song's lyrics. Hey. Whatever! I wanted to see it on MTV!

I heard my song for the very first time while driving across the Bay Bridge from a horn session in Oakland. It was a sunny, beautiful day in the Bay Area. *Perfect World* sounded unbelievable. They'd taken the song to new heights, for sure. Huey's vocal rocked. The Tower of Power horns were doing my horn lines. The backing vocal parts were magical. It was a smash recording. I pulled through the tollbooth, a very proud and happy fellow. This song came closest to reflecting my soul, my music. It stood a very good chance of being a number one song. It was like the flip side of my L.A. nightmare, a wonderful dream come true. I couldn't believe it had really happened.

Then came the high-stress part: watching the charts as the song climbed. Week by week it had to advance. Even though it was Huey Lewis and the News at the top of their careers, there were no guarantees. Huey had had a couple of number ones, like *Power of Love*, but most of his singles had just missed. On the Hot 100 or any other chart, retreat is defeat. It had to move up steadily, hopefully not too fast. We wanted the maximum number of weeks on the charts to get all that airplay. That's where the big radio money comes from. Every week that a song makes a jump upwards, it gets its bullet. On the Billboard's Hot 100 chart, there is a colored dot over the number of the song.

Perfect World was climbing up. It kept its bullet week after week. It got to the top twenty, then the teens, and then it was in the Top Ten. This is where the money is: It's also where the competition is fiercest. Other top songs were battling it for number one. Promotional money was being spent and wheels and palms, the hands that spin the wheels, were being greased, no doubt. *Perfect World* inched up. It got into the top five. It reached number three. It stayed there, *with its bullet*, for three weeks. Every Tuesday when the charts were announced, I called Huey's office to talk to his administrator, Carol, who'd give me the critical week's news.

After the three weeks at number three, the following chart day was hyper-crucial. It had to go up or it most likely, it had peaked and would then go down. I called Carol, my heart in my throat as usual. She said, "Sorry, we lost our bullet." Well, that was it. *Simply Irresistible* by Robert Palmer leapfrogged over *Perfect World* to number one. Too bad! So close! But not a bad run at all. Top Five is where the big bucks are. At least it got aced out by a cool song by an artist I really dug, by a song that was a classic hit. Huey's album, *Small World*, was still selling briskly, though not as well as the previous two records. There was some feeling out there that this album was too jazzy. It was a break from the party-hearty mode of the other albums. Huey and the guys knew it. But they'd wanted to do this record. *Small World* was also the title of the other single, which featured jazz legend Stan Getz on sax. It was very cool, but it wasn't *The Heart of Rock-n-Roll*, which is what radio and the punters expected and wanted.

Huey was pissed at his label. He thought they'd dropped the ball in terms of promotion. He told me, "There's no way that song isn't a number one song."

I was sorry to see the song slowly fall off the charts, but I knew I could count on some good royalties and airplay money. I couldn't wait to see my BMI check for radio play.

Small World went platinum, but that was it. *Perfect World* was Huey's last Top Five single. Later on I would jokingly call it the "kiss of death." Huey wouldn't record any more of my songs. The News gradually went into a very slow decline, though they'd never go away. They still make piles of dough playing. They're still one of the top bands for corporate events, twenty years after they started. But by the early '90s, they wouldn't have a major record deal any longer. What have you done for me lately?: Part 5,999.

Perfect World was nominated for best song of the year at the Bay Area Music Awards. *867-5309* had won it in 1982. Maybe

I'd be a two-time winner. Huey pulled some strings for me and I got to perform it at the show with my band, Real Life.

I had been doing taekwondo and I was in the best shape of my life. I was thirty-nine, but I could pass for twenty-nine. I could kick higher than my head. I had a great version of my band then, including burning lead-master Mark Karan on guitar. At the awards show we played a couple of songs, *Blue Avenue* and *Perfect World*. The unfortunate highlight came when the horn guys failed to play their big solo piece in *Perfect World*, as their chart was somehow off right at that part of the song by eight bars. The silence was deafening, though I'm not sure how many of the jovially inebriated attendees noticed or cared.

Perfect World didn't win. That honor went to Neil Young for *This Note's for You*, a song that didn't even get any airplay. It was bullshit. BAM must have been trying to get Neil to show up for the event. Boz Skaggs had a great, classy song, *Heart of Mine*, which should have come in number two after *Perfect World*. Or at least vice versa. When they announced Neil Young had won, there was a bit of a surprised reaction. That's my story, and I'm stickin' to it.

BAM had full page ads run by BMI and ASCAP, congratulating the nominees. Huey had just jumped from BMI to ASCAP, probably over a dispute about performance royalties with BMI and a promise of better treatment by ASCAP. So BMI left Huey and *Perfect World* out of their ads in BAM Magazine.

Radio play at that time was estimated by a survey of radio stations, not counted by computer. So there could be serious variances between BMI and ASCAP on the amount that was paid to the writers. When there are two writers on a song, one affiliated with BMI and one with ASCAP, there could be comparisons of royalty statements. Adjustments were frequently made to the parties who were shorted. The two performance societies vied with each other for the accounts of major artists and writers. Huey had made the switch, I'm guessing for ASCAP's promise of higher royalties than BMI could estimate. I was a BMI writer and had been for almost twenty years. I'd always felt that my performance money on *867–5309* wasn't fair, but I didn't have any way of comparing what ASCAP might have paid, as my co-writer Jim Keller was also a BMI writer.

When BMI left *Perfect World* and therefore me–out of their congratulatory ads in BAM, I was pissed off and hurt. I won in '82 for *867–5309*, and I was nominated again. I felt they were ignoring me as a writer. Also, I'd recently met ASCAP's Loretta Munoz and her husband Peter Lienheiser at the Northern California Songwriter's Conference. Loretta is a very winning artist liaison. She took me and several others out to dinner on ASCAP's dime a couple of times. So right then, I was inclined to like ASCAP.

My first performance statement from BMI for *Perfect World* was very nice, though not as much as my ten percent of *Power of Love* had been, and I was the only writer and had half the publishing. It seemed more than a little light. I called BMI and asked for an estimate of the next quarter's earnings. I was told a certain amount, about half of what the last check had been. When the next quarter's check arrived, it was for only one-third of that amount. I was outraged. I was trying to figure out how to make my life work. These checks wouldn't come in forever, and I needed to know what I should or shouldn't do with the money.

I called up BMI and raged a bit. They promised to make it up to me on the next check. I was dissatisfied. It's was a cumulative thing: short-changed on the *867–5039* and Benatar money, and now this, plus being left out of the BAM ads. In a fit of pique, I decided to jump to ASCAP.

This might not have been the best move. After all, BMI would always collect and pay my performance royalties for the hits I already had, including *867–5309, Little Too Late,* and *Perfect World. Power of Love* money came directly from Huey's office, as I wasn't listed as a writer on the copyright. Perhaps over time BMI would pay me less than I should have been paid. This is still something I think happened. More than a few seasoned songwriters and music publishers have agreed with me. But at the time I was so caught up in being offended that I just jumped. I figured that I'd have more hits as an ASCAP writer, and they'd pay me better and treat me better. I'd continue to have my doubts about BMI. One thing that bothered me is that they'd never grant *867–5309* "Million Play" status, which is absolutely absurd. Country songs you've never heard of have those BMI certificates. That's got to be payback for me jumping to ASCAP.

Despite this stuff, 1988 had been a big year for me. I had money in the bank. I had songs out there that would earn me royalties for the rest of my life. I'd been running down my dream now for twenty-two years. I'd had a lot of tough times, but I also had more than my share of unforgettable memories. I wouldn't have traded any of it for the world, except for my personal failings in my L.A. years. I'd had the great good fortune to be in Clover, a band of brothers, something that you can't buy. Now I had my own cool band and I was playing songs I'd written that everyone had heard on the radio.

The San Rafael *Independent Journal*, the biggest local Marin daily paper, put my picture on its front page along with eighty-seven other people as one of their "88 in'88." George Lucas and Senator Barbara Boxer were on the same page. I had a couple of pretty big in-depth write-ups for the I.J. and the *San Francisco Chronicle*. I was sober and in fantastic physical shape. I was just turning forty, but I looked like I was thirty. L.A. was in my rearview mirror and I'd flipped the mirror to dim. I saw a future of more hits and, who knows? Maybe even another record.

Ain't life grand? Heck, it was a *Perfect World*.

867-5309, Back to the Future

Jenny, Jenny, who can I turn to...

Tommy Tutone

Life is what happens to you when you're busy making other plans. Wasn't it John Lennon who said that?

Nashville 2010.

The more things change, the more they stay the same. After many years of financial freedom afforded by my handful of major hits, I find myself once again poised at the edge of being hero or a zero, this time in that distant land called Tennessee. But that, as they say, is another story.

867–5309/Jenny almost disappeared money-wise for a few years. By the mid '90s, it was only earning me a few thousand dollars a year. *Power of Love* was still making solid money. Then something funny happened. I went to my mailbox at Muir Beach, at the nice house up on the hill made affordable when Dede sold her home-grown paralegal placement business. I was hoping that my Warner-Chappell royalty statement would be at least a thousand dollars for *867–5309*. Instead it was fifteen grand.

Jenny had started having her fifteen year reunion. Kids who were calling up *Jenny* in high school in '82 were now working at ad agencies, choosing the songs to be included on those "as seen on TV," record compilations. *867–5309* was on over forty of them, some of which sold hundreds of thousands of copies. *Best Hits of the Eighties, Worst Hits of the Eighties, Eighties Rock, 80s Rock Party, Permed Jennies of the 80s, Songs You Puked To, etc.*

Arnold Schwarzenegger put it on his *Workout with Arnold* and "Beavis and Butthead" had a snigger-along to the dirty lyrics version on theirs. The Goo Goo Dolls played it live, as did Blink-182. Everclear put it out as a single, which flopped, but hey, they can't all be hits. Country love hunk Keith Urban does the best version of the song ever in his live shows, but he'll never put it out. Will you, Keith? Like, please.

The song somehow stayed in the popular consciousness all these years. My son James's many friends from his years at Tam High knew the song, and not from me but from radio and TV. They called me "telephone-number man." Even younger kids know it. It's a strange cultural phenomenon. *867–5309* is just part of the American landscape. The song made the national network news when a guy with the number in New York City put it on eBay and the bidding got to $80,000 before Verizon said he couldn't sell the use of "their" number. Then companies started using it for radio and TV ads, everyone from Cingular Wireless to Ben Franklin Plumbing, for heaven's sake. A young man sold his DJ business with the transferable Vonage number on eBay. The auction got to $434,000 in two days, but unfortunately for the guy with the bright idea, it was a seven-day auction. He settled for $186,000 by the end of the week. No cut for me. I must have owed the guy $186,000 from another lifetime. I had a nice interview in the Sunday *New York Times* and pieces on CNN, MSNBC, and FOX Headline News. Stewie or Brian on "The Family Guy" made a snide comment about Jenny's reputation. The song now makes more money than when it was on the charts in '82.

I hear many stories about the song. Some people who have had the number have chucked it because yahoos keep calling, asking if Jenny is there. But one extended family from Florida loves it and uses 5309 as the last four digits on all their cell phones, wherever they live around the country. Emergency rooms at hospitals use 867–5309 on a security code on their entry keypads. Over a hundred women have told me that they've used it as a brush-off number. The guy wakes up, a bit hung-over perhaps, but he's got this girl's name and number on a bar napkin. "Shit. It's Jenny. 867–5309."

Ha ha, he's been had. So the song does have some redeeming social value.

I'd almost disowned *867–5309 Jenny* for years. I didn't want to be known as the writer of a novelty song. I want to be known as a writer of beautiful, meaningful music, like *Perfect World*. But I have comfortably settled for the notion and semi-notoriety of being the writer of the song about the girl's number on the bathroom wall. When I started going to Nashville to write in '92, I constantly heard "My band played y'all's song five hun'erd times."

I said to myself, "hey play the cards you're dealt, sucker."

People included me in its thirtieth anniversary issue, on the same page as the guy who came up with, "Where's the beef?" Perfect. It's been mentioned on both "The Simpsons" and "South Park." It doesn't get any bigger than that.

When will *867–5309* die away? When all those living today are gone, it will be too, just like everything else. Still, it's a bit of rock immortality, for what that's worth. It's instantly recognizable from the guitar lick, like my all-time favorite rock song, *Satisfaction*. I know many very successful songwriters here in Nashville who don't have as recognizable a song. I was talking to John McFee about famous guitar players and he said, "I could play circles around those guys." And that is totally true. It takes a hacker like me to come up with a guitar lick dumb enough that people can instantly recognize it. When I play, I always close the show with *867–5309*, even though my fellow performers are famous and have lots more hits. There's just no following it.

Huey is still going strong. HLN plays a lot of very lucrative corporate dates every year, in addition to their public concerts. Huey's been in many TV shows and movies as an actor. He's just finished a run on Broadway, in *Chicago*. He and I both ended up with places in the Bitterroot Valley in Montana. His is a bit bigger, like a hundred times bigger. He needs the executive weed trimmer. My eight acres of wilderness—trout stream, with its log house and starry Big Sky view—ended up being sold. Broke my heart, but like I said, life goes on and things change. Huey and I stay in touch.

John McFee is still a Doobie Brother. He also does a lot of production and sessions. John is nationally regarded as one of the best guitar players around. He still maintains a sense of humility he needn't maintain. He's long ago outpaced his old guitar heroes.

Johnny Ciambotti had a good run as manager and bass player for Carlene Carter and Lucinda Williams. He was instrumental in getting Dwight Yoakum signed to his first record deal. He went back to UCLA and became a very successful doctor of chiropractic in L.A. Johnny unfortunately passed away suddenly last year.

Keith Knudsen also died recently of everything but a generous heart.

Mitch Howie is playing drums and doing well.

Kevin Wells is an award-winning high school music teacher in a small Native American reservation town in the mountains of northern California.

Sean Hopper, of course, plays keys with HLN. He collects fine things like fast cars and even faster motorcycles and rare bottles of exceptional port.

Mickey Shine is a mural painter who has spent a lot of years on Native American reservations as well, doing artwork and community service.

Jim Keller is the music publishing coordinator for the famous composer Philip Glass.

Jake Riviera is still managing Nick Lowe, I believe.

Ron Nevison has had a fabulous career producing hit records.

Elvis Costello is Elvis Costello.

Tommy Tutone and *Jenny* are firmly established on VH1's *One Hit Wonders*. The song keeps moving up. It's at number four now, I believe. It was at number sixty-nine a few years ago, so maybe we'll finally end up with number one someday. It's also in the top thirty of VH1's Hits of the '80s. Considering the competition, that's a big honor for a backyard, plum-tree song.

My son James, who eventually became quite popular, recognized by his high school peers for his original brilliance and creativity, lives in New York City, where he's gotten a degree in music production at CCNY. He studied theater at NYU, but quit after a couple of years to do music. I think he only went back to school to find out how Steely Dan got that bass and kick sound, so he could use it in his recordings. He's a brilliant music writer and artist. I call him the "block off the old chip." His seizure disorder went away for several years and then resurfaced in his late teens, but is now under control.

Dede and I divorced in 1997.

I moved to Nashville shortly thereafter to see how I'd do up against the best songwriters in the world.

I kind of ran my course with that one. Shoot, man, I jest ain't country. I've recently produced and co-written an album for a genius healthcare innovator named Quint Studer. His message, which resonates so well with me and my wife, Lisa, who sings with me, is that people should follow their passion in life, whether it's in music or in healthcare. I play around the country for Quint's healthcare conferences, sometimes by myself, sometimes with a vocal-driven band of wonderful singers and players. I'm a regular Springsteen for nurses.

There is a lot more to this part of the story, but that's for another time. Suffice it to say, life doesn't carry on in one straight line. There are boulders on the mountainsides out there, and sometimes lightning strikes them and knocks them loose, and sometimes you dislodge them yourself. They can roll down on you or you might ride them. Sometimes you find a gold nugget while clearing out a drainage ditch. Other times, meteors plummet from out of deep space and knock you right off your skateboard.

I used to go see this old gypsy fortune-teller in Greenwich Village when I found myself in New York. A few years ago, she told me I had another son. I said, "Fair enough. I was once out on the road, I was a hippie. I suppose I could have another son."

But she meant I had another son to come. She was right! His name is Aidan and he's now a young baseball whiz and has enough talent on the violin that we won't let him stop taking lessons. His mommy is my love, Lisa Carrie. Lisa is a wonderful singer who has had a long career singing with Eddie Arnold, Micky Gillie, Wayne Newton, and Charlie Louvin. Aidan fortunately inherited her good looks. I'm brainwashing him with my sense of humor and love of history, baseball, and the great outdoors. He sees me working away endlessly at my creative projects, both my music and prose writing. I've written several novels now, including a baseball tale that has movie talk swirling around it, and an epic historical novel about the man who might have built Stonehenge.

So life begins again, as it always does. I need to get lucky again. I'm good looking for lucky, so I can once again be that hit act Good & Lucky. Will another *Jenny* show up? I wouldn't mind, because once again, my ass needs saving, but I'm happy to be leaving my boys a legacy of creative work. I hope they appreciate that, since they won't get much money!

For the last ten years I've been playing in an open G tuning, tuned way down to a C on the low string: C-G-D-G-B-D. Try it: you'll like it. It's wonderful thing for a hacker like me. I never could learn to finger-pick and all that fancy stuff. This tuning makes me sound like I know what I'm doing. In the G tuning you're always making a chord. There are ringing grace notes that make my Taylor guitar, "Little Darlin," sound very full. It's much better than the illogical standard tuning for guitar. I sound pretty damn good when I play "in the rounds" with my fellow writers or at hotel ballroom healthcare conferences. *867–5309 Jenny* sounds like it was written in this tuning.

People nowadays think I'm a good guitar player, but really, I'm just sliding my hand around the neck, playing like I did the first night I picked up that beat-up old two-string guitar at age eleven after the dance.

A FEW WORDS ABOUT ALEX CALL

Alex grew up in Mill Valley, California, in the 1950s, the third child of well-educated, musical parents. His father was a charming man who was also an alcoholic packrat who couldn't finish building their house. Alex lived in a dingy basement room co-inhabited by spiders and rats. He was afraid of the critters, the dark, and the H-bombs they told him about at school. He took refuge in baseball, Superman, and the songs he heard at night on the radio when his parents thought he was sleeping. Alex discovered at an early age that he loved music and that he could escape the tough-guy world of the early 60s by singing in rock bands. He lucked out in going to a progressive high school where he started his first band, was exposed to Dylan, the Beatles, and the Stones, and was given a glimpse of what it might be like to be an agent of positive change in the world. Alex was signed to a record deal at age nineteen as the lead singer and songwriter of his legendary San Francisco country rock band **Clover**, whose members included **Huey Lewis** and **John McFee** of the **Doobie Brothers**. Clover gained a local following in San Francisco and made two albums for **Fantasy Records**, which unknown to Clover became cult classics in the U.K. Then Clover lost their deal and fell on hard times. They fought their way back and in 1976, thanks to meeting British pub-rock-hero **Nick Lowe**, a fan of the early Clover records.

Clover toured England with **Thin Lizzy** and **Lynyrd Skynyrd**, made two more albums on Phonogram/Mercury produced by Mutt Lange, and backed **Elvis Costello** on his famed first album, My Aim is True.

When Clover broke up in 1978, Alex fell into despair. He had been at the edge of the big time, but now he was on his own, down and out. At rock bottom he found his salvation by writing a series of classic rock songs, including *867–5309 Jenny*, one of the most iconic songs of the last thirty years. In 1982, as *867–5309 Jenny* was making its way up the charts, he quit his temporary construction job and signed a record deal with **Arista Records** and a major publishing deal. But his travails were far from over. His album failed to catch on and he learned the hard way about the duplicity of people in the music business. Alex took a plunging and bucking ride on the rollercoaster of fame and rejection, persevered, and once again reached the top of the charts with more big hits for his old band mate **Huey Lewis and the News, Pat Benatar,** and others. In the 1990s Alex began going on writing to trips to Nashville, where he moved in 1998. He has written songs for country artists and made two albums. In addition to songwriting and making videos for YouTube, Alex has written several books including a humorous novel about an aging band titled Second Childhood which will be released by Charles River Press in 2012. He also has written a baseball story, a sci-fi thriller, an historical epic about the early Bronze Age, and an adventure series for adolescents. Alex lives in Nashville with his wife, singer Lisa Carrie, his second son, Aidan, three dogs, and two cats. His older son, James Call, is a budding music star in New York. Alex is a lifelong student of history and loves baseball, fly fishing, and politics. *867–5309 Jenny: The Song that Saved Me* is always captivating. Heartbreaking, insightful, and funny in turns, his lively and deeply descriptive personal narrative takes you for a ride in cold vans, onto arena and club stages, backstage with some of the most influential musicians of the 60s 70s and 80s, behind the scenes with double-dealing music biz people, and into crazy situations where a sense of humor, a song, his band mates, and a willingness to keep on trying against long odds were his best companions.

CPSIA information can be obtained at www.ICGtesting.com
Printed in the USA
BVOW031143050612

291295BV00010B/2/P